150 Crochet Blocks

CHARTS, INSTRUCTIONS, TOOLS & TECHNIQUES

Sarah Hazell

Search Press

A QUARTO BOOK

Published in 2015 by
Search Press Ltd
Wellwood
North Farm Rd
Tunbridge Wells
Kent TN2 3DR

ISBN: 978-1-78221-270-6

Conceived, designed and produced by
Quarto Publishing plc
The Old Brewery
6 Blundell Street
London N7 9BH

QUAR.TFCB

Senior Editor:Chelsea Edwards
Senior Art Editor: Emma Clayton
Designer: Tanya Devonshire-Jones
Illustrator: Kuo Kang Chen
Photographers: Nicki Dowey (location)
and Phil Wilkins (studio)
Proofreader: Liz Jones
Pattern Checker: Rachel Atkinson
Design Assistant: Martina Calvio
Indexer: Helen Snaith

Art Director: Caroline Guest
Creative Director: Moira Clinch
Publisher: Paul Carslake

Colour separation in Singapore by
Pica Digital Pte Limited

Printed by Hung Hing Off-set Printing Co. Ltd,
China

10 9 8 7 6 5 4 3 2 1

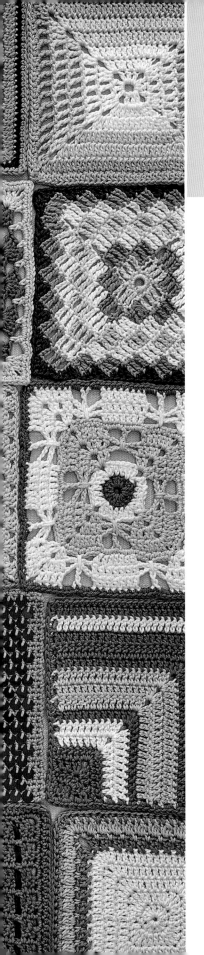

Contents

6   Sarah's World
7   About This Book

8 **CHAPTER 1:** ALL-TIME FAVOURITE COLLECTION

10   Traditional
12   Textures
16   Lace & Mesh
20   Shape Changers

24   Crosses
28   Colourwork
32   Flowers
36   Special Techniques

40 **CHAPTER 2:** THE PATTERNS

42   Traditional
48   Textures
60   Lace & Mesh
74   Shape Changers

86   Crosses
98   Colourwork
108   Flowers
124   Special Techniques

138 **CHAPTER 3:** THE PROJECTS

140   Floor Cushion
142   Vase Cover
143   Journal Cover

144   Baby Block
145   Lap Blanket

146   Techniques
154   Symbols & abbreviations

158   Index
160   Credits

Sarah's World

There is something very special about being able to take a hook and some odd bits of yarn and transform them into something beautiful and useful! Crochet can take you on many journeys—backwards and forwards as well as up, down and round and round. I particularly like working with blocks, because they are manageable if you are short on time, space, or are traveling. They are incredibly versatile and can be combined in all sorts of ways to make different kinds of projects. They are a great way to experiment with unusual colour combinations and textures of yarn. Perhaps one of the most significant things about blocks is their huge appeal. So, whether you are working on a project for yourself or for someone else, your efforts will always be admired and stand the test of time.

About This Book

This book presents a classic collection of 150 crochet blocks, which are sure to become some of your firm favorites. It includes large colour-coded charts and row-by-row instructions for every pattern—and a selection of unique crochet projects to put your completed squares to good use.

8-39 CHAPTER 1: ALL-TIME FAVOURITE COLLECTION

The All-time Favourite Collection showcases the 150 stunning designs featured in this book. Flick through this colourful visual guide, select your desired design and then turn to the relevant page of instructions to create your chosen block.

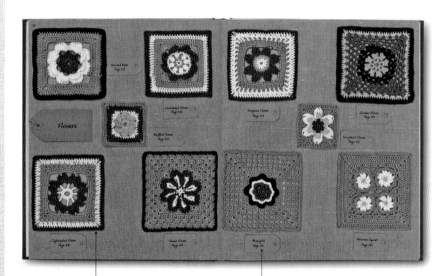

Each design is shown in proportion to the others on the page, which gives you an idea of scale.

Each block is labeled with its name and page number so that you can easily find the pattern.

Photographs show
the complete design

Pattern name

Skill level gives a rough
guide to difficulty

40-137 CHAPTER 2: THE PATTERNS

The selection of 150 designs forms the
heart of this book. The patterns cover
everything from traditional Afghan blocks
to textured clusters, floral designs, and
colourwork. Find detailed instructions,
charts, and beautiful colour combinations
for each pattern, and discover a wealth of
new crochet square styles.

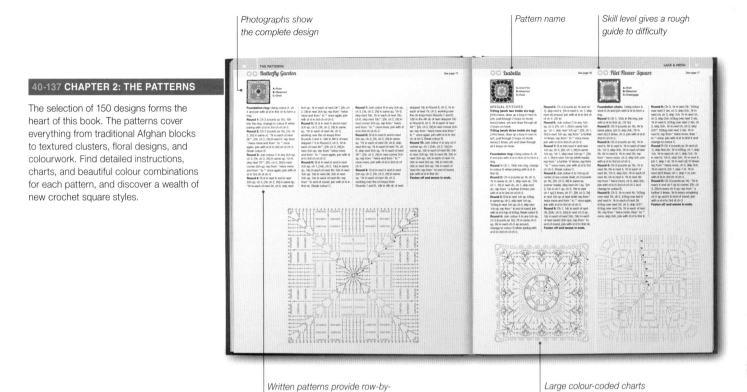

Written patterns provide row-by-
row instructions from start to finish

Large colour-coded charts
to keep you on course

Project title

Tools, materials
and measurements

138-145 CHAPTER 3: THE PROJECTS

This chapter features five gorgeous
projects to put your crochet squares and
skills to use. Instructions explain how to
join your blocks together, and each project
provides advice on additional tools,
materials, and expert finishing techniques
to create something unique for yourself or
to give as a gift.

How to work
the crochet

Guidance on
finishing techniques

Large photographs illustrate
the finished project

1

All-time Favourite Collection

This collection displays all 150 blocks in beautiful, stitch-themed groups.
Flip through for inspiration, then turn to the relevant page in the Patterns
chapter to make the block.

Four-patch
Granny
Page 44

Alternative
Granny
Page 46

Rectangle
Granny
Page 43

Traditional

Plain Granny
Page 42

Granny in
the Middle
Page 42

Nine-patch
Granny
Page 47

Granny
Stripes
Page 43

Mitered
Granny
Page 45

Flower Granny
Page 45

Raised Flower
Granny
Page 47

Celtic Cable
Page 53

Bobble Stripes
Page 51

Textures

Textured Stripes
Page 48

Big Bloom
Page 59

Diagonal
Raised Treble
Page 54

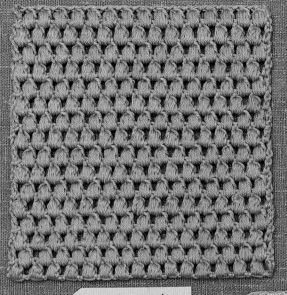

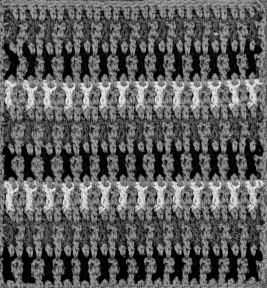

Pineapple
Cluster
Page 55

Tricolour Trinity
Page 56

Alternating
Bobbles
Page 50

Aligned
Railing Block
Page 57

Winter Blueberry
Patch
Page 52

14

Lemon Peel
Page 49

Two-colour
Raised Ripple
Page 56

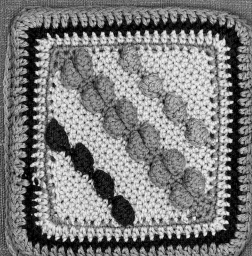

Bobbles on the
Diagonal
Page 52

Striped Knot
Page 49

Honeycomb
Page 55

Candy Stripe
Bobbles
Page 50

Classic Cable
Page 58

Basket Weave
Page 54

Fine Texture
Page 48

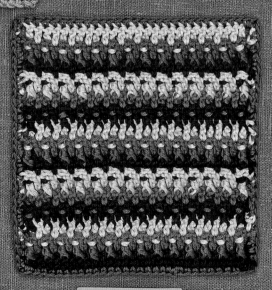

Interwoven Block
Page 57

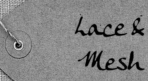

Lace &
Mesh

Spiralling
Lace
Page 72

Openwork
Page 60

Queen Anne's
Lace
Page 63

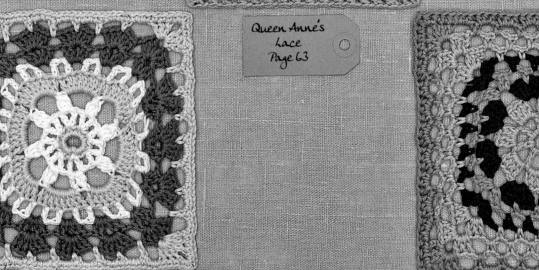

Isabella
Page 67

Lacy Wheel
Page 61

Old Vienna
Page 62

Butterfly
Garden
Page 66

Picot Rose
Page 69

Filet Flower
Square
Page 67

Victorian
Lace
Page 62

Daisy Chain
Square
Page 71

Filet Mesh
Center
Page 73

Popcorn Square
Page 69

Pineapple Lace
Page 65

Belgian Lace
Page 60

Eyelet Lace
in the Round
Page 64

Sunshine Lace
Page 70

Fleur
Page 68

Double Filet
Mesh
Page 73

Popcorns & Lace
Page 68

Shapé
Changers

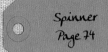

Spinner
Page 74

Circle in a
Hexagon
Page 84

Cluster Circle
Page 76

Starflower
Circle
Page 77

Framed Circle
Page 78

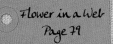
Double
Diamonds
Page 85

Starburst
in a Square
Page 75

Flower in a Web
Page 79

Fretwork Circle
Page 76

Star in a Square
Page 80

Squaring
the Circle
Page 75

Diamonds
Page 83

Octagon Framed
Flower
Page 82

Edwardian
Fancy
Page 81

Hexagon in a
Square
Page 84

Diamond in a
Square
Page 80

Mitered Curve
Page 83

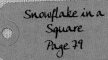

Octagon Tile
Page 82

Snowflake in a
Square
Page 79

Circle in a
Square
Page 74

Italian Cross
Page 89

St. Petersburg
Page 97

Crosses

Embossed Cross
Page 91

Sunray Cross
Page 87

Wisteria
Page 95

Double Popcorn
Cross
Page 94

Gothic Square
Page 92

Interlocking Cross
Page 90

Seville
Page 88

Lacy Cross
Page 86

Catherine Wheel
Page 92

Compass Cross
Page 94

Looped Cross
Page 90

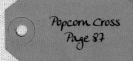

Popcorn Cross
Page 87

Treble Cross
Page 93

Danish
Diamond
Page 96

Criss Cross
Page 86

Crossroads
Page 91

Anemone
Page 88

Tricolour Square
Page 97

Hourglass
Page 103

Random Patches
Page 99

Colourwork

Florentine Tile
Page 105

Seminole
Page 100

Intarsia Steps
Page 98

Dip Stitch Cross
Page 107

Trio
Page 103

Spiky Square
Page 107

Jaquard Stripes
Page 101

Half and Half
Page 102

Tuscan Tile
Page 106

Rose of Sharon
Page 106

Flying Carpet
Page 104

Quartet
Page 98

Darts
Page 102

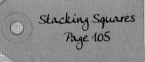

Interlocking
Stripes
Page 100

Zig Zag
Page 99

Stacking Squares
Page 105

Bold Block
Page 104

Jaquard Checks
Page 101

Raised Rose
Page 113

Cartwheel Flower
Page 110

Flowers

Ruffled Flower
Page 113

Eight-petal Flower
Page 108

Flame Flower
Page 117

Origami Flower
Page 111

Cluster Flower
Page 114

Six-petal Flower
Page 112

Marigold
Page 116

Primrose Square
Page 120

Poppy
Page 115

Poinsettia
Page 123

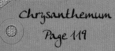

Chrysanthemum
Page 119

Filet Flower
Page 121

Lacy Daisy
Page 115

Raised Petal
Flower
Page 112

Framed Flower
Page 109

Rosetta
Page 122

American
Beauty
Page 118

Waterlily
Page 121

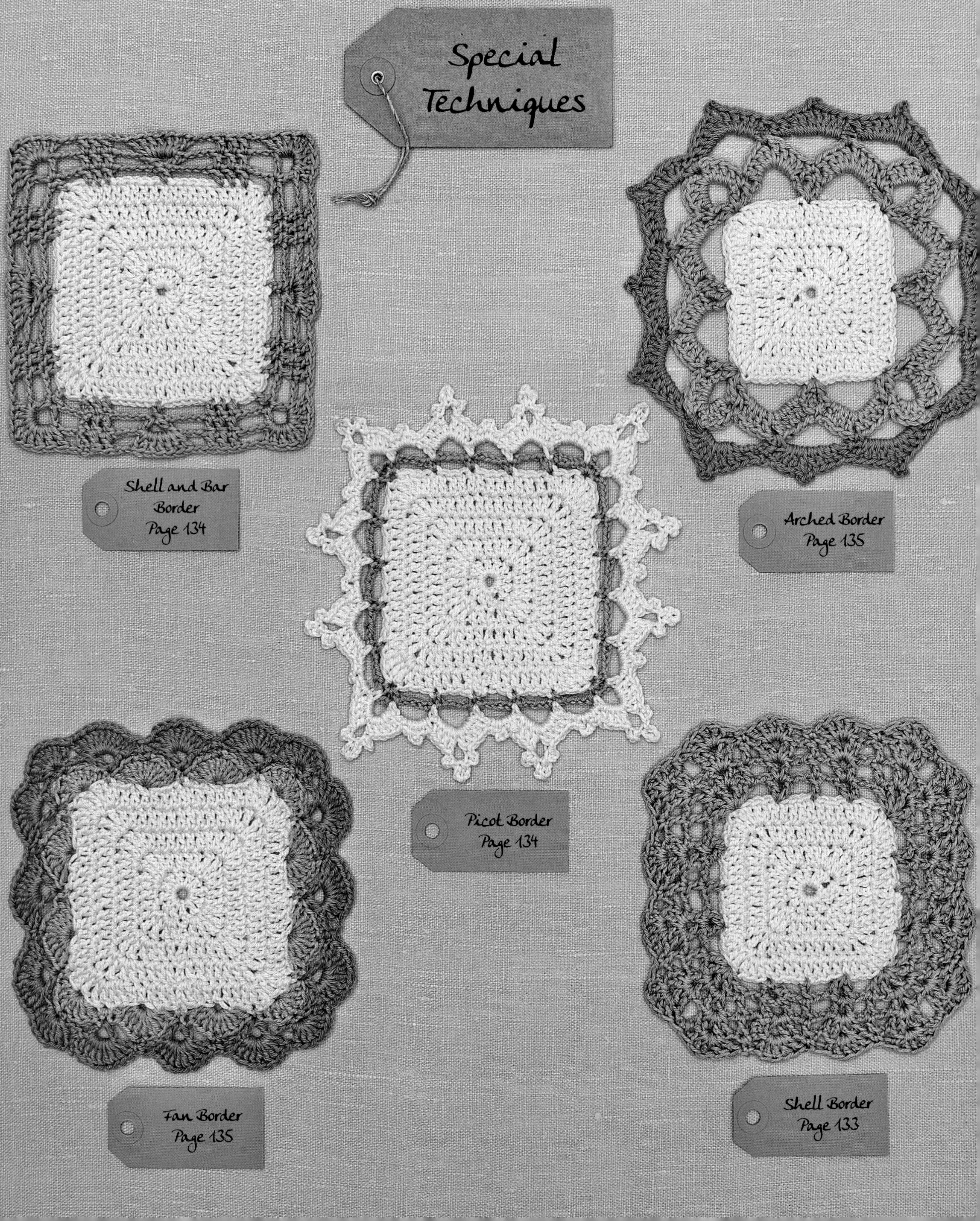

Special Techniques

Shell and Bar
Border
Page 134

Arched Border
Page 135

Picot Border
Page 134

Fan Border
Page 135

Shell Border
Page 133

Vertical woven
Block
Page 126

Mitered
Increase
Page 124

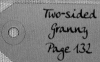

Two-sided
Granny
Page 132

Mitered
Decrease
Page 125

Horizontal
Woven Block
Page 131

Harlequin
Page 131

Loop Stitch
Columns
Page 130

Chain Loops
Flower
Page 130

Beaded Double
Crochet
Page 129

Sequined Double
Crochet
Page 129

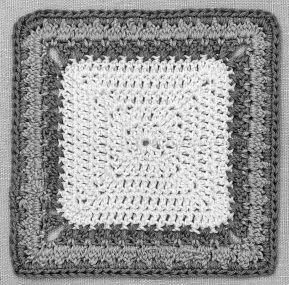

Cross-stitched
Border
Page 137

Log Cabin Granny
Page 126

Log Cabin
Page 128

Corner Log
Cabin
Page 127

Cluster Border
Page 136

2

Patterns

Organised by theme, this chapter contains patterns and charts for all of the 150 blocks featured in this book.

⭐ *Plain Granny*

See page 10

A=Lavender

Foundation ring: Using colour A, ch 6 and join with sl st in first ch to form a ring.

Round 1: Ch 3, (counts as 1tr), 2tr in ring, ch 3, *3tr in ring, ch 3; rep from * twice more, join with sl st in 3rd ch of first ch-3.

Round 2: Sl st in each of next 2tr, sl st in ch-3 corner sp, ch 3, [2tr, ch 3, 3tr] in same sp to make corner, *ch 1, [3tr, ch 3, 3tr] in next ch-3 sp; rep from * twice more, ch 1, join with sl st in 3rd ch of first ch-3.

Round 3: Sl st in each of next 2tr, sl st in ch-3 corner sp, ch 3, [2tr, ch 3, 3tr] in same sp to make corner, *ch 1,

3tr in ch-sp, ch 1, [3tr, ch 3, 3tr] in next ch-3 sp; rep from * twice more, ch 1, 3tr in ch-sp, ch 1, join with sl st in 3rd ch of first ch-3.

Round 4: Sl st in each of next 2tr, sl st in ch-3 corner sp, ch 3, [2tr, ch 3, 3tr] in same sp to make corner, *[ch 1, 3tr in each ch-sp] along the side of the square, ch 1, [3tr, ch 3, 3tr] in next ch-3 sp; rep from * twice more, [ch 1, 3tr in each ch-sp] along the side of the square, ch 1, join with sl st in 3rd ch of first ch-3.

Rounds 5–9: As Round 4.

Fasten off and weave in ends.

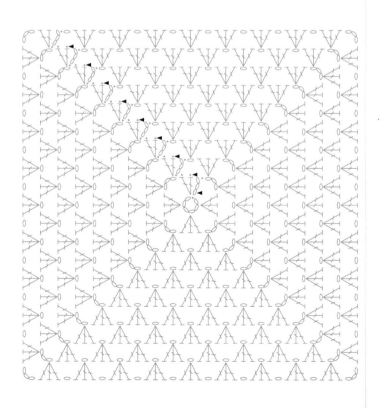

⭐ *Granny in the Middle*

See page 10

A=Blackcurrant
B=Persimmon
C=Ecru
D=Greengage
E=Lavender

Foundation ring: Using colour A, work 6 ch and join with sl st in first ch to form a ring.

Round 1: Ch 3, (counts as 1tr), 2tr in ring, ch 3, *3tr in ring, ch 3; rep from * twice more, join with sl st in 3rd ch of first ch-3. Break colour A.

Round 2: Join colour B to any ch-3 corner sp with a sl st, ch 3, [2tr, ch 3, 3tr] in same sp to make corner, *ch 1, [3tr, ch 3, 3tr] in next ch-3 sp; rep from * twice more, ch 1, join with sl st in 3rd ch of first ch-3. Break colour B.

Round 3: Join colour C to any ch-3 corner sp with a sl st, ch 3, [2tr, ch 3, 3tr] in same sp to make corner, *ch 1, 3tr in ch-sp, ch 1, [3tr, ch 3, 3tr] in next ch-3 sp; rep from * twice more, ch 1, 3tr in ch-sp, ch 1, join with sl st in 3rd ch of first ch-3. Break colour C.

Round 4: Join colour D to any ch-3 corner sp with a sl st, ch 3, [2tr, ch 3, 3tr] in same sp to make corner, *[ch 1, 3tr in each ch-sp] along the side of the square, ch 1, [3tr, ch 3, 3tr] in next ch-3 sp; rep from * twice more, [ch 1, 3tr in each ch-sp] along the side of the square, ch 1, join with sl st in 3rd ch of

first ch-3. Break colour D.

Round 5: Join colour E and work as Round 4. Break colour E.

Round 6: Join colour A with a sl st to any tr of previous round. Ch 1, 1dc in every tr and ch-sp of previous round, working 5dc in each ch-3 corner sp, join with sl st in first ch.

Round 7: Ch 1, 1dc in every dc of previous round, working 3dc in centre st of the 5dc corner groups, join with sl st in first ch, changing to colour B at last yrh.

Round 8: Ch 2, 1htr in every dc of previous round, working 3htr in centre st of the 3dc corner groups, join with sl st in 2nd ch of first ch-2, changing to colour C at last yrh.

Round 9: Ch 2, 1htr in every htr of previous round, working 3htr in centre st of the 3htr corner groups, join with sl st in 2nd ch of first ch-2, changing to colour D at last yrh.

Round 10: Ch 1, 1dc in every htr of previous round, working 3dc in centre st of the 3htr corner groups, join with sl st in first ch.

Fasten off and weave in ends.

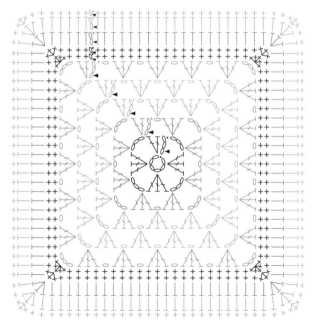

⭐ *Rectangle Granny*

See page 10

A=Lavender
B=Ecru
C=Persimmon
D=Blackcurrant
E=Greengage

Foundation ring: Using colour A, work 12 ch.

Round 1: [2tr, ch 2, 3tr, ch 2, 3tr] in 4th ch from hook, ch 2, skip next 2ch, 1tr in each of next 3ch, ch 2, skip next 2ch, [3tr, ch 2, 3tr, ch 2 3tr] all in last ch, ch 2, skip next 2 ch on opposite side of foundation ch, 1tr in each of next 3ch, ch 2, skip next 2ch, join with sl st in 3rd of ch-3. Break colour A.

Round 2: Join colour B to the last ch-2 sp made, ch 3 (counts as 1tr), 2tr in same sp, ch 2, *[3tr, ch 2, 3tr, ch 2] in next 2 ch-2 sps (2 corners made), [3tr in next ch-2 sp, ch 2] twice; rep from * once again, join with sl st in 3rd of ch-3. Break colour B.

Round 3: Join colour C to the first ch-2 sp of last round, ch 3 (counts as 1tr), 2tr in same sp, ch 2, *[3tr, ch 2, 3tr] in next ch-2 sp (corner), ch 2, 3tr in next ch-2 sp, ch 2, [3tr, ch 2, 3tr] in next ch-2 sp (corner), [ch 2, 3tr] in each of next 3 ch-2sps, ch 2; rep from * once more, omitting last [3tr, ch 2], join with sl st in 3rd of ch-3. Break colour C.

Round 4: Join colour D to the first ch-2 sp of last round, ch 3 (counts as 1tr), 2tr in same sp, *ch 2, [3tr, ch 2, 3tr] in next ch-2 sp (corner), [ch 2, 3tr in every ch-2 sp] along the short side of the rectangle, ch 2, [3tr, ch 2, 3tr] in next ch-2 sp (corner), [ch 2, 3tr] in every ch-2 sp along the long side of the rectangle, ch 2; rep from * once more, omitting last [3tr, ch 2], join with sl st in 3rd of ch-3. Break colour D.

Round 5: As Round 4 in colour E. Break colour E.

Round 6: As Round 4 in colour A.
Fasten off and weave in ends.

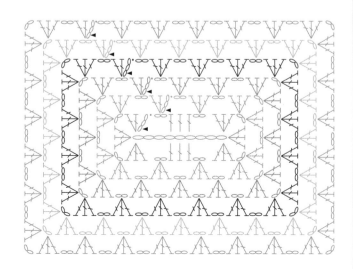

⭐ *Granny Stripes*

See page 11

A=Blackcurrant
B=Ecru
C=Persimmon

Foundation chain: Using colour A, work 38 ch.

Foundation row (RS): 1dc in 2nd ch from hook, 1dc in each ch to end, turn. (37 dc)

Row 1: Ch 3 (counts as 1tr), 1tr in same place, [skip 2dc, 3tr in next dc] to last 3dc, skip 2dc, 2tr in last dc, turn.

Row 2: Ch 3 (counts as 1tr), [3tr in next sp between tr groups] to end of row, 1tr in 3rd ch of ch-3 from previous row, turn. Break colour A.

Row 3: Join colour B. Ch 3 (counts as 1tr), 1tr in same place, [3tr in next sp between tr groups] to end of row, 2tr in 3rd ch of ch-3 from previous row, turn.

Row 4: Ch 3 (counts as 1tr), [3tr in next sp between tr groups] to end of row, 1tr in 3rd of ch-3, turn. Break colour B.

Rows 5–6: Using colour C, work as Rows 3-4.

Row 7: Using colour A, work as Row 3.

Row 8: Using colour B, work as Row 4.

Rows 9–10: Using colour C, work as Rows 3-4.

Row 11: Using colour B, work as Row 3.

Row 12: Using colour A, work as Row 4.

Rows 13–14: Using colour C, work as Rows 3-4.

Rows 15–16: Using colour B, work as Rows 3-4.

Rows 17–18: Using colour A, work as Rows 3-4.

Row 19: Ch 1, 1dc in every tr to end of row.

Fasten off and weave in ends.

Four-patch Granny

See page 10

A=Greengage
B=Ecru
C=Lavender

FIRST MOTIF

Foundation ring: Using colour A, work 6 ch and join with sl st in first ch to form a ring.

Round 1: Ch 3 (counts as 1tr), 2tr in ring, ch 3, *3tr in ring, ch 3; rep from * twice more, join with sl st in 3rd ch of first ch-3. Break colour A.

Round 2: Join colour B to any ch-3 corner sp with a sl st, ch 3, [2tr, ch 3, 3tr] in same sp to make corner, *ch 1, [3tr, ch 3, 3tr] in next ch-3 sp; rep from * twice more, ch 1, join with sl st in 3rd ch of first ch-3. Break colour B.

Round 3: Join colour C to any ch-3 corner sp with a sl st, ch 3, [2tr, ch 3, 3tr] in same sp to make corner, *ch 1, 3tr in ch-sp, ch 1, [3tr, ch 3, 3tr] in next ch-3 sp; rep from * twice more, ch 1, 3tr in ch-sp, ch 1, join with sl st in 3rd ch of first ch-3. Break colour C.

Round 4: Join colour B to any ch-3 corner sp with a sl st, ch 3, [2tr, ch 3, 3tr] in same sp to make corner, *[ch 1, 3tr in each ch-sp] along the side of the square, ch 1, [3tr, ch 3, 3tr] in next ch-3 sp; rep from * twice more, [ch 1, 3tr in each ch-sp] along the side of the square, ch 1, join with sl st in 3rd ch of first ch-3.
Fasten off.

Make one more motif as above and two motifs reversing the position of colours A and C.

SECOND MOTIF

Foundation ring: Using colour C, work 6 ch and join with sl st to form a ring.

Round 1: Ch 3 (counts as 1tr), 2tr in ring, ch 3, *3tr in ring, ch 3; rep from * twice more, join with sl st in 3rd ch of first ch-3. Break colour C.

Round 2: Join colour B to any ch-3 corner sp with a sl st, ch 3, [2tr, ch 3, 3tr] in same sp to make corner, *ch 1, [3tr, ch 3, 3tr] in next ch-3 sp; rep from * twice more, ch 1, join with sl st in 3rd ch of first ch-3. Break yarn B.

Round 3: Join colour A to any ch-3 corner sp with a sl st, ch 3, [2tr, ch 3, 3tr] in same sp to make corner, *ch1, 3tr in ch-sp, ch 1, [3tr, ch 3, 3tr] in next ch-3 sp; rep from * twice more, ch 1, 3tr in ch-sp, ch 1, join with sl st in 3rd ch of first ch-3. Break colour A.

Round 4: Join colour B to any ch-3 corner sp with a sl st, ch 3, [2tr, ch 3, 3tr] in same sp to make corner, [ch 1, 3tr in each ch-sp] along side of the square, ch 1, 3tr, in next ch-3 sp, sl st

in any ch-3 corner sp of first motif, 3tr in same ch-3 corner sp as previous cluster, [join through next ch-1 sp of first motif with sl st, 3tr in next ch-1 sp of current motif] twice, join through next ch-1 sp of first motif with sl st, 3tr, in next ch-3 sp, sl st in next ch-3 corner sp of first motif, 3tr in same ch-3 corner sp as previous cluster, *[ch 1, 3tr in each ch-sp] along side of the square**, ch 1, [3tr, ch 3, 3tr] in next ch-3 sp; rep from * once more, [ch 1, 3tr in each ch-sp] along side of the square, ch 1, join with sl st in 3rd ch of first ch-3. Fasten off.

THIRD MOTIF

Work Rounds 1-3 of first motif.

Round 4: Join colour B to any ch-3 corner sp with a sl st, ch 3, [2tr, ch 3, 3tr] in same sp to make corner, [ch 1, 3tr in each ch-sp], along side of the square, ch 1, 3tr in next ch-3 sp, sl st in bottom LH corner of ch-3 corner sp of second motif, 3tr in same ch-3

corner sp as previous cluster, [join through next ch-1 sp of second motif with a sl st, 3tr in next ch-1 sp of current motif] twice, join through next ch-1 sp of second motif with a sl st, 3tr, in next ch-3 sp, sl st in next ch-3 corner sp of second motif, 3tr in same ch-3 corner sp as previous cluster, *[ch 1, 3tr in each ch-sp] along side of the square**, ch 1, [3tr, ch 3, 3tr] in next ch-3 sp; rep from * once more, [ch1, 3tr in each ch-sp] along side of the square, ch 1, join with sl st in 3rd ch of first ch-3. Fasten off.

FOURTH MOTIF

Work Rounds 1-3 of second motif.

Round 4: Join colour B to any ch-3 corner sp with a sl st, ch 3, [2tr, ch 3, 3tr] in same sp to make corner, [ch 1, 3tr in each ch-sp] along side of the square, ch 1, 3tr in next ch-3 sp, sl st in bottom LH corner of ch-3 corner sp of first motif, 3tr in same ch-3 corner sp as previous cluster, [join through

next ch-1 sp of first motif with a sl st, 3tr in next ch-1 sp of current motif] twice, join through next ch-1 sp of first motif with a sl st, 3tr in next ch-3 sp, sl st in next ch-3 corner sp of third motif, 3tr in same ch-3 corner sp as previous cluster, [join through next ch-1 sp of third motif with a sl st, 3tr in next ch-1 sp of current motif] twice, join through next ch-1 sp of third motif with a sl st, 3tr, in next ch-3 sp, sl st in next ch-3 corner sp of third motif, 3tr in same ch-3 corner sp as previous cluster, [ch 1, 3tr in each ch-sp] along side of the square**, ch 1, [3tr, ch 3, 3tr] in next ch-3 sp, ch 1, 3tr in each ch-sp] along side of the square, ch 1, join with sl st in 3rd ch of first ch-3. Fasten off.

Border: Join colour A to any tr. Ch 1, 1dc in same place, 1dc in every tr and ch-1 sp and 3dc in each ch-3 corner sp to end of round. Join with sl st in first dc.

Fasten off and weave in ends.

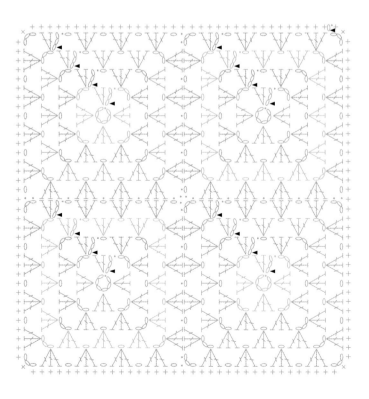

Mitered Granny

See page 11

A=Persimmon
B=Ecru
C=Lavender
D=Greengage

Foundation ring: Using colour A, work 6 ch and join with sl st in first ch to form a ring.

Round 1: Ch 3 (counts as 1tr), 2tr in ring, ch 3, *3tr in ring, ch 3; rep from * twice more, join with sl st in 3rd ch of ch-3.

Round 2: Sl st in each of next 2tr, sl st in ch-3 corner sp, ch 3, [2tr, ch 3, 3tr] in same sp to make corner, *ch 1, [3tr, ch 3, 3tr] in next ch-3 sp; rep from * twice more, ch 1, join with sl st in 3rd of ch-3. Break colour A.

Row 3: Join colour B to any ch-3 corner sp with a sl st, ch 3, 2tr in same place, *[ch 1, 3tr in each ch-sp] along the side of the square**, ch 1, [3tr, ch 3, 3tr] in next ch-3 sp; rep from * to **, ch 1, 3tr in 2nd ch of ch-3 corner sp, turn.

Row 4: Ch 3 (counts as 1tr), *[ch 1, 3tr in each ch-sp] along the side of the square**, ch 1, [3tr, ch 3, 3tr] in ch-3 corner sp; rep from * to **, ch 1, 1tr in 3rd ch of ch-3 from previous row. Break colour B.

Row 5: Using colour C, ch 3 (counts as 1tr), 2tr in same place, *[ch 1, 3tr in each ch-sp] along the side of the square**, ch 1, [3tr, ch 3, 3tr] in next ch-3 sp; rep from * to **, ch 1, 3tr in 3rd ch of ch-3 from previous row, turn.

Row 6: Ch 3 (counts as 1tr), *[ch 1, 3tr in each ch-sp] along the side of the square**, ch 1, [3tr, ch 3, 3tr] in next ch-3 sp; rep from * to **, ch 1, 1tr in 3rd ch of ch-3 from previous row. Break colour C.

Rows 7–8: Using colour B, work as rows 5-6. Break colour B.

Rows 9–10: Using colour D, work as rows 5-6. Break colour D.

Rows 11–12: Using colour B, work as rows 5-6. Break colour B.

Round 13: Using colour A, ch 3 (counts as 1tr), 2tr in same place, *[ch 1, 3tr in each ch-sp] along the side of the square**, ch 1, [3tr, ch 3, 3tr] in next ch-3 sp; rep from * twice more then from * to ** once, ch 3, join with sl st in 3rd ch of ch-3.

Round 14: Ch 2 (counts as 1htr), 1htr in each tr and ch-1 sp and [1htr, 1tr, 1htr] in every ch-3 sp to end of round, join with sl st in 2nd ch of ch-2.

Fasten off and weave in ends.

Flower Granny

See page 11

A=Persimmon
B=Blackcurrant
C=Greengage
D=Lavender
E=Ecru

SPECIAL STITCHES

Beg cl: Work two tr sts to the last "yrh, pull through," yrh once again and draw through all three loops on the hook.

Cl: Work three tr sts to the last "yrh, pull through," yrh once again and draw through all four loops on the hook.

Foundation ring: Using colour A, work 6 ch and join with sl st in first ch to form a ring.

Round 1: Ch 3 (counts as 1tr), beg cl in ring, ch 3, [cl in ring, ch 3] seven times, join with a sl st in top of beg cl. Break colour C.

Round 2: Join colour B to any ch-3 sp, ch 3 (counts as 1tr), [beg cl, ch 3, cl] in same ch-3 sp, ch 1, *[cl, ch 3, cl] in next ch-3 sp, ch 1; rep from * a further six times, join with sl st in top of beg cl. Break colour B.

Round 3: Join colour C to any ch-3 corner sp, ch 3, [2tr, ch 3, 3tr] in same sp to make corner, *ch 1, 3tr in ch-sp, ch 1, [3tr, ch 3, 3tr] in next ch-3 sp; rep from * twice more, ch 1, join with sl st in 3rd ch of ch-3.

Round 4: Sl st in each of next 2tr, sl st in ch-3 corner sp, ch 3, [2tr, ch 3, 3tr] in same sp to make corner, *[ch 1, 3tr in each ch-sp] along the side of the square, ch 1, [3tr, ch 3, 3tr] in next ch-3 sp; rep from * twice more, ch 1, join with sl st in 3rd ch of ch-3.

Round 5: Join colour D to any ch-3 corner sp with a sl st, ch 3, [2tr, ch 3, 3tr] in same sp to make corner, *[ch 1, 3tr in each ch-sp] along the side of the square, ch 1, [3tr, ch 3, 3tr] in next ch-3 sp; rep from * twice more, ch 1, join with sl st in 3rd ch of ch-3.

Round 6: As Round 4. Break colour D.

Round 7: Using colour C, work as Round 5. Break colour C.

Round 8: Using colour A, work as Round 5. Break colour A.

Round 9: Join colour B to any tr, ch 1, 1dc in same place, 1dc in every tr and ch-1 sp of previous round, working [1dc, 1htr, 1dc] in every ch-3 corner, join with sl st to first dc.

Fasten off and weave in ends.

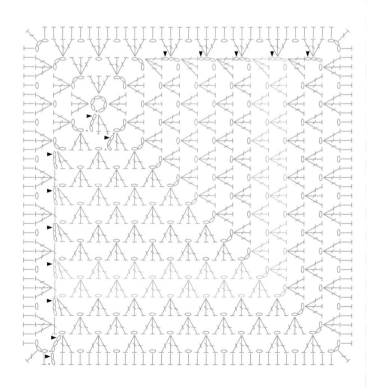

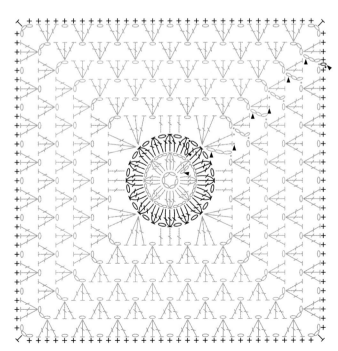

⊛ *Alternative Granny*

See page 10

A=Greengage
B=Blackcurrant
C=Ecru
D=Lavender
E=Persimmon

Foundation ring: Using colour A, work 4 ch and join with sl st in first ch to form a ring.

Round 1: Ch 3 (counts as 1tr), 2tr in ring, ch2, *3tr in ring, ch2; rep from * twice more, join with sl st in 3rd ch of ch-3. Break colour A.

Round 2: Join colour B to any ch-2 corner sp with sl st, ch 1, [1dc, ch 3, 1tr] in same sp, *ch 3, [1tr, ch 3, 1tr] in next ch-2 sp; rep from * twice more, ch 3, join with sl st to first tr. Break colour B.

Round 3: Join colour C to any corner sp with sl st, ch 3, [2tr, ch 3, 3tr] in same sp, ch 1, *3tr in next ch-3 sp, ch 1, *[3tr, ch 3, 3tr] in next ch-3 sp, ch 1, 3tr in next ch-3 sp, ch 1; rep from * twice more, join with sl st in 3rd ch of ch-3. Break colour C.

Round 4: Join colour B to any ch-3 corner sp with sl st, ch 1, [1tr, ch 3, 1tr] in same sp, ch 3, [1tr in next ch-1 sp, ch 3] twice more, *[1tr, ch 3, 1tr] in next ch-3 corner sp, ch 3, [1tr in next ch-1 sp, ch 3] twice more, join with sl st in first tr. Break colour B.

Round 5: Join colour D to any ch-3 corner sp with sl st, ch 3, [2tr, ch 3, 3tr] in same sp, ch 1, [3tr in next ch-3 sp, ch 1] 3 times, *[3tr, ch 3, 3tr] in next ch-3 sp, ch 1, [3tr in next ch-3 sp, ch 1] three times; rep from * twice more, join with sl st in 3rd ch of ch-3. Break colour D.

Round 6: Join colour B to any ch-3 corner sp with sl st, ch 1, [1tr, ch 3, 1tr] in same sp, ch 3, [1tr in next ch-1 sp, ch 3] four times, *[1tr, ch 3, 1tr] in next ch-3 corner sp, ch 3, [1tr in next ch-1 sp, ch 3] four times; rep from * twice more, join with sl st in first tr. Break colour B.

Round 7: Join colour E to any ch-3 corner sp with sl st, ch 3, [2tr, ch 3, 3tr] in same sp, ch 1, [3tr in next ch-3 sp, ch 1] five times, *[3tr, ch 3, 3tr] in next ch-3 sp, ch 1, [3tr in next ch-3 sp, ch 1] five times; rep from * twice more, join with sl st in 3rd ch of ch-3. Break colour E.

Round 8: Join colour B to any ch-3 corner sp with sl st, ch 1, [1tr, ch 3, 1tr] in same sp, ch 3, [1tr in next ch-1 sp, ch 3] six times, *[1tr, ch 3, 1tr] in next ch-3 corner sp, ch 3, [1tr in next ch-1 sp, ch 3] six times; rep from * twice more, join with sl st in first tr. Break colour B.

Round 9: Join colour C to any ch-3 corner sp with sl st, ch 3, [2tr, ch 3, 3tr] in same sp, ch 1, [3tr in next ch-3 sp, ch 1] seven times, *[3tr, ch 3, 3tr] in next ch-3 sp, ch 1, [3tr in next ch-3 sp, ch 1] seven times; rep from * twice more, join with sl st in 3rd ch of ch-3. Break colour C.

Round 10: Join colour A to any tr with sl st, ch 1, 1tr in same place, 1tr in every tr and ch-1 sp from previous round, working 3tr in every ch-3 corner sp, join with sl st in 3rd ch of ch-3.

Fasten off and weave in ends.

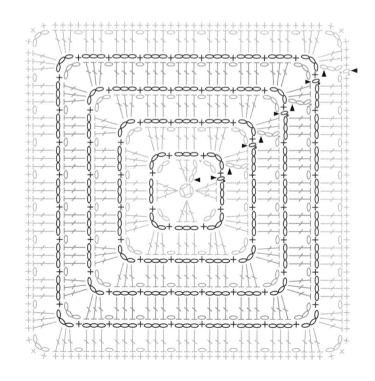

Raised Flower Granny
See page 11

A=Ecru
B=Greengage
C=Blackcurrant

Nine-patch Granny
See page 11

A=Persimmon
B=Ecru
C=Lavender
D=Greengage
E=Blackcurrant

SPECIAL STITCHES

pc (popcorn): Work 5tr in designated st, remove hook from last loop, and insert hook from front to back in top of first tr, pick up the dropped loop and pull this through the loop on the hook to complete the popcorn.

Foundation ring: Using colour A, work 6 ch and join with sl st in first ch to form a ring.

Round 1: Ch 3 (counts as 1tr), 15tr in ring, join with sl st in 3rd ch of ch-3. (16 tr)

Round 2: Ch 3 (counts as 1tr), 1tr in same place, 2tr in each tr to end of round, join with sl st in 3rd ch of ch-3. (32 tr)

Round 3: Ch 3 (counts as 1tr), 1pc in next tr, [1tr in next tr, 1pc in next tr] 15 times, join with sl st in 3rd ch of ch-3. (16 pc, 16 tr)

Round 4: Ch 1, 1dc in first tr (3rd ch of ch-3 from previous row), *ch 2, skip next pc, 1dc in next tr; rep from * a further 14 times, ch 2, join with sl st in first dc. (16 ch-2 sp)

Round 5: Sl st in next ch-2 sp, ch 3 (counts as 1tr), 2tr in ch-2 sp, *[ch 1, 3tr] in next ch-2 sp; rep from * a

further 14 times, ch 1, 1dc in 3rd ch of ch-3, (instead of last ch-1 sp). (16 ch-1 sps.) Break colour A.

Round 6: Join colour B to any ch-1 sp with sl st, ch 3, [2tr, ch 3, 3tr] in same sp to make corner, *[ch 1, 3tr in each ch-sp] three times, ch 1, [3tr, ch 3, 3tr] in next ch-1 sp; rep from * twice more, [ch 1, 3tr in each ch-sp] three times, ch 1, join with sl st in 3rd ch of ch-3. Break colour B.

Round 7: Sl st in each of next 2tr, sl st in ch-3 corner sp, ch 3, [2tr, ch 3, 3tr] in same sp to make corner, *[ch 1, 3tr] in each ch-sp along the side of the square, ch 1, [3tr, ch 3, 3tr] in next ch-3 sp; rep from * twice more, [ch 1, 3tr] in each ch-sp along the side of the square, ch 1, join with sl st in 3rd ch of ch-3. Break colour B.

Round 8: Using colour A, work as Round 7. Break colour A.

Round 9: Using colour B, work as Round 7. Break colour B.

Round 10: Join colour C to any tr, ch 1, 1dc in same place, 1dc in each tr and ch from previous round, working 3dc in every ch-3 corner sp, joining with sl st in 3rd ch of ch-3.

Fasten off and weave in ends.

Foundation ring: Using colour A, work 6 ch and join with sl st in first ch to form a ring.

Round 1: Ch 3 (counts as 1tr), 2tr in ring, ch 3, *3tr in ring, ch 3; rep from * twice more, join with sl st in 3rd ch of ch-3. Break colour A.

Round 2: Join colour B to any ch-3 corner sp with a sl st, ch 3, [2tr, ch 3, 3tr] in same sp to make corner, *ch 1, [3tr, ch 3, 3tr] in next ch-3 sp; rep from * twice more, ch 1, join with sl st in 3rd ch of ch-3. Break colour B. Work 3rd, 7th, and 9th motifs in colour A, the 2nd and 8th motifs in C, and the 4th and 6th motifs in 5th motif in D

for Round 1 and one with colour E for Round 1. Use the photograph as a guide to join as you go on Round 2 as described for Four-patch Granny.

Border

Round 1: Join D to any tr with sl st, ch 3 (counts as 1tr), 1tr in every tr and ch sp and [1tr, 1dtr, 1tr] in every ch-3 corner sp from previous round, join with sl st in 3rd ch of ch-3. Break colour D.

Round 2: Using E, work 1tr in every tr from previous round and 3tr in each corner dtr, join with sl st in 3rd ch of ch-3.

Fasten off and weave in ends.

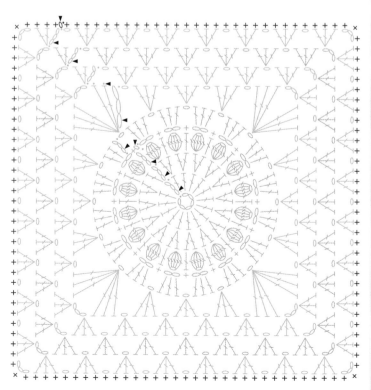

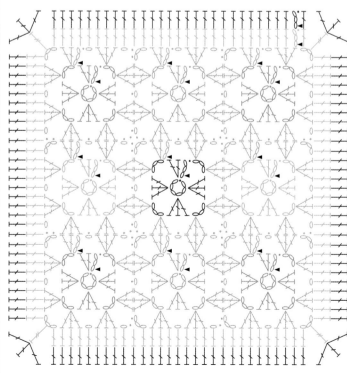

Fine Texture

See page 15

A=Persimmon
B=Toffee

Foundation chain: Using colour A, work 32 ch.
Foundation row (RS): 1dc in 2nd ch from hook, 1dc in every ch to end, turn. (31 dc)
Row 1: Ch 1, 1dc in first dc, *ch 1, skip next dc, 1dc in next dc; rep from * to end, turn.
Row 2: Ch 1, 1dc in first dc, *1tr in next ch-1 sp, 1dc in next dc; rep from * to end, turn.
Row 3: Ch 1, 1dc in first dc, *ch 1, skip next dc, 1dc in next dc; rep from * to end, turn.
Rep Rows 2 and 3 a further 11 times ending with Row 3.

Next row: Ch 1, 1dc in every st to the end of the row. Fasten off.
Border
Round 1: Join colour B to any ch along Foundation edge. 1ch, 1dc in same place, 1dc in every ch, to corner, *[1dc, 1htr, 1dc] in corner, work 22dc evenly along row-end edge, [1dc, 1htr, 1dc] in corner**, 1dc in each of next 29ch; rep from * to ** once more, 1dc in every ch to end of round, join with sl st in first dc.
Fasten off and weave in ends.

Textured Stripes

See page 12

A=Toffee
B=Persimmon
C= Bleached

Foundation chain: Using colour A, work 29 ch.
Foundation row (WS): [1dc, 1ch, 1dc] in 2nd ch from hook, *skip 1ch, [1dc, 1ch, 1dc] in next ch; rep from * to last ch, 1dc in last dc, turn.
Row 1: Ch 1, *[1dc, 1ch, 1dc] in first dc of each group of sts from previous row; rep from * to last st, 1dc in last st changing to colour B on last pull though, turn. Do not break A.
Row 2: Ch 1, *[1dc, 1ch, 1dc] in first dc of each group of sts from previous row; rep from * to last st, 1dc in last st changing to colour C on last pull though, turn. Do not break B.
Row 3: Ch 1, *[1dc, 1ch, 1dc] in first dc of each group of sts from previous row; rep from * to last st, 1dc in last st changing to colour A on last pull though, turn. Do not break C.
Rep Rows 1–3 a further 8 times then Row 1 only once more. Fasten off.
Border
Round 1: Join colour B to any ch along Foundation edge. Ch 1, 1dc in same place, 1dc in every ch, to corner, *[1dc, 1htr, 1dc] in corner, work 26dc evenly along row-end edge, [1dc, 1htr, 1dc] in corner**, 1dc in each of next 26tr; rep from * to ** once more, 1dc in every ch to end of round, join with sl st to first dc.
Fasten off and weave in ends.

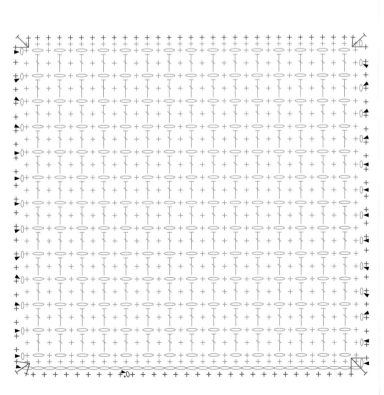

Striped Knot

See page 14

A=Bleached
B=Persimmon
C=Toffee

Foundation row: Using C, make 29ch.

Row 1: 1dc in 2nd ch from hook, 1dc in every ch to end, turn. Break colour C. (28 dc)

Row 2: Join A, ch 1, 1dc in next dc, *1tr in next dc, 1dc in next dc; rep from * to last st, 1dc in last dc, turn. Break colour A.

Row 3: Using B, ch 1, 1dc in every st to end of row, turn. Break colour B.

Row 4: Using C, ch 1, 1dc in next 2dc, *1tr in next dc, 1dc in next dc; rep from * to last 2 sts, 1dc in each of last 2dc, turn. Break colour C.

Row 5: Using A, ch 1, 1dc in every st to end of row, turn.

Keeping the stripe sequence as set,

rep Rows 2–5, a further 5 times, ending with Row 5 in colour B. Fasten off.

Border: Join colour A with sl st to any dc on Foundation row edge.

Round 1: Ch 1, 1dc in every st and row end and 3dc in each corner to end of round, join with sl st to first dc. Break colour A.

Round 2: Using B, ch 1, 1dc in every dc of previous round and, 3dc in centre st of 3dc at each corner to end of round, join with sl st to first dc. Break colour B.

Round 3: Using C, ch 1, 1dc in every dc of previous round and, 3dc in centre st of 3dc at each corner, to end of round, join with sl st to first dc.

Fasten off and weave in ends.

Lemon Peel

See page 14

A=Toffee
B=Ecru
C=Persimmon

Foundation chain: Using colour A, work 31 ch.

Foundation row (RS): 1dc in 3rd ch from hook, *1tr in next ch, 1dc in next ch; rep from * to end, turn.

Row 1: Ch 1, 1dc in first tr, 1tr in next dc, *1dc in next tr, 1tr in next dc; rep from * to end.

Rep Row 1 a further 23 times.
Fasten off.

Border

Round 1: Join colour B to any ch along Foundation edge. Ch 1, 1dc in

same place, 1dc in every ch, to corner, *[1dc, 1htr, 1dc] in corner, work 24dc evenly along row-end edge, [1dc, 1htr, 1dc] in corner**, 1dc in each of next 29 sts; rep from * to **, 1dc in every ch to end of round, changing to colour C when joining with sl st to first dc.

Round 2: Ch 1, 1dc in blo of every dc and [1dc, 1htr, 1dc] in every htr from previous round, join with sl st to first dc.

Fasten off and weave in ends.

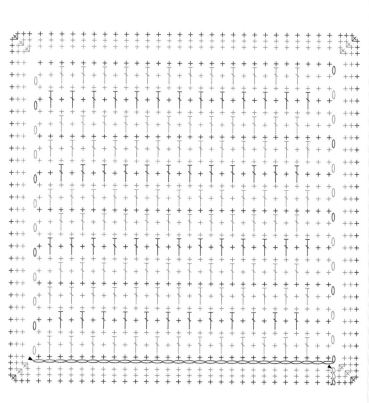

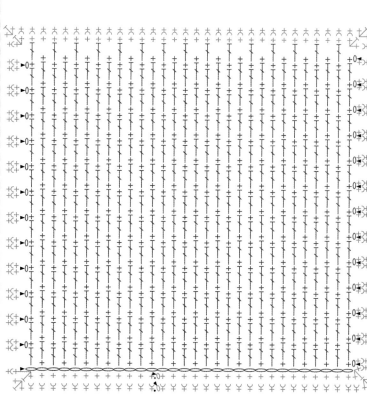

Alternating Bobbles   *See page 13*

A=Oyster
B=Nightshade
C=Persimmon

SPECIAL STITCHES

MB (Make bobble): Work four treble stitches together: Working into the same stitch, [yarn round hook, draw up a loop, yarn round hook, pull through two loops on the hook] four times, yarn round hook and pull through all five loops on hook.

Foundation chain: Using colour A, work 28ch.

Row 1 (WS): 1dc in 2nd ch from hook, 1dc in every ch to end of row, turn. (27 dc)

Rows 2–4: Ch 1, 1dc in every dc to end of row, turn.

Row 5: Ch 1, 1dc in each of next 4dc, [MB, 1dc in each of next 5dc] 3 times, MB, 1dc in each of next 4dc, turn.

Rows 6–8: As Rows 2-4.

Row 9: Ch 1, 1dc in each of next 7dc, [MB, 1dc in each of next 5dc] twice, MB, 1dc in each of next 7dc, turn.

Rep Rows 2–9 twice more, then Rows 2–8 only once more.
Fasten off.

Border

Round 1: Join colour B to any ch along Foundation edge. Ch 1, 1dc in same place, 1dc in every ch, to corner, *[1dc, 1htr, 1dc] in corner, work 25dc evenly along row-end edge, [1dc, 1htr, 1dc] in corner**, 1dc in each of next 27ch; rep from * to **, 1dc in every ch to end of round, changing to colour C when joining with sl st in first dc.

Round 2: Ch 1, 1dc in every dc and [1dc 1htr, 1dc] in every corner htr to end of round, changing to colour B when joining with sl st in first dc.

Round 3: Ch 2 (counts as 1htr), 1htr in every dc and [1htr, 1tr, 1htr] in every corner htr, to end of round, join with sl st to first dc.

Fasten off and weave in ends.

 Candy Stripe Bobbles   *See page 15*

A=Nightshade
B=Sky
C=Oyster
D=Bleached
E=Toffee

SPECIAL STITCHES

MB (Make bobble): Work four treble stitches together: Working into the same stitch, [yarn round hook, draw up a loop, yarn round hook, pull through two loops on the hook] four times, yarn round hook and pull through all five loops on hook.

Foundation chain: Using colour A, work 28ch.

Foundation row (WS): 1dc in 2nd ch from hook, 1dc in every ch to end, turn. (27 dc)

Row 1: Ch 1, 1dc in every dc to end of row, turn.

Row 2: Ch 1, 1dc in each of next 10dc, [MB, 1dc in each of next 2dc] twice, MB, 1dc in each of next 10dc, turn.

Rep last 2 rows according to the following sequence:
Using colour B, work Row 1, 3 times.
Using colour C, work Row 2, then Row 1 twice.
Using colour D, work Row 1, Row 2, Row 1.
Using colour B, work Row 1 twice and then Row 2.

Using colour C, work Row 1, 3 times.
Using colour B, work Row 2 and then Row 1 twice.
Using colour D, work Row 1, Row 2, Row 1.
Using colour C, work Row 1 twice and then Row 2.
Using colour B, work Row 1, 3 times.
Using colour A, work Row 2 and then Row 1 twice.
Fasten off.

Border

Round 1: Join colour E to any ch along Foundation edge. Ch 2 (counts as 1htr), 1htr in every ch, to corner, *[1htr, 1tr, 1htr] in corner, work 24htr evenly along row-end edge, [1htr, 1tr, 1htr] in corner**, 1htr in each of next 25dc; rep from * to **, 1dc in every ch to end of round, changing to colour A when joining with sl st in 2nd ch of ch-2.

Round 2: Ch 1, 1dc in every htr and [1dc, 1htr, 1dc] in every corner tr, to end of round, join with sl st in first dc.

Fasten off and weave in ends.

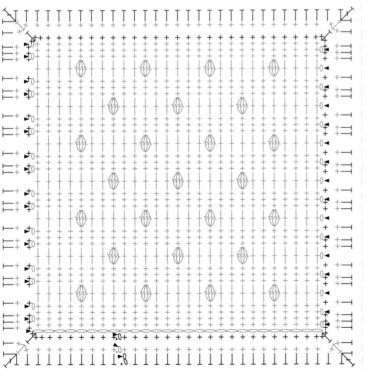

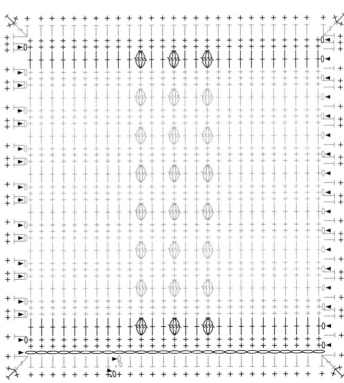

Bobble Stripes

See page 13

A=Oyster
B=Toffee
C=Persimmon
D=Bleached
E=Sky

SPECIAL STITCHES

MB (Make bobble): Work four treble stitches together: Working into the same stitch, [yarn round hook, draw up a loop, yarn round hook, pull through two loops on the hook] four times, yarn round hook and pull through all five loops on hook.

Foundation chain: Using colour A, make 28ch.

Row 1 (WS): 1dc in 2nd ch from hook, 1dc in every ch to end of row, turn. (27 dc)

Row 2: Ch 1, 1dc in every dc to end of row, turn.

Rows 3–4: As Row 2, changing to colour B when working last dc, turn.

Row 5: Ch 1, 1dc in next dc, [MB, 1dc in each of next 5dc] 4 times, MB, 1dc in next dc changing to colour A when working last pull through, turn.

Rows 6–10: As Row 2, changing to colour C when working last dc of Row 10, turn.

Row 11: As Row 5, changing to colour A when working last dc, turn.

Rows 12–16: As Row 2, changing to colour D when working last dc of Row 16, turn.

Row 17: As Row 5, changing to colour A when working last dc, turn.

Rows 18–22: As Row 2, changing to colour E when working last dc of Row 22, turn.

Row 23: As Row 5, changing to colour A when working last dc, turn.

Rows 24–28: As Row 2, changing to colour F when working last dc of Row 28, turn.

Row 29: As Row 5, changing to colour A when working last dc, turn.

Rows 30–33: As Row 2.
Fasten off.

Border

Round 1: Join colour D to any ch along Foundation edge. Ch 2 (counts as 1htr), 1htr in every ch to corner, *[1htr, 1tr, 1htr] in corner, work 27htr evenly along row-end edge, [1htr, 1tr, 1htr] in corner**, 1htr in each of next 25dc; rep from * to **, 1htr in every ch to end of round, changing to colour B when joining with sl st in 2nd ch of ch-2.

Round 2: Ch 1, 1dc in every htr and [1dc, 1htr, 1dc] in every corner tr to end of round, join with sl st in first dc.

Fasten off and weave in ends.

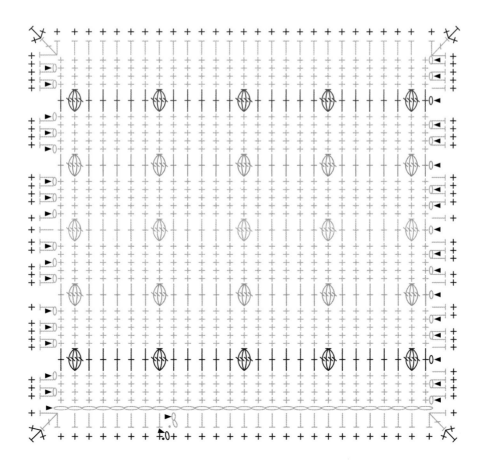

Winter Blueberry Patch
See page 13

A=Sky
B=Ecru
C=Persimmon
D=Oyster

SPECIAL STITCHES
MB (Make bobble): Work four double treble stitches together: Working into the same stitch, [(yarn round hook) twice, draw up a loop, yarn round hook, pull through two loops on the hook] four times, yarn round hook and pull through all five loops on hook.

Foundation chain: Using colour A, make 12ch.
Row 1 (RS): 1dc in 2nd ch from hook, 1dc in every ch to end of row, turn. (11 dc)
Row 2: Ch 3 (counts as 1tr), 1tr in next st, MB in next st, 1tr in next 2 sts] 3 times, turn.
Row 3: Ch 1, 1dc in every st to end of row, turn.
Rows 4–7: Rep Rows 2–3 twice more.
Commence working in the round as follows:
Round 1: Join colour B to corner st, ch 1, 1dc in same st, *[1dc in base of dc, 2dc around post of tr] 3 times, 1dc in base of dc**, 2dc in first foundation ch, 1dc in next 9 foundation ch, 2dc in last foundation ch; rep from * to ** once more, 1dc in next 10 sts, changing to colour C when joining with sl st in first dc made. Break B. (44 sts)
Round 2: Ch 1, *[1dc, 1htr, 1dc] in same st, 1dc in next 10 sts; rep from *

a further 3 times, changing to colour D when joining with sl st in first dc made. Break C. (52 sts)
Round 3: Ch 1, 1dc in same st, *[1dc, 1htr, 1dc] in htr of corner**, 1dc in each st to next htr; rep from * twice more then from * to ** once again, 1dc in each st to end of round, changing to colour B when joining with sl st in first dc made. Break D. (60 sts)
Round 4: As Round 3 in B.
Round 5: As Round 3 in D.
Round 6: As Round 3 in A.
Round 7: As Round 3 in C, changing to colour D when joining with sl st in first dc.
Round 8: Ch 3, (counts as 1tr), 1tr in every st from previous round, working 3tr in every corner htr to end of round, changing to colour B, when joining with sl st in 3rd ch of ch-3.
Round 9: Ch 3, (counts as 1tr), 1tr in every st from previous round, working 3tr into centre tr of each 3tr corner cluster to end of round, changing to colour A, when joining with sl st in 3rd ch of ch-3.
Round 10: Ch 3, (counts as 1tr), 1tr in every st from previous round, working 3tr in centre tr of each 3tr corner cluster to end of round, join with sl st in 3rd ch of ch-3.
Fasten off and weave in ends.

Bobbles on the Diagonal
See page 14

A=Oyster
B=Nightshade
C=Persimmon
D=Sky

SPECIAL STITCHES
MB (Make bobble): Work five double treble sts tog: [(yrh) twice, draw up a loop in next st, (yrh, pull through two loops on hook) twice] 5 times, yrh and pull through all six loops on hook.
dc3tog: Work 3dc over 3 sts to last yrh, yrh and pull through all 4 loops on hook. (2 sts decreased)

Foundation row: Using colour A, make 2ch.
Row 1: 3dc in 2nd ch from hook, turn. (3 sts)
Row 2: Ch 1, 2dc in first st, 1dc in each st to last st, 2dc in last st, turn. (5 sts)
Rows 3-4: As Row 2. (9 sts)
Row 5: Ch 1, 1dc in every dc, turn.
Rows 6-8: As Row 2. (15 sts)
Row 9: As Row 2, change to colour B in last dc of row, turn.
Row 10: Ch 1, 2dc in first st, [MB in each of next 3 sts] 3 times, 2dc in last dc, turn. Break colour B. (17 sts)
Rows 11: Join colour A and rep Row 2. (19 sts)
Row 12: As Row 2. (21 sts)
Row 13: As Row 5.
Rows 14-15: As Row 2. Fasten off colour A. (25 sts)
Row 16: Join colour C, ch 1, 2dc in first st, 1dc in next st, [MB in each of next 3 sts] 5 times, MB, 1dc in next st, 2dc in last dc, turn. (27 sts)
Row 17: As Row 2. (29 sts)
Row 18: Ch 1, skip 1 st, 1dc in each of next 3 sts, [MB, 1dc in each of next 3 sts] 5 times, MB, 1dc in each of next 2 sts, skip 1 st, 1dc in last st, turn. Fasten off colour C. (27 sts)
Row 19: Join colour A, ch 1, skip 1 st,

1dc in each st to last 2 sts, skip 1 st, 1dc in last st, turn. (25 sts)
Row 20: As Row 19. (23 sts)
Row 21: As Row 5. (23 sts)
Rows 22-24: As Row 19. (17 sts)
Row 25: As Row 5. Fasten off colour A (17 sts)
Row 26: Join colour D, ch 1, skip 1 st, 1dc in next st, [MB, 1dc in each of next 3 sts] 3 times, MB, 1dc in last dc, turn. Fasten off colour D. (15 sts)
Rows 27: Join colour A and rep Row 19. (13 sts)
Row 28: As Row 19. (11 sts)
Row 29: As Row 5. (11 sts)
Rows 30-33: As Row 19. (3 sts)
Row 34: Dc3tog. (1 st)
Fasten off.
Border
Round 1: Join colour C to any ch along in any row-end or corner. Ch 1, 1dc in same place, 1dc in every row-end to corner, *[1dc, 1htr, 1dc] in corner, work 17dc evenly along row-end edge, [1dc, 1htr, 1dc] in corner**, 1dc in each of next 17 row-ends; rep from * to **, 1dc in every ch to end of round, changing to colour A when joining with sl st in first dc.
Round 2: Ch 1, 1dc in every dc and [1dc 1htr, 1dc] in every corner htr to end of round, changing to colour B when joining with sl st in first dc.
Round 3: Ch 1, 1dc in every dc and [1dc 1htr, 1dc] in every corner htr to end of round, changing to colour D when joining with sl st in first dc.
Round 4: Ch 2 (counts as 1htr), 1htr in every dc and [1htr 1tr, 1htr] in every corner htr, to end of round, join with sl st to first dc.

Fasten off and weave in ends.

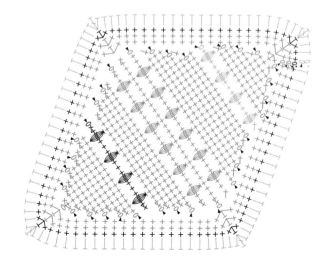

Celtic Cable

See page 12

A=Persimmon
B=Oyster

SPECIAL STITCHES

FPtr (Front Post treble): Yrh, insert hook from front to back around post of designated st, yrh and pull up a loop, (yrh and pull through 2 loops on hook) twice. Skip the dc behind the FPtr.

Foundation chain: Using colour A, make 26 ch.

Row 1: 1dc in 2nd ch from hook, 1dc in every ch to end of row, turn. (25 sts)

Row 2 and all WS rows: Ch 1 (does not count as st), 1dc in every dc to end of row, turn.

Row 3: Ch 1, 1dc in each of first 7 sts, work FPtr around dc one row below next dc, [1dc in next dc, work FPtr around dc one row below next dc] 5 times, 1dc in each of last 7dc, turn.

Row 5: Ch 1, 1dc in each of first 8 sts, work FPtr around next FPtr, 1dc in next dc, work FPtr around next FPtr, skip next FPtr, work FPtr around next FPtr, 1dc in next dc, working behind FPtr just made, work FPtr around the skipped FPtr, work FPtr around next FPtr, 1dc in next dc, work FPtr around next FPtr, 1dc in each of last 8 dc, turn.

Row 7: Ch 1, 1dc in each of first 9 sts, work FPtr around next FPtr, skip next FPtr, work FPtr around next FPtr, working in front of FPtr just made, work FPtr around the skipped FPtr, 1dc in next dc, skip next FPtr, work FPtr around next FPtr, working in front of FPtr just made, work FPtr around the skipped FPtr, work FPtr around next FPtr, 1dc in each of last 9 dc, turn.

Row 9: Ch 1, 1dc in each of next 9dc, *skip next FPtr, work FPtr around next FPtr, working behind FPtr just made, work FPtr around the skipped FPtr; rep from * twice more, 1dc in each of last 9 dc, turn.

Row 11: Ch 1, 1dc in each of next 8dc, work FPtr around next FPtr, 1dc in next dc, *skip next FPtr, work FPtr around next FPtr, working in front of FPtr just made, work FPtr around the skipped FPtr, 1dc in next dc; rep from * once more, work FPtr around next FPtr, 1dc in each of last 8 dc, turn.

Row 13: Ch 1, 1dc in each of next 7dc, [work FPtr around next FPtr, 1dc in next dc] twice, skip next FPtr, work FPtr around next FPtr, 1dc in next dc, working behind FPtr just made, work FPtr around the skipped FPtr, [1dc in next dc, work FPtr around next FPtr] twice, 1dc in each of last 7dc, turn.

Rows 15, 17, 19: Ch 1, 1dc in each of first 7dc, work FPtr around next FPtr, [1dc in next dc, 1FPtr around next FPtr] 5 times, 1dc in each of last 7dc, turn.

Row 20: Ch 1, 1dc in every dc to end of row, turn.

Rep Rows 5–15.

Next row: Ch 1, 1dc in every dc to end of row. Do not turn.

Side edges

First edge

Row 1: Working down the first set of row-ends, ch 2 (counts as 1htr), work 23htr evenly along row edge, turn. (24 htr)

Row 2: Ch 2 (counts as 1htr), 1htr in every htr to end of row. Fasten off. Join colour A to second side edge and work as for First edge.

Border

Join colour B to any ch along Foundation edge.

Round 1: Ch 1, 1dc in same place, 1dc in every ch to first row end edge, 2dc in this row end, [1dc, 1htr, 1dc] in second row end, *1dc in every htr to next row end edge, [1dc, 1htr, 1dc] in first row end edge, 2dc in next row end, *1dc in every dc to next row end edge, 2dc in next row end, [1dc, 1htr, 1dc] in second row end; rep from * to * once more, 1dc in every ch along Foundation edge to end of round, join with sl st in first dc.

Round 2: Ch 1, 1dc in every dc and 3dc in every middle dc of corner 3dc to end of round, change to colour A when joining with sl st in first dc.

Round 3: Ch 1, 1dc in every dc and 3dc in every middle dc of corner 3dc to end of round, join with sl st in first dc.

Round 4: As Round 3.

Fasten off and weave in ends.

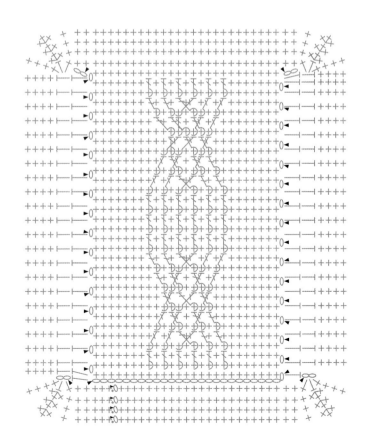

Basket Weave

See page 15

A=Sky

SPECIAL STITCHES

FRtr (Front Raised treble crochet):
Yarn round hook, insert hook from front to back around the post of designated stitch, yarn round hook, pull up a loop, [yarn round hook, pull through two loops on the hook] twice more.

BRtr (Back Raised treble crochet):
Yarn round hook, insert hook from back to front around the post of designated stitch, yarn round hook, pull up a loop, [yarn round hook, pull through two loops on the hook] twice more.

Foundation chain: Using colour A, make 37ch.
Row 1: 1tr in 4th ch from hook, 1tr in every ch to end of row, turn. (34 tr)
Row 2: Ch 2, skip first tr, *1FRtr around each of next 3tr, 1BRtr around each of next 3tr; rep from * to last 3 sts, 1FRtr in each of last 3tr, 1tr in 3rd ch of ch-3, turn.
Row 3: Ch 2, skip first tr, *1BRtr around each of next 3 FRtr, 1FRtr around each of next 3 BRtr; rep from * to last 3 sts, 1BRtr in each of last 3 FRtr, 1tr in 2nd ch of ch-2, turn.
Row 4: Ch 2, skip first tr, *1BRtr around each of next 3 BRtr, 1FRtr around each of next 3 FRtr; rep from * to last 3 sts, 1BRtr in each of last 3 BRtr, 1tr in 2nd ch of ch-2, turn.
Row 5: Ch 2, skip first tr, *1FRtr around each of next 3 BRtr, 1BRtr around each of next 3 FRtr; rep from * to last 3 sts, 1FRtr in each of last 3 BRtr, 1tr in 2nd ch of ch-2, turn.
Row 6: Ch 2, skip first tr, *1FRtr around each of next 3 FRtr, 1BRtr around each of next 3 BRtr; rep from * to last 3 sts, 1FRtr in each of last 3 FRtr, 1tr in 2nd ch of ch-2, turn.
Rep Rows 3-6, a further 4 times, then Rows 3-4 only once more.
Fasten off and weave in ends.

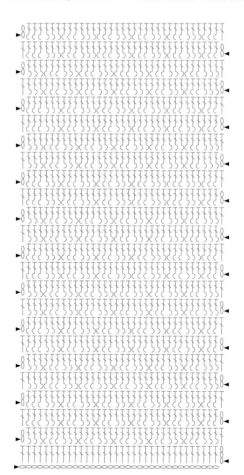

Diagonal Raised Double Treble

See page 12

A=Sky

SPECIAL STITCHES

FRtr (Front Raised treble crochet):
Yarn round hook, insert hook from front to back around the post of designated stitch, yarn round hook, pull up a loop, [yarn round hook, pull through two loops on the hook] twice more.

BRtr (Back Raised treble crochet):
Yarn round hook, insert hook from back to front around the post of designated stitch, yarn round hook, pull up a loop, [yarn round hook, pull through two loops on the hook] twice more.

Foundation chain: Using colour A, make 40ch.
Row 1: 1tr in 4th ch from hook, 1tr in every ch to end of row, turn.
Row 2: Ch 2, skip first tr, *1FRtr around each of next 2tr, 1BRtr around each of next 2tr; rep from * to end of row, 1tr in 3rd ch of ch-3, turn.
Row 3: Ch 2, skip first tr, *1FRtr around first BRtr, *1BRtr around each of next 2 sts, 1FRtr around each of next 2 sts; rep from * to last 3 sts, 1BRtr around each of next 2 sts, 1FRtr around last st, 1tr in 2nd ch of ch-2, turn.
Row 4: Ch 2, skip first tr, *1BRtr around each of next 2 sts, 1FRtr around each of next 2 sts; rep from * to end of row, 1tr in 2nd ch of ch-2, turn.
Row 5: Ch 2, skip first tr, 1BRtr around first FRtr, *1FRtr around each of next 2 sts, 1BRtr around each of next 2 sts; rep from * to last 3 sts, 1FRtr around each of next 2 sts, 1BRtr in last BRtr, 1tr in 2nd ch of ch-2, turn.
Row 6: As Row 2 to end of row, 1tr in 2nd ch of ch-2, turn.
Rep Rows 3-6 a further 4 times.
Fasten off and weave in ends.

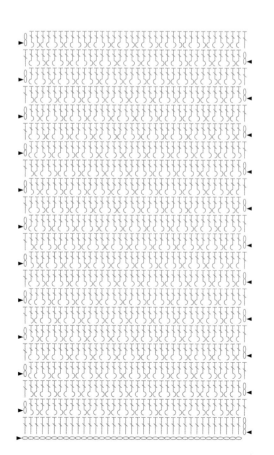

⊛⊛ *Pineapple Cluster*

See page 13

A=Persimmon

SPECIAL STITCHES
PS (Pineapple stitch): [Yarn round hook, insert hook in designated stitch or space, draw a loop through] 4 times in same place, yarn round hook, draw loop through first 8 loops on hook, yarn round hook, draw through two remaining loops.

Foundation chain: Using colour A, work 34ch.
Row 1: 1PS in 4th ch from hook, ch 1, *miss 1ch, 1PS in next ch, ch 1; rep from * to last 2 ch, miss 1 ch, 1tr in last ch, turn.
Row 2: *Miss 1ch, 1PS in next ch, ch1; rep from * to last 2ch, miss 1ch, 1dtr in last ch, turn.
Row 3: Ch 3, miss first tr, 1PS in first ch-sp, *ch 1, miss 1 PS, 1PS in next ch-sp; rep from * to last PS, ch 1, miss last PS, 1dtr in the 3rd ch of ch-3, turn.
Rep Row 3 a further 13 times.
Fasten off and weave in ends.

⊛⊛ *Honeycomb*

See page 14

A=Persimmon

Foundation ring: Using colour A, make 26ch.
Row 1: 1tr into 2nd ch from hook, 1tr into every ch to end, turn.
Row 2: Ch 1, 1tr in each of first 2tr,*tr5tog into next tr, 1tr in each of next 2tr; rep from * to last tr, tr5tog into last tr, turn.
Row 3: Ch 1, * 1tr into top of the first cl, 1tr in each of next 2tr; repeat from * to end of row, turn.
Row 4: Ch 1, tr5tog into next tr, *1tr in each of next 2tr, tr5tog into next tr; repeat from * to last 2 ch, 1tr into each of last 2tr, turn
Row 5: Ch 1, 1tr in each of first 2tr * 1tr into top of the first cl, 1tr in each of next 2tr; repeat from * to last cl, 1tr into top of the last cl, turn.
Rep rows 2–5, 7 times more.
Fasten off and weave in ends.

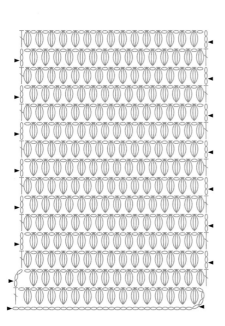

Tricolour Trinity

See page 13

A=Nightshade
B=Toffee
C=Oyster

SPECIAL STITCHES
Cl (Cluster): Work three double crochet stitches together: Insert hook and draw up a loop in each of the 3 designated sts, yarn round hook and draw through all 4 loops on hook.

Foundation chain: Using colour A, work 30ch.

Row 1: 1dc in 2nd ch from hook, dc3tog inserting hook in same ch as first dc and then in next 2ch, *ch 1, dc3tog inserting hook in same ch as 3rd leg of previous cluster and then in next 2ch; rep from * to last ch, changing to colour B when working 1dc in same ch as 3rd leg of previous cluster, turn.

Row 2: Ch 1, 1dc in first st, dc3tog inserting hook in same place as first dc, then in top of next cl and then in next ch-sp, *ch 1, dc3tog inserting hook in same place as 3rd leg of previous cl, then in top of next cl and then in next ch-sp; rep from * to end working 3rd leg of last cluster in last dc, changing to colour C when working 1dc in same place, turn.

Row 3: Rep Row 2 changing to next colour at end of row as given in the sequence below.
Continue to rep Row 2 using the following colour stripe sequence: [A, B, C] 6 times.
Fasten off.

Border
Round 1: Join colour B to any ch along Foundation edge. Ch 1, 1dc in same place, 1dc in every ch to corner, *[1dc, 1htr, 1dc] in corner, work 20dc evenly along row-end edge, [1dc, 1htr, 1dc] in corner**, 1dc in each of next 25cl and ch-sp; rep from * to **, 1dc in every ch to end of round, changing to colour C when joining with sl st in first dc. (98dc, 4htr)

Round 2: Ch 2 (counts as 1htr), 1htr in every dc and [1htr, 1tr, 1htr] in every corner htr to end of round, changing to colour A when joining with sl st in 2nd ch of ch-2.

Round 3: Ch 3 (counts as 1tr), 1tr in every htr and 3tr in every corner tr to end of round, join with sl st in 3rd ch of ch-3.
Fasten off and weave in ends.

Two-colour Raised Ripple

See page 14

A=Toffee
B=Oyster

SPECIAL STITCHES
FRtr (Front Raised treble crochet):
Yarn round hook, insert hook from front to back around the post of designated stitch, yarn round hook, pull up a loop, [yarn round hook, pull through two loops on the hook] twice more.

BRtr (Back Raised treble crochet):
Yarn round hook, insert hook from back to front around the post of designated stitch, yarn round hook, pull up a loop, [yarn round hook, pull through two loops on the hook] twice more.

Foundation chain: Using colour A, work 31ch.

Row 1: 1tr in 4th ch from hook, 1tr in every ch to the end of the row, turn.
Row 2: Ch 1, skip first st, 1dc in every tr to end of row, 1dc in 3rd ch of ch-3, turn.
Row 3: Ch 3, skip first dc, *skip next dc and work 1FRtr around tr in row below skipped dc, 1tr in next dc; rep from * to end of row, changing to colour B when working 1tr in ch-1, turn.
Row 4: As Row 2.
Row 5: Ch 3, skip first dc, *1tr in next dc, 1 FRtr around the tr in the row below the skipped dc; rep from * to last tr, change to colour A when working 1 FRtr around the tr in the row below ch-1, turn.
Rep Rows 2-5 a further 5 times.
Fasten off.

Row-end edge: With RS of work facing, join yarn A to top LH corner of block. Ch 1, 1tr in same place, work 32tr evenly along edge. Fasten off. Rep for other edge, joining yarn at bottom RH corner and working 31tr evenly along edge. Do not break yarn.

Top edge: 3tr in corner, 1tr in every ch along last row of block, 2tr in corner, join with sl st to first tr.
Fasten off.

Fasten off and weave in ends.

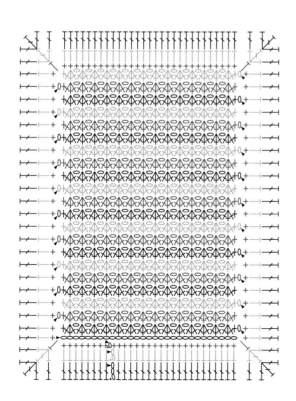

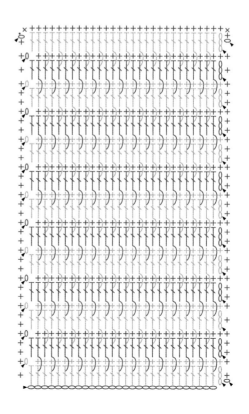

Interwoven Block

See page 15

A=Nightshade
B=Toffee
C=Oyster

SPECIAL STITCHES

FRdtr (Front Raised double treble crochet): Yarn round hook, insert hook from front to back around the post of designated stitch, yarn round hook, pull up a loop, [yarn round hook, pull through two loops on the hook] twice more.

Foundation chain: Using colour A, work 31ch.

Row 1 (RS): 1tr in 4th ch from hook, 1tr in every ch to end of row, changing to colour B at end of last tr, turn. (28 tr)

Row 2: Ch 3 (counts as 1tr), skip first st, *1FRdtr around next st, 1tr in next st; rep from * changing to colour C when working last tr in 3rd ch of

ch-3, turn.

Row 3: Rep Row 2 changing to next colour at end of row as given in the sequence below.
Continue to rep Row 2 using the following colour stripe sequence: [A, B, C] 4 times.
Fasten off.

Border

Round 1: Join colour B to any ch along Foundation edge. Ch1, 1dc in same place, 1dc in every ch, to corner, *[1dc, 1htr, 1dc] in corner, work 26dc evenly along row-end edge, [1dc, 1htr, 1dc] in corner**, 1dc in each of next 27 sts; rep from * to **, 1dc in every ch to end of round, join with sl st in first dc.

Fasten off and weave in ends.

Aligned Railing Block

See page 13

A=Persimmon
B=Nightshade
C=Toffee
D=Oyster
Additional Notions: Stitch holder or safety pin

SPECIAL STITCHES

FRdtr (Front Raised double treble crochet): Yarn round hook, insert hook from front to back around the post of designated stitch, yarn round hook, pull up a loop, [yarn round hook, pull through two loops on the hook] twice more.

Foundation chain: Using colour A, work 31ch.

Row 1: 1tr in 4th ch from hook, 1tr in every ch to end of row, turn. (28 ch)

Row 2: Ch 3 (counts as 1tr), skip next st, 1tr in every tr to end of row, 1tr in 3rd ch of ch-3.

Row 3: Place working loop on a stitch holder and draw a loop of colour B through top of last completed background stitch, ch 1, work 1FRdtr around stem of 2nd st in second to last row, *ch 1, skip 1 st, 1FRtr around

stem of next st in second to last row; rep from * ending with sl st in 3rd ch of ch-3 at beg of last background row. Fasten off, but do not turn the work.

Row 4: Replace hook in working loop of colour A, ch 3, work 1tr inserting hook through top of raised st and background st at the same time, *work 1tr inserting hook under contrast colour ch and top of next st in colour A at the same time, work 1tr inserting hook under top of next raised st and next st in colour A as before; rep from * to end, 1tr in 3rd ch of ch-3, turn.

Row 5: Ch 3 (counts as 1tr), skip next st, 1tr in every tr to end of row, 1tr in 3rd ch of ch-3.
Rep Rows 3-5 a further 7 times using the following colour stripe sequence for Row 3: [C, D, B] twice.

Fasten off and weave in ends.

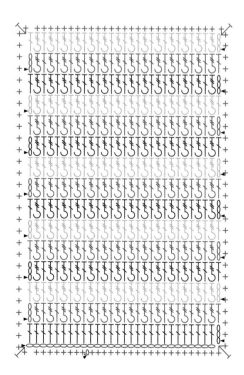

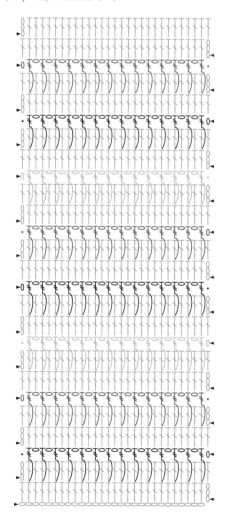

Classic Cable

See page 15

A=Oyster

SPECIAL STITCHES

FPdtr (front post double treble):
[Yrh] twice, insert hook from front to back around the post of designated stitch, yrh, pull up a loop, then [yrh, pull through two loops on the hook] three times.

BPdtr (Back post double treble):
[Yrh] twice, insert hook from back to front around the post of designated stitch, yrh, pull up a loop, then [yrh, pull through two loops on the hook] three times.

Foundation chain: Using colour A, make 30ch.

Row 1: 1dc in 2nd ch from hook, 1dc in every ch to end of row, turn.

Row 2: Ch 2, 1htr in every dc to end of row, turn.

Row 3: Ch 2, 1htr in each of next 3htr, *[1FPdtr in next st, 1htr in next st] twice, 1FPdtr in each of next 4 sts, 1htr in next st; rep from * once, [1FPdtr in next st, 1htr in next st] twice, 1htr in each of last 3htr, turn.

Row 4: Ch 2, 1htr in each of next 3htr, *[1BPdtr in next st, 1htr in next st] twice, 1BPdtr in each of next 4 sts, 1htr in next st; rep from * once, 1BPdtr in next st, 1htr in next st] twice, 1htr in each of last 3htr, turn.

Row 5: Ch 2, 1htr in each of next 3htr, [1FPdtr in next st, 1htr in next st] twice, *skip next 2 sts, 1FPdtr in each of next 2 sts, working in front of the 2 sts just worked, 1FPdtr in each of the 2 sts just skipped, 1htr in next st; rep from * once, 1FPdtr in next st, 1htr in next st] twice, 1htr in each of last 3htr, turn.

Row 6: As Row 4.
Row 7: As Row 3.
Row 8: As Row 4.
Row 9: As Row 5.
Row 10: As Row 4.
Row 11: As Row 3.
Row 12: As Row 4.
Row 13: As Row 5.
Row 14: As Row 4.
Row 15: As Row 3.
Row 16: As Row 4.
Row 17: As Row 5.
Row 18: Ch 2, 1htr in every st to end of row, turn.

Row 19: Ch 1, 1dc in every htr to end of row, do not turn or fasten off.

**Row-end edge 1: Ch 2, 1htr in every row end edge to end of row. (18 htr)

Row-end edge 2: Ch 2, 1htr in every htr to end of row. Fasten off.**
Join yarn with a sl st to bottom right hand corner.
Repeat from ** to **.

Border
Round 1: Ch 1, 1dc in every st around working [1dc, ch 1, 1dc] in each corner to end of round, join with sl st in first dc.
Fasten off and weave in ends.

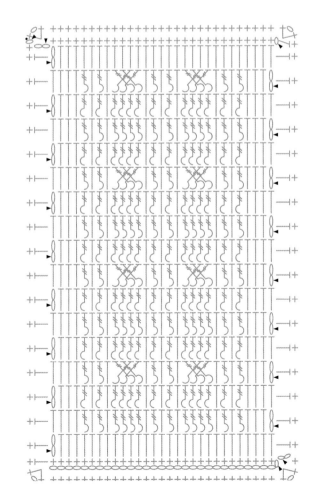

 **Big Bloom**

See page 12

A=Persimmon
B=Bleached
C=Oyster
D=Blackcurrant

Foundation ring: Using A, make a Magic Ring (see page 153).

Round 1: Ch 2 (counts as 1htr), 11htr in the ring, join with sl st in flo of 2nd ch of ch-2. (12 htr)

Round 2: *Ch 7, sl st in flo of next htr; rep from * a further 10 times, ch 7, join with sl st in blo of 2nd ch of ch-2 from Round 1. (12 ch sp)

Round 3: Ch 2 (counts as 1htr), 1htr in blo in same place, 2htr in blo of every st to end of round, join with sl st in blo of 2nd ch of ch-2 from Round 2. Break colour A. (24 sts)

Round 4: Using B, *ch 7, sl st in flo of next htr; rep from * a further 22 times, ch 7, join with sl st in blo of 2nd ch of ch-2 from Round 3. (24 ch sps)

Round 5: Ch 2 (counts as 1htr), *2htr in blo of next st, 1htr in blo of next st;

rep from * a further 11 times, 2htr in blo of next st, join with sl st through back loop of 2nd ch of ch-2 from Round 4. Break colour B. (36 sts)

Round 6: Using C, *ch 7, sl st in flo of next htr; rep from * a further 34 times, ch 7, join with sl st in blo of 2nd ch of ch-2 from Round 5. Break colour C. (36 ch sp)

Round 7: Join D in blo, ch 1 and 1dc in blo of same space *1dc in blo of next st, 1htr in blo of next st, 1tr in blo of next 2 sts, [1tr, 1dtr, 1tr] in next st, 1tr in blo of next 2 sts, 1htr in blo of next st**, 1dc in blo of next st; rep from * twice more, then from * to ** once more, join with sl st to first dc. (44 sts)

Round 8: Ch 3 (counts as 1tr), *1tr in each st across to corner dtr, [1tr, 1dtr,

1tr] in dtr; rep from * a further 3 times, 1tr in each st to end of round, join with sl st to 3rd ch of ch-3. (52 sts)

Round 9: Work as Round 8. Break colour D. (60 sts)

Round 10: Using C, ch 1, 1dc in same place, *1dc in each st across to corner dtr, [1dc, 1htr, 1dc] in dtr; rep from * a further 3 times, 1dc in each st to end of round, join with sl st to first dc. Break colour C. (68 sts)

Round 11: Using A, ch 1, 1dc in same place, *1dc in each st across to corner htr, [1dc, 1htr, 1dc] in htr; rep from * a further 3 times, 1dc in each st to end of round, join with sl st to first dc. Break colour A. (76 sts)

Round 12: Using C, work as Round 11. Break colour C. (84 sts)

Round 13: Using D, ch 3 (counts as

1tr), *1tr in each st across to corner htr, [1tr, 1dtr, 1tr] in htr; rep from * a further 3 times, 1tr in each st to end of round, join with sl st to 3rd ch of ch-3. Break colour D. (92 sts)

Round 14: Using C, ch 3 (counts as 1tr), *1tr in each st across to corner htr, [1tr, 1dtr, 1tr] in dtr; rep from * a further 3 times, 1tr in each st to end of round, join with sl st to 3rd ch of ch-3. Break colour C. (100 sts)

Round 15: Using D, ch 2 (counts as 1htr), *1htr in each st across to corner dtr, [1htr, 1tr, 1htr] in dtr; rep from * a further 3 times, 1htr in each st to end of round, join with sl st to 2nd of ch-2. (108 sts).

Fasten off and weave in ends.

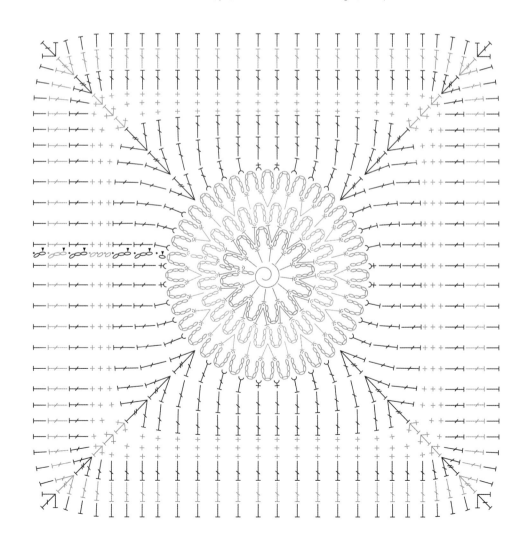

Openwork

See page 16

A=Shell
B=Bleached
C=Rose

Foundation chain: Using colour A, work 36 ch.

Row 1 (RS): 1dc in 2nd ch from hook, 1dc in every ch to end, turn. (34 dc)

Row 2: Ch 4 (counts as 1tr and 1ch), skip 1dc, 1tr in next dc, *ch 1, skip next dc, 1tr in next dc; rep from * to end, turn. (17 ch-1 sp)

Row 3: Ch 1, 2dc in every ch-1 sp to end, 2dc in ch-1 sp created by turning ch, turn. (33 dc)

Row 4: Ch 1, 1dc in every dc to end of row, turn.

Rep Rows 2-4 a further 6 times. Fasten off.

Border

Round 1: Join colour B to any dc along previous row, ch 1, 1dc in same place, 1dc in every dc and row-end, working 3dc in each corner, join with sl st to first dc. Break colour B.

Round 2: Join colour C to any dc along previous row, ch 2, 1htr in every dc to end of round, working [1htr, 1tr, 1htr] in 2nd dc of each 3dc corner group, join with sl st to 2nd of ch-2.

Fasten off and weave in ends.

Belgian Lace

See page 18

A=Lavender

SPECIAL STITCHES

Beg cl (Beginning cluster): Work 3 tr sts tog to the last "yrh, pull through," yrh once again and draw through all four loops on the hook.

Cl (cluster): Work 4 tr sts tog to the last "yrh, pull through," yrh once again and draw through all five loops on the hook.

Foundation ring: Using colour A, work 8 ch and join with sl st to form a ring.

Round 1: Ch 3 (counts as 1tr), 6tr in ring, [ch 7, 7tr in ring] 3 times, ch 4, 1tr in 3rd ch of ch-3. (4 ch-7 sp)

Round 2: Ch 10 (counts as 1tr and ch 7), skip next 3tr, *1dc in next tr, ch 7, skip next 3tr**, 7tr in next ch-7 sp, ch 7, skip next 3tr; rep from * twice more and from * to ** once again, 6tr in next ch-7 sp, join with sl st in 3rd ch of ch-10. (8 ch-7 sp)

Round 3: Sl st to centre of next ch-7 sp, beg cl in same space, *ch 3, cl in next ch-7 sp, ch 11, skip next 3tr, 1tr in next tr, ch 11**, cl in next ch-7 sp; rep from * twice more and from * to ** once again, join with sl st in 3rd ch of ch-3.

Round 4: Sl st in next ch-3 sp, beg cl in same sp, *ch 8, 7tr in each of next two 11-ch sps, ch 8**, cl in next ch-3 sp; rep from * twice more and from * to ** once again, join with sl st to top of beg cl.

Round 5: Ch 4 (counts as 1dtr), 2dtr in first cluster (half corner made), *4tr in next ch-8 sp, skip 1tr, 1tr in next 12tr, skip 1tr, 4tr in next ch-8 sp**, [3dtr, ch 4, 3dtr] in top of next cl (corner made); rep from * twice more and from * to ** once again, 3dtr in top of beg cl from previous round, ch 4, join with sl st to 4th ch of beg ch-4.

Fasten off and weave in ends.

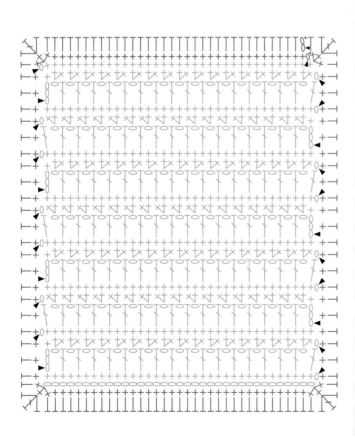

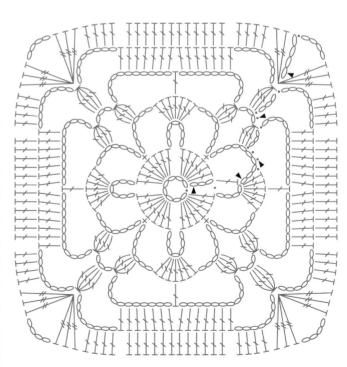

✪ Lacy Wheel

See page 16

A=Dawn Grey
B=Nightshade
C=Lavender

Foundation ring: Using colour A, work 8 ch and join with sl st in first ch to form a ring.

Round 1: Ch 6 (counts as 1tr and 3ch), [1tr in ring, ch 3] seven times, join with sl st in 3rd ch of ch-6. (8 spaced tr)

Round 2: Sl st in next ch-3 sp, ch 3 (counts as 1tr), 3tr in same sp, [ch 2, 4tr in next ch-3 sp] 7 times, ch 2, join with sl st in 3rd ch of ch-3. Break colour A.

Round 3: Join colour B to any ch-2 sp, ch 3 (counts as 1tr), 5tr in same sp, *ch 1, 6tr in next ch-2 sp, ch 3**, 6tr in next ch-2 sp; rep from * twice more and from * to ** once again, join with sl st in 3rd ch of ch-3. Break colour A.

Round 4: Join colour C to any ch-3 sp, ch 1, 1dc in same sp, *ch 3, 1dc between 3rd and 4th tr of next 6tr group, ch 3, [2tr, ch 3, 2tr] in next ch-3 sp, ch 3, 1dc between 3rd and 4th tr of next 6tr group, ch 3**, 1dc in next ch-3sp; rep from * twice and from * to ** once again, join with sl st in first dc. Break colour C.

Round 5: Join colour B to any ch-3 corner sp, ch 3 (counts as 1tr), [1tr, ch 3, 2tr] in same sp, *[ch 3, 1dc in next ch-3 sp] four times, ch 3**, [2tr, ch 3, 2tr] in next ch-3 corner sp; rep from * twice more, and from * to ** once again, join with sl st in 3rd ch of ch-3. Break colour B.

Round 6: Join colour A to any ch-3 corner sp, ch 3 (counts as 1tr), [2tr, ch 3, 3tr] in same sp, *[ch 3, 1dc in next ch-3 sp] five times, ch 3**, [3tr, ch 3, 3tr] in next ch-3 corner sp; rep from * twice more, and from * to ** once again, join with sl st in 3rd ch of ch-3.

Round 7: Sl st in next 2tr and in next ch-3 corner sp, ch 3 (counts as 1tr), [2tr, ch 3, 3tr] in same sp, *[ch 3, 1dc in next ch-3 sp] six times, ch 3**, [3tr, ch 3, 3tr] in next ch-3 corner sp; rep from * twice more, and from * to ** once again, join with sl st in 3rd ch of ch-3. Break colour A.

Round 8: Join colour C to any ch-3 corner sp, ch 3 (counts as 1tr), [2tr, ch 3, 3tr] in same sp, *[ch 3, 1dc in next ch-3 sp] seven times, ch 3**, [3tr, ch 3, 3tr] in next ch-3 corner sp; rep from * twice more, and from * to ** once again, join with sl st in 3rd ch of ch-3.

Round 9: Sl st in next 2tr and in next ch-3 corner sp, ch 2 (counts as 1htr), [1tr, 1htr] in same sp, *1htr in each of next 3tr, 3htr in every ch-3 sp to corner, [1htr, 1tr, 1htr] in next ch-3 corner sp; rep from * twice more, 1htr in each of next 3tr, 3htr in every ch-3 sp to corner, 1htr in each of next 3tr, join with sl st in 2nd ch of ch-2.
Fasten off and weave in ends.

Victorian Lace

See page 17

A=Shell

Old Vienna

See page 17

A=Rose

SPECIAL STITCHES

dtr2tog: Work two dtr sts to the last "yrh, pull through," yrh once again and draw through all three loops on the hook.

Beg cl (Beginning cluster): Work two tr sts to the last "yrh, pull through," yrh once again and draw through all three loops on the hook.

Cl (cluster): Work three tr sts to the last "yrh, pull through," yrh once again and draw through all four loops on the hook.

Foundation ring: Work 10 ch and join with sl st in first ch to form a ring.

Round 1: Ch 4 (counts as 1dtr), 1dtr in ring, ch 2, [dtr2tog in ring, ch 2] 11 times, join with sl st in 4th ch of ch-4.

Round 2: Sl st in next tr and in next ch-2 sp, ch 3 (counts as 1tr), beg cl in same sp, ch 3, [cl in next ch-2 sp, ch 2] 11 times, join with sl st to top of beg cl.

Round 3: Ch 5, (counts as 1htr and ch 3), skip next ch-3 sp, [cl, ch 2, cl, ch 4, cl, ch 2, cl] in next ch-3 sp, ch 3, *skip next ch-3 sp, 1htr in top of next cl, ch 3, skip next ch-3 sp, [cl, ch 2, cl, ch 4, cl, ch 2, cl] in next ch-3 sp, ch 3; rep from * twice, join with sl st in 2nd ch of ch-5.

Round 4: Sl st in next ch-3 sp, ch 4, (counts as 1tr and ch 1), 1tr in same sp, *ch 1, 1tr in top of next cl, ch 1, 1tr

in next ch-2 sp, ch 1, [cl, ch 2, cl, ch 4, cl, ch 2, cl] in next ch-4 sp, ch 1, 1tr in next ch-2 sp, ch 1, 1tr in top of next cl, ch 1, 1tr in next ch-3 sp, ch 1**, 1tr in next htr, ch 1, 1tr in next ch-2 sp; rep from * twice and from * to ** once again, join with sl st in 3rd ch of ch-4.

Round 5: Ch 4 (counts as 1tr and ch 1), [1tr in next tr, ch 1] three times, *1tr in top of next cl, ch 1, 1tr in next ch-2 sp, ch 1, [cl, ch 2, cl, ch 4, cl, ch 2, cl] in next ch-4 sp, ch 1, 1tr in next ch-2 sp, ch 1, 1tr in top of next cl, ch 1**, [1tr in next tr, ch 1] seven times; rep from * twice and from * to ** once again, [1tr in next tr, ch 1] three times, join with sl st in 3rd ch of ch-4.

Round 6: Ch 4 (counts as 1tr and ch 1), [1tr in next tr, ch 1] five times, *1tr in top of next cl, ch 1, 1tr in next ch-2 sp, ch 1, 5tr in next ch-4 sp, ch 1, 1tr in next ch-2 sp, ch 1, 1tr in top of next cl, ch 1**, [1tr in next tr, ch 1] 11 times; rep from * twice and from * to ** once again, [1tr in next tr, ch 1] five times, join with sl st in 3rd ch of ch-4.

Round 7: Ch 2 (counts as 1htr), 1htr in every tr and ch-1 sp, working [1htr, 1tr, 1htr] in 3rd tr of 5tr corner group, join with sl st to 2nd ch of ch-2.

Fasten off and weave in ends.

Foundation ring: Work 8 ch and join with sl st in first ch to form a ring.

Round 1: Ch 3 (counts as 1tr), 2tr in ring, ch 5, *3tr in ring, ch 5; rep from * a further 3 times, join with sl st in 3rd ch of ch-3.

Round 2: Sl st in next 2tr and in next ch-5 sp, ch 3, (counts as 1tr), [2tr, ch 5, 3tr] in same sp, *ch 3, [3tr, ch 5, 3tr] in next ch-5 sp; rep from * twice, ch 3, join with sl st in 3rd ch of ch-3.

Round 3: Ch 3, (counts as 1tr), 1tr in each of next 2tr, *[3tr, ch 5, 3tr] in next ch-5 sp, ch 3, 1tr in next ch-3 sp ch 3**, 1tr in each of next 3tr; rep from * twice more and from * to ** once again, join with sl st in 3rd ch of ch-3.

Round 4: Sl st in next 3tr, ch 3, (counts as 1tr), 1tr in each of next 2tr, *[3tr, ch 5, 3tr] in next ch-5 sp, 1tr in each of next 3tr, ch 3, [1dc in next ch-3 sp, ch 3] twice**, skip next 3tr, 1tr in each of next 3tr; rep from * twice more and from * to ** once again, join with sl st in 3rd ch of ch-3.

Round 5: Ch 3, (counts as 1tr), 1tr in each of next 2tr, ch 2, skip 3tr, *[3tr, ch 5, 3tr] in next ch-5 sp, ch2, skip next 3tr, 1tr in each of next 3tr, [2tr in

next ch-3 sp, ch 1] twice, 2tr in next ch-3 sp**, 1tr in each of next 3tr, ch 2; rep from * twice more and from * to ** once again, join with sl st in 3rd ch of ch-3.

Round 6: Sl st in next 2tr and next ch-2 sp, ch 3, (counts as 1tr), 2tr in same ch-2 sp ch 2, skip next 3tr, *[3tr, ch 5, 3tr] in next ch-5 sp, ch 2, skip next 3tr, 3tr in next ch-2 sp, ch 3, skip next 3tr, [1tr in next 2tr, ch 1] twice, 1tr in next 2tr, ch 3, skip next 3tr**, 3tr in next ch-2 sp, ch 2; rep from * twice more and from * to ** once again, join with sl st in 3rd ch of ch-3.

Round 7: Ch 3 (counts as 1tr), 1tr in next 2tr, 2tr in next ch-2 sp, *1tr in each of next 3tr, [1tr, ch 1, 1dtr, ch 1, 1tr] in ch-5 corner sp, 1tr in each of next 3tr, 2tr in next ch-2 sp, 1tr in each of next 3tr, 3tr in next ch-3 sp, [1tr in next 2tr, 1tr in next ch-1sp] twice, 1tr in next 2tr, 3tr in next ch-3 sp**, 2tr in next ch-2 sp; rep from * twice more and from * to ** once again, join with sl st in 3rd ch of ch-3.

Fasten off and weave in ends.

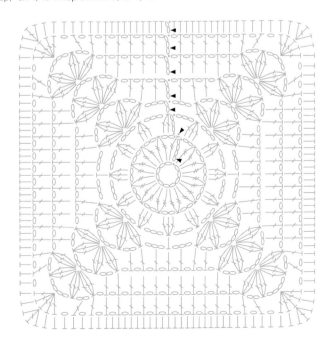

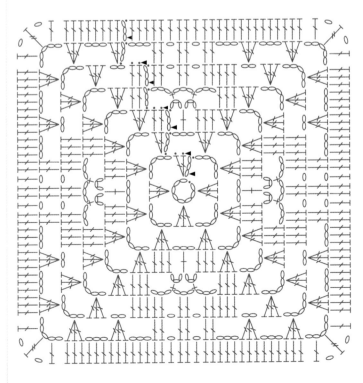

Queen Anne's Lace

See page 16

A=Dawn Grey
B=Bleached

SPECIAL STITCHES

Beg cl (Beginning cluster): Work three tr sts to the last "yrh, pull through," yrh once again and draw through all four loops on the hook.

Cl (cluster): Work four tr sts to the last "yrh, pull through," yrh once again and draw through all five loops on the hook.

Foundation ring: Using colour A, work 6 ch and join with sl st in first ch to form a ring.

Round 1: Ch 1, 12dc in ring, join with sl st in first dc.

Round 2: Ch 4 (counts as 1tr and ch 1), [1tr in next dc, ch 1] 11 times, join with sl st in 3rd ch of ch-4.

Round 3: Sl st in next ch-1 sp, ch 3 (counts as 1tr), 2tr in same sp, ch 1, [3tr in next ch-1 sp, ch 1] 11 times, join with sl st in 3rd ch of ch-3.

Round 4: Sl st in next 2tr and in next ch-1 sp, ch 3 (counts as 1tr), beg cl in same sp, *ch 2, skip 1tr, 1tr in next tr, ch 2, cl in next ch-1 sp; rep from * a further 10 times, ch 2, join with sl st to top of beg cl.

Round 5: Sl st in next ch-2 sp, ch 1, 3dc in same sp, 3dc in every ch-2 sp to end of round, join with sl st in first dc.

Round 6: Ch 3 (counts as 1tr), [1tr, ch 2, 2tr] in same place, *[ch 2, skip next 3dc group, 1dc in sp between next two 3dc groups] five times, ch 2**, [2tr, ch 2, 2tr] in sp above next cl; rep from * twice more and from * to ** once again, join with sl st in 3rd ch of ch-3.

Round 7: Ch 3 (counts as 1tr), 1tr in next tr, *[2tr, ch 2, 2tr] in next ch-2 corner sp, 1tr in each of next 2tr, [1tr, 1htr] in next ch-2 sp, 1htr in next dc, [2dc in next ch-2 sp, 1dc in next dc] three times, 2dc in next ch-2 sp, 1htr in next dc, [1htr, 1tr] in next ch-2 sp**, 1tr in each of next 2tr; rep from * twice more and from * to ** once again, join with sl st in 3rd ch of ch-3. Break colour A.

Round 8: Join colour B 2 sts to the left of any corner st, ch 1, 1dc in same place, ch 1, skip next st, *[1dc in next st, ch 1, skip next st] to 2-ch corner sp, [1dc, ch 1, 1dc] in 2-ch corner sp, ch 1, skip next st; rep from * to end of round, join with sl st to first dc. Break colour B.

Round 9: Join colour A to any ch-1 corner sp, ch 3 (counts as 1tr), [1dtr, 1tr] in same sp, *[ch 1, skip next dc, 1tr in next ch-1 sp] to corner**, [1tr, 1dtr, 1tr] in ch-1 corner sp; rep from * twice more and from * to ** once again, ch 1, join with sl st to 3rd ch of ch-3.

Fasten off and weave in ends.

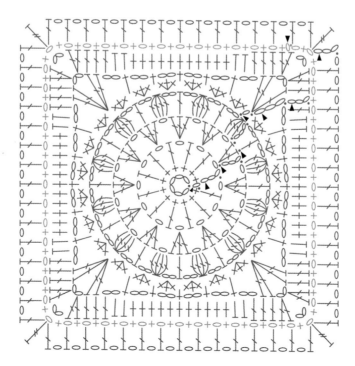

Eyelet Lace in the Round

See page 19

A=Lavender
B=Bleached
C=Dawn Grey

Foundation ring: Using colour A, work 4 ch and join with sl st in first ch to form a ring.

Round 1: Ch 3 (counts as 1tr), 2tr in ring, ch 2, [3tr in ring, ch 2] 3 times, join with sl st in 3rd of ch-3. Break colour A.

Round 2: Join colour B to any ch-2 sp, ch 3 (counts as 1tr), [2tr, ch 3, 3tr] in same sp, [(3tr, ch 3, 3tr) in next ch-2 sp] 3 times, join with sl st in 3rd ch of ch-3.

Round 3: Sl st in next 2tr and in next ch-3 sp, ch 3 (counts as 1tr), [2tr, ch 3, 3tr] in same sp, *ch 1, skip next 2tr, 1tr in each of next 2tr, ch 1, skip next 2tr**, [3tr, ch 3, 3tr] in next ch-3 sp; rep from * twice more and from * to ** once again, join with sl st in 3rd ch of ch-3.

Round 4: Sl st in next 2tr and in next ch-3 sp, ch 3 (counts as 1tr), [2tr, ch 3, 3tr] in same sp, *ch 1, skip next 2tr, 1tr in next tr, 1tr in next ch-1 sp, 1tr in each of next 2tr, 1tr in next ch-1 sp, 1tr in next tr, ch 1, skip next 2tr**, [3tr, ch 3, 3tr] in next ch-3 sp; rep from * twice more and from * to ** once again, join with sl st in 3rd ch of ch-3. Break colour B.

Round 5: Join colour C to any ch-3 corner sp, ch 3 (counts as 1tr), [2tr, ch 3, 3tr] in same sp, *ch 1, skip next 2tr, 1tr in next tr, ch 1, 1tr in next 6tr, ch 1, 1tr in next tr, ch 1, skip next 2tr**, [3tr, ch 3, 3tr] in next ch-3 sp; rep from * twice more and from * to ** once again, join with sl st in 3rd ch of ch-3.

Round 6: Sl st in next 2tr and in next ch-3 sp, ch 3 (counts as 1tr), [2tr, ch 3, 3tr] in same sp, *ch 1, skip next 2tr, 1tr in next tr, [ch 1, 1tr in next tr] twice, ch 1, skip next tr, 1tr in each of next 2tr, ch 1, skip next tr, 1tr in next tr, [ch 1, 1tr in next tr] twice, ch 1**, [3tr, ch 3, 3tr] in next ch-3 sp; rep from * twice more and from * to ** once again, join with sl st in 3rd ch of ch-3.

Round 7: Sl st in next 2tr and in next ch-3 sp, ch 3 (counts as 1tr), [2tr, ch 3, 3tr] in same sp, *1tr in each of next 3tr, [ch 1, 1tr in next tr] four times, 1tr in each of next 3tr**, [3tr, ch 3, 3tr] in next ch-3 sp; rep from * twice more and from * to ** once again, join with sl st in 3rd ch of ch-3. Break colour C.

Round 8: Join colour B to any ch-3 corner sp, ch 3 (counts as 1tr), [2tr, ch 3, 3tr] in same sp, *ch 1, skip next 2tr, 1tr in each of next 4tr, [ch 1, 1tr in next tr] 4 times, [1tr in next tr, ch 1] 4 times, 1tr in each of next 4tr, ch 1**, [3tr, ch 3, 3tr] in next ch-3 sp; rep from * twice more and from * to ** once again, join with sl st in 3rd ch of ch-3. Break colour B.

Round 9: Join colour A to any tr from previous round, ch 2, 1htr in every tr and ch-1 sp from previous round, working [1htr, 1tr, 1htr] in each ch-3 corner sp, join with a sl st in 2nd ch of ch-2.

Fasten off and weave in ends.

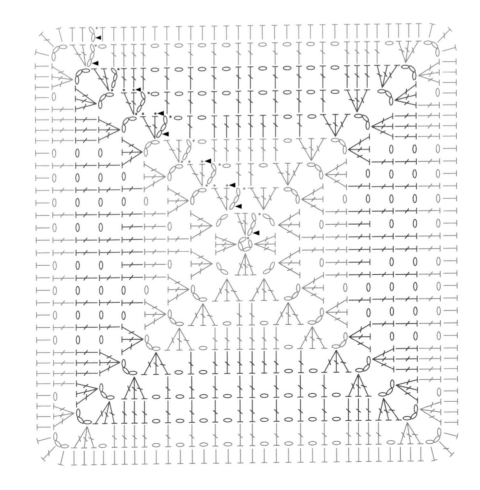

✪✪ Pineapple Lace

See page 18

A=Bleached
B=Shell

Foundation ring: Using colour A, work 4 ch and join with sl st to form a ring.

Round 1: Ch 3 (counts as 1tr), 2tr in ring, [ch 3, 3tr in ring] 3 times, ch 3, join with sl st in 3rd ch of ch-3.

Round 2: Sl st in next 2tr and in ch-3 sp, ch 3 (counts as 1tr), [2tr, ch 3, 3tr] in same sp, ch 1, *[3tr, ch 3, 3tr] in next ch-3 corner sp, ch 1; rep from * twice more, join with sl st in 3rd ch of ch-3. Fasten off.

Round 3: Sl st in next 2tr and ch-3 corner sp, ch 3 (counts as 1tr), [1tr, ch 3, 2tr] in same sp, *ch 2, [(1tr, ch 1) 5 times, 1tr in next ch-1 sp, ch 2**, [2tr,

ch 3, 2tr] in next ch-3 sp; rep from * twice more, then from * to ** again, join with sl st in 3rd ch of ch-3.

Round 4: Sl st in next 2tr and ch-3 corner sp, ch 3 (counts as 1tr), [1tr, ch 3, 2tr] in same sp, *1tr in next 2tr, ch 2, [1dc in next ch-1 sp, ch 3] 4 times, 1dc in next ch-1 sp, ch 2, 1tr in next 2tr**, [2tr, ch 3, 2tr] in ch-3 sp; rep from * twice more, then from * to ** once again, join with sl st in 3rd ch of ch-3. Break colour A.

Round 5: Join colour B to any ch-3 corner sp, ch 3 (counts as 1tr), 1tr in same sp, *1tr in next 4tr, ch 2, 1dc in next ch-1 sp, [ch 3, 1dc in next ch-1

sp] 3 times, ch 2, 1tr in next 4tr**, [2tr, ch 3, 2tr] in next ch-3 sp; rep from * twice more, then from * to ** once again, 2tr in ch-3 sp, ch 3, join with sl st in 3rd ch of ch-3.

Round 6: Ch 3 (counts as 1tr), 1tr in same sp, *1tr in next 6tr, ch 2, [1dc in next ch-3 sp, ch 3] twice, 1dc in next ch-3 sp, ch 2, 1tr in next 6tr**, [2tr, ch 3, 2tr] in next ch-3 sp; rep from * twice more, then from * to ** once again, 2tr in ch-3 sp, ch 3, join with sl st in 3rd ch of ch-3.

Round 7: Ch 3 (counts as 1tr), 1tr in same sp, 1tr in next 8tr, ch 2, 1dc in next ch-3 sp, ch 3, 1dc in next ch-3,

ch 2, 1tr in next 8tr**, [2tr, ch 3, 2tr] in next ch-3 sp; rep from * twice more, then from * to ** once again, 2tr in ch-3 sp, ch 3, join with sl st in 3rd ch of ch-3.

Round 8: Ch 2 (counts as 1htr), 1htr in same sp, *1htr in next 10tr, ch 3, 1dc in next ch-3 sp, ch 3, 1htr in next 10tr**, [2htr, ch 3, 2htr] in next ch-3 sp; rep from * twice more, then from * to ** once again, 2htr in ch-3 sp, ch 3, join with sl st in 2nd ch of ch-2.

Fasten off and weave in ends.

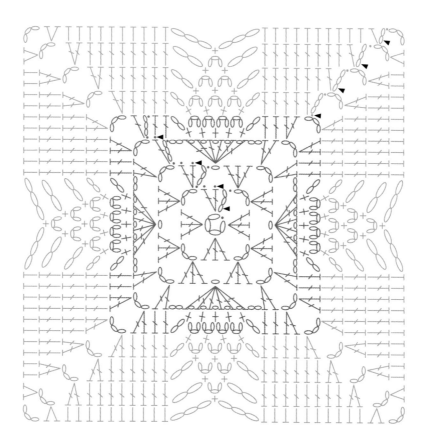

Butterfly Garden

See page 17

A=Rose
B=Bleached
C=Shell

Foundation ring: Using colour A, ch 4 and join with sl st in first ch to form a ring.

Round 1: Ch 3 (counts as 1tr), 15tr into the ring, change to colour B when joining with sl st in 3rd ch of ch-3.

Round 2: Ch 3 (counts as 1tr), [1tr, ch 2, 2tr] in same st, *1tr in each of next 3tr**, [2tr, ch 2, 2tr] in next tr; rep from * twice more and from * to ** once again, join with sl st in 3rd ch of ch-3. Break colour B.

Round 3: Join colour C in any 2ch-sp, ch 3, [1tr, ch 2, 2tr] in same sp, *ch 6, skip next 7tr**, [2tr, ch 2, 2tr] in next corner 2ch-sp; rep from * twice more and from * to ** once again, join with sl st in 3rd ch of ch-3.

Round 4: Sl st in next tr and in next 2ch-sp, ch 3, [1tr, ch 2, 2tr] in same sp, *1tr in each of next 2tr, ch 6, skip next 6ch-sp, 1tr in each of next 2tr**, [2tr, ch 2, 2tr] in next 2ch-sp; rep from * twice more and from * to ** once again, join with sl st in 3rd ch of ch-3.

Round 5: Sl st in next tr and in next 2ch-sp, ch 3, [1tr, ch 2, 2tr] in same sp, *1tr in each of next 4tr, ch 3, working over the ch-loops from Rounds 3 and 4, 1dtr in 4th tr of next skipped 7 tr in Round 2, ch 3, 1tr in each of next 4tr**, [2tr, ch 2, 2tr] in next 2ch-sp; rep from * twice more and from * to ** once again, join with sl st in 3rd ch of ch-3.

Round 6: Sl st in next tr and in next 2ch-sp, ch 3, [1dc, ch 2, 1dc] in same sp, 1dc in each of next 6tr, 3dc in next 3ch-sp, 1dc in next dtr, 3dc in next 3ch-sp, 1dc in each of next 6tr; rep from * to end of round, join with sl st in first dc. Break colour C.

Round 7: Join colour B in any 2ch-sp, ch 3, [1tr, ch 2, 2tr] in same sp, *ch 6, skip next 7dc, 1tr in each of next 7dc, ch 6, skip next 7dc**, [2tr, ch 2, 2tr] in next corner 2ch-sp; rep from * twice and from * to ** once more, join with sl st in 3rd ch of ch-3.

Round 8: Sl st in next tr and in next 2ch-sp, ch 3, [1tr, ch 2, 2tr] in same sp, *1tr in each of next 2tr, ch 6, skip next 6ch-sp, 1tr in each of next 7tr, ch 6, skip next 6ch-sp, 1tr in each of next 2tr**, [2tr, ch 2, 2tr] in next corner 2ch-sp; rep from * twice and from * to ** once more, join with sl st in 3rd ch of ch-3.

Round 9: Sl st in next tr and in next 2ch-sp, ch 3, [1tr, ch 2, 2tr] in same sp, *1tr in each of next 4tr, ch 3, working over the ch-loops from Rounds 7 and 8, 1dtr in 4th dc of next skipped 7dc in Round 6, ch 3, 1tr in each of next 7tr, ch 3, working over the ch-loops from Rounds 7 and 8, 1dtr in the 4th dc of next skipped 7dc in Round 6, ch 3, 1tr in each of next 4tr**, [2tr, ch 2, 2tr] in next corner 2ch-sp; rep from * twice more and from * to ** once again, join with sl st in 3rd ch of ch-3. Break colour B.

Round 10: Join colour A to any ch-2 corner sp, ch 1, [1dc, ch 2, 1dc] in same sp, 1dc in each of next 6tr, 3dc in next 3ch-sp, 1dc in next dtr, 3dc in next 3ch-sp, 1dc in each of next 7tr, 3dc in next 3ch-sp, 1dc in next dtr, 3dc in next 3ch-sp, 1dc in each of next 6tr; rep from * to end of round, join with sl st in first dc.

Fasten off and weave in ends.

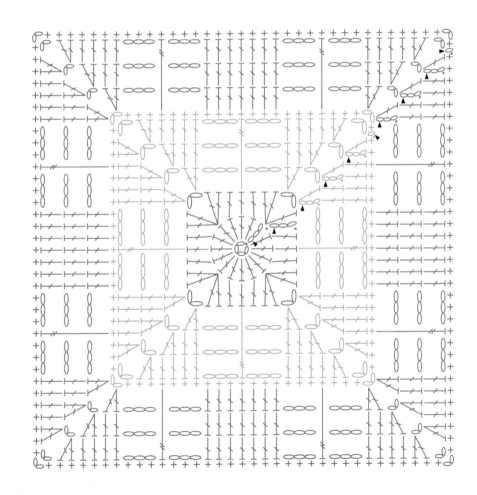

⭐⭐ Isabella

See page 16

A=Shell Pink
B=Bleached
C=Rose

SPECIAL STITCHES

Tr2tog (work two treble sts tog):
[(Yrh) twice, draw up a loop in next st, (yrh, pull through 2 loops on hook) twice] twice, yrh and draw through all 3 loops on hook.

Tr3tog (work three treble sts tog):
[(Yrh) twice, draw up a loop in next st, (yrh, pull through 2 loops on hook) twice] 3 times, yrh and draw through all 4 loops on hook.

Foundation ring: Using colour A, ch 6 and join with sl st in first ch to form a ring.

Round 1: Ch 1, 16dc into ring, change to colour B when joining with sl st to first dc.

Round 2: Ch 4 (counts as 1tr, ch 1), 1tr in same st, ch 1, skip next dc, *[1tr, ch 1, 1tr] in next dc, ch 1, skip next dc; rep from * a further 6 times, join with sl st in 3rd ch of ch-3.

Round 3: Sl st in next 1ch-sp, tr2tog in same sp, ch 5, skip next 1ch-sp, *tr3tog in next 1ch-sp, ch 5, skip next 1ch-sp; rep from * to end of round, join with sl st in top of tr2tog. Break colour B.

Round 4: Join colour A to any 5ch-sp, ch 3 [counts as 1tr], 7tr in same ch-5 sp, 8tr in each ch-5 sp around, change to colour B when joining with sl st in 3rd ch of ch-3.

Round 5: Ch 4 [counts as 1tr and ch 1], skip next tr, [1tr in next tr, ch 1, skip next st] around, join with sl st in 3rd ch of ch-4. (32 tr)

Round 6: Join colour C to any 1ch-sp, ch 3, [1tr, ch 1, 2tr] in same 1ch-sp, *ch 1, skip next 1ch-sp**, [2tr, ch 1, 2tr] in next 1ch-sp; rep from * a further 14 times; rep from * to ** once more, join with sl st in 3rd ch of ch-3.

Round 7: Sl st into next tr and next 1ch-sp, ch 3, [2tr, ch 1, 3tr] in same 1ch-sp, *ch 1, skip next 1ch-sp **, [3tr, ch 1, 3tr] in next 1ch-sp (shell made); rep from * a further 14 times; rep from * to ** once more, join with sl st in 3rd ch ch-3. Break colour C.

Round 8: Join colour A to 1ch-sp at centre of any corner shell, ch 3 (counts as 1tr), [2tr, ch 3, 3tr] in same sp, (corner made), skip next ch-1 sp, *[ch 3, 1dc in ch-1 sp, ch 3, 1htr in next ch-1 sp] 3 times, ch 3**, [3tr, ch 3, 3tr] in next 1ch-sp of next shell; rep from * twice more and from * to ** once again, join with sl st in 3rd ch of ch-3.

Round 9: Ch 1, 1dc in each of next 3tr, [2dc, ch 3, 2dc] in next ch-3 sp, 1dc in each of next 3dc, 3dc in each of next seven 3ch-sps; rep from * to end of round, join with sl st to first dc.
Fasten off and weave in ends.

⭐⭐ Filet Flower Square

See page 17

A=Shell
B=Bleached
C=Greengage

Foundation chain: Using colour A, work 6 ch and join with sl st to form a ring.

Round 1: Ch 1, 12dc in the ring, join with sl st to first dc. (12 dc)

Round 2: Ch 3 (counts as 1tr), 4tr in same place, [ch 3, skip 2dc, 5tr in next dc] 3 times, ch 3, join with sl st in 3rd ch of ch-3.

Round 3: Ch 3 (counts as 1tr), 1tr in next tr, 5tr in next tr, 1tr in each of next 2tr, *ch 3, skip 3ch, 1tr in each of next 2tr, 5tr in next tr, 1tr in next 2tr; rep from * twice more, ch 3, skip 3ch, join with sl st in 3rd ch of ch-3.

Round 4: Ch 3 (counts as 1tr), 1tr in next 3tr, 5tr in next tr, 1tr in each of next 4tr, *ch 3, skip 3ch, 1tr in each of next 4tr, 5tr in next tr, 1tr in next 4tr; rep from * twice more, ch 3, skip 3ch, join with sl st in 3rd ch of ch-3 and change to colour B.

Round 5: Ch 3, 1tr in next 4tr, *tr2tog over next 2tr, ch 5, tr2tog over last tr and next tr, 1tr in each of next 3tr, tr2tog over next 2tr, ch 5, skip 3ch**, tr2tog over next 2tr, 1tr in each of next 3tr; rep from * twice more, then * to ** once, skip 3ch, join with sl st to first tr.

Round 6: Ch 3, 1tr in next 2tr, *tr2tog over next 2 sts, cn 3, skip 2ch, 1tr in next ch, ch 3, skip 1ch, 1tr in next ch, ch 3, skip 2ch, 1tr in next ch, ch 3, skip 1ch, 1tr in next ch, tr2tog over next 2 sts, 1tr in next tr, tr2tog over next 2 sts, ch 3, skip 2ch, 1tr in next ch, ch 3, skip 2ch**, tr2tog over next 2 sts, 1tr in next tr; rep from * twice more, then * to ** once, join with sl st to first tr and change to colour C.

Round 7: Ch 4 (counts as 1tr and ch 1), skip first 2tr, 1tr in tr2tog, ch 1, skip 1ch, 1tr in next ch, ch 1, skip 1ch, 1tr in next tr, *ch 5, skip 3ch, 1tr in next tr, [ch 1, skip 1 st, 1tr in next st] 10 times; rep from * once, ch 5, skip 3ch, 1tr in next tr, [ch 1, skip 1 st, 1tr in next st] 6 times, ch 1, skip 1 st, join with sl st in 3rd ch of ch-4.

Round 8: Ch 3 (counts as 1tr), *1tr in every tr and ch-1 sp to corner, [2tr, ch 3, 2tr] in every ch-5 sp; rep from * a further 3 times, 1tr in every remaining ch-2 sp and tr to end of round, join with a sl st to 3rd of ch-3.
Fasten off and weave in ends.

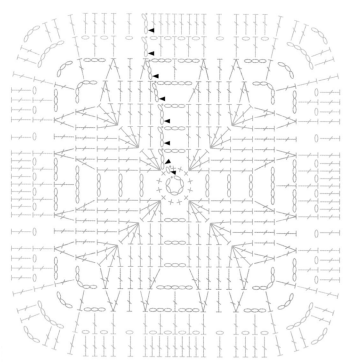

Popcorns & Lace

See page 19

A=Dawn Grey

Fleur

See page 19

A=Greengage

SPECIAL STITCHES

Beg cl (Beginning cluster): Ch 3, [(yarn round hook) twice, insert hook, yarn round hook, draw a loop through, yarn round hook, draw through 2 loops] 3 times in same stitch or space, yarn round hook, draw through all 4 loops on hook.

Cl (Cluster): [(Yarn round hook) twice, insert hook, yarn round hook, draw a loop through, yarn round hook, draw through 2 loops] 4 times in same stitch or space, yarn round hook, draw through all 5 loops on hook

Beg PC (Beginning popcorn): Ch 3 (counts as 1tr), 4tr in same stitch or space, remove hook from loop, insert hook in 3rd ch of beg ch-3, pick up the dropped loop and pull yarn through.

PC (Popcorn): 5tr in same stitch or space, remove hook from loop, insert hook into first of 5tr just made, pick up the dropped loop and pull yarn through.

Foundation chain: Using colour A, ch 8 and join with sl st in first ch to form a ring.

Round 1: Beg cl in ring, *ch 3, cl into ring, ch 5**, cl into ring; rep from * twice more and from * to ** once again, join with sl st in 3rd ch of ch-3.

Round 2: Sl st in centre of next ch-3 sp, ch 1, 1dc in same sp, *9tr in next ch-5 sp, 1dc in next ch-3 sp; rep from * to end of round, omitting last dc and join with sl st in first dc.

Round 3: Beg PC in first dc, *ch 2, skip next 2tr, 1tr in next tr, ch 2, skip next tr, [2dc, ch 3, 2dc] in next tr, ch 2, skip next tr, 1tr in next tr, ch 2, skip next 2tr**, 1PC in next dc; rep from * twice more and from * to ** once again, join with sl st in top of first PC.

Round 4: Ch 3 (counts as 1tr), *[2tr in ch-2 sp, 1tr in next tr] twice, 1tr in next tr, [2tr, ch3, 2tr] in next ch-3 sp, 1tr in next tr, [1tr in next tr, 2tr in next ch-2 sp] twice**, 1tr in next PC; rep from * twice more and from * to ** once again, join with sl st in 3rd ch of ch-3.

Round 5: Ch 6 (counts as 1tr, ch 3), 1tr in same st at base of ch 6, *skip next 2tr, 1tr in next tr, 1PC in next tr, 1tr in each of next 3tr, [2tr, ch3, 2tr] in next ch-3 sp, 1tr in each of next 3tr, 1PC in next tr, 1tr in each of next 3tr, skip next 2tr**, [1tr, ch3, 1tr] in next tr; rep from * twice more and from * to ** once again, join with sl st in 3rd ch of ch-6.

Round 6: Sl st to 2nd ch of next ch-3 sp, ch 4 (counts as 1tr, ch 1), skip next tr, *1tr in next tr, [ch 1, skip next st, 1tr in next st] 4 times, [2tr, ch 3, 2tr] in next ch-3 sp, [1tr in next tr, ch 1, skip next st] 5 times**, 1tr in 2nd ch of next ch-3 sp, ch 1; rep from * twice more and from * to ** once again, join with sl st in 3rd ch of ch-4.

Fasten off and weave in ends.

Foundation ring: Using colour A, ch 6 and join with sl st in first ch to form a ring.

Round 1: Ch 1, [1dc, ch 3, 1dtr, ch 3, 1dtr, ch 3] 4 times into ring, join with sl st in first dc. (4 petals made)

Round 2: Sl st back in last dtr made (to the left of any ch-3 sp), ch 1, 1dc in same dtr, *1dc in 3rd ch of next ch-3 sp, 2tr in next dc between petals, 1dc in 3rd ch of ch-3 sp, 1dc in next dtr, 1dc in first ch of next ch-3 sp, ch 3, skip next ch, 1dc in next ch**, 1dc in next dtr; rep from * twice more and from * to ** once again, join with sl st to first dc.

Round 3: Ch 3 (counts as 1tr), 1tr in each of next 6 sts, *[1tr, ch 3, 1tr] in next ch-3 sp (corner made)**, 1tr in each of next 8 sts; rep from * twice more and from * to ** once again, 1tr in next st, join with sl st in 3rd ch of ch-3.

Round 4: Sl st in next ch-3 corner sp, ch 3 (counts as 1tr), 2tr in same sp (half corner made), *[ch 2, skip next 2tr, 1tr in each of next 2tr] twice, ch 2, skip next 2tr**, [3tr, ch 3, 3tr] in next ch-3 corner sp; rep from * twice more and from * to ** once again, 3tr in same ch-3 sp as first half corner, ch 3, join with sl st in 3rd ch of ch-3.

Round 5: Sl st in next ch-3 corner sp, ch 3 (counts as 1tr), 2tr in same sp (half corner made), *1tr in each of next 3tr, 2tr in ch-2 sp, [1tr in each of next 2tr, 2tr in next ch-2 sp] twice, 1tr in each of next 3tr**, [3tr, ch 3, 3tr] in next ch-3 sp (corner made); rep from * twice more and from * to ** once again, 3tr in same ch-3 sp as first half corner, ch 3, join with sl st in 3rd ch of ch-3.

Fasten off and weave in ends.

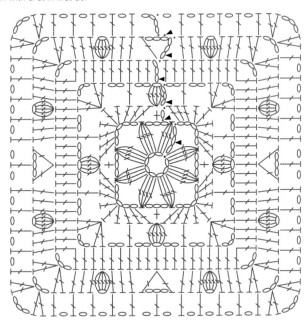

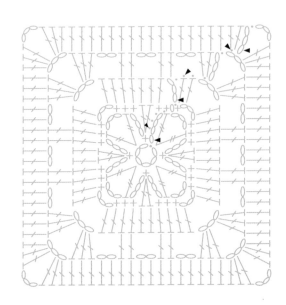

⭐⭐ *Picot Rose*

See page 17

A=Dawn Grey

⭐⭐ *Popcorn Square*

See page 18

A=Greengage

SPECIAL STITCHES

P (Picot): Ch 4, sl st into 4th ch from hook.

Foundation ring: Using colour A, ch4 and join with sl st in first ch to form a ring.

Round 1: Ch 5 (counts as 1tr, ch 2), [1tr, ch 2] 7 times into ring, join with sl st in 3rd ch of ch-5. (8ch-2 sps, 8tr)

Round 2: Sl st in next ch-2 sp, ch 4 (counts as 1tr, ch 1), [picot, ch 1] twice, [1tr in next ch-2 sp, [ch 1, picot] twice, ch 1] 7 times, join with sl st in 3rd ch ch-4.

Round 3: Sl st in next ch-1 sp between 2 picots, ch 1, 1dc in same sp, *ch 7, skip 2 picots**, 1dc in next ch-1 sp between 2 picots; rep from * 6 times more, then from * to ** once again, join with sl st in first dc.

Round 4: Sl st in next ch-7 sp, ch 1,

[1dc, 1htr, 9tr, 1htr, 1dc] in each ch-7 sp to end of round, join with sl st to first dc.

Round 5: Sl st in to next sp between 2dc in Round 4, ch 4 (counts as 1dtr), 1dtr in same sp, (half corner made), *ch3, skip next 4 sts, 1dc in each of next 5tr, skip next 8 sts, 1dc in each of next 5tr, ch 3 skip next 4 sts**, [2dtr, ch 3, 2dtr] in space between last skipped and next dc (corner made); rep from * twice more and from * to ** once again, 2dtr in same sp as first half corner, ch 3, join with sl st in 3rd ch ch-3.

Round 6: Ch 1, 1dc in first dtr, *[3dc in next ch-3 sp, 1dc in each of next 5dc] twice, 3dc in next ch-3 sp, 1dc in each of next 2dtr, [2dc, ch 3, 2dc] in next ch-3 sp**, 1dc in each of next 2dtr; rep from * twice more and from * to ** once again, join with sl st in first dc.

Fasten off and weave in ends.

SPECIAL STITCHES

Beg PC (Beginning Popcorn): Ch 2 (counts as 1htr), 4htr in same stitch or space, remove hook from loop, insert hook in 2ch of beg ch-2, pick up the dropped loop and pull yarn through.

PC (Popcorn): 5htr in same stitch or space, remove hook from loop, insert hook into first of 5htr just made, pick up the dropped loop and pull yarn through.

Foundation ring: Using colour A, ch 10 and join with sl st in first ch to form a ring.

Round 1: Ch 1, 16dc into ring, join with sl st in first dc. (16 dc)

Round 2: Beg PC in first dc, ch 3, skip next dc, [PC in next dc, ch3, skip next dc] 7 times, join with a sl st in beg PC. (8PC, 8ch-3 sps)

Round 3: Sl st in top of next PC, ch 1, 1dc in same st, [(ch 6, 1dc) in each

PC] 7 times, ch 3, join with 1tr in first dc.

Round 4: Ch 3, 4tr in same sp (half corner), *ch 3, 1dc in next ch-6 sp, ch3**, [5tr, ch 3, 5tr] in next ch-6 sp (corner); rep from * twice more and from * to ** once again, join with sl st in 3rd ch of ch-3.

Round 5: Ch 7 (counts as 1tr, ch 4), *1dc in next ch-3 sp, ch 3, 1dc in next ch-3 sp, ch 4**, [5tr, ch3, 5tr] in next ch-3 sp (corner made), ch 4; rep from * twice more and from * to ** once again, [5tr, ch 3, 4tr] in next ch-3 sp, join with sl st in 3rd ch of ch-6.

Round 6: Sl st back to last ch-3 corner sp, ch 3, 2tr in same sp (half corner made), *[ch 2, 3tr] in each of next ch-3 sp, ch 2**, [3tr, ch 3, 3tr] in next ch-3 sp (corner made); rep from * twice more and from * to ** once again, join with sl st in 3rd ch of ch-3.

Fasten off and weave in ends.

⭐⭐ Sunshine Lace

See page 19

A=Lavender

Foundation ring: Using colour A, work 8 ch and join with sl st in first ch to form a ring.

Round 1: Ch 1, 12dc in ring, join with sl st to first dc. (12 dc)

Round 2: Ch 6 (counts as 1dtr and 2 ch), [1dtr in next st, ch 2] 11 times, join with sl st in 4th ch of ch-6. (12 spaced dtr)

Round 3: Ch 5 (counts as 1tr and 2 ch), *[1dc in next ch-2 sp, ch 2] twice, [3tr, ch 2, 3tr] in next ch-2 sp, ch 2; rep from * a further 3 times omitting 1tr, ch 2 at end of last rep, join with sl st in 3rd ch of ch-5.

Round 4: Ch 1, *[1dc in next ch-2 sp, ch 2] 3 times, [3tr, ch 2, 3tr] in ch-2 corner sp, ch 2; rep from * 3 more times, join with sl st to first dc.

Round 5: Sl st in first ch-2 sp, ch 1, 1dc in same sp, ch 2, [1dc in next ch-2 sp, ch 2] twice, *[3tr, ch 2, 3tr] in ch-2 corner sp, ch 2**, [1dc in next ch-2 sp, ch 2] 4 times; rep from * twice more and from * to ** once again, 1dc in next ch-2 sp, ch 2, join with sl st to first dc.

Round 6: Sl st in next ch-2 sp, ch 3 (counts as 1tr), 1tr in same sp, 2tr in each ch-2 sp on previous round, working 1tr in each tr and [3tr, ch 2, 3tr] in each ch-2 corner sp, join with sl st in 3rd ch of ch-3.

Round 7: Ch 3 (counts as 1tr), 1tr in each tr on previous round working 5tr in each ch-2 corner sp, join with a sl st in 3rd of ch-3.

Round 8: Ch 3 (counts as 1tr), 1tr in each tr on previous round working 3tr in 3rd tr of 5tr cluster on previous round, join with sl st in 3rd ch of ch-3.

Fasten off and weave in ends.

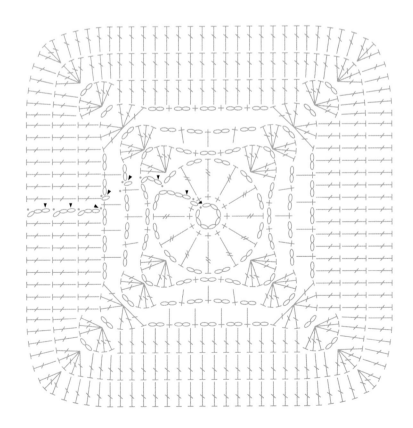

✪✪ Daisy Chain Square

See page 18

A=Lavender
B=Ecru

Foundation ring: Using colour A, work 5 ch and join with sl st to form a ring.

Round 1: Ch 4 (counts as 1tr and ch 1), [1tr in ring, ch 1] 7 times, sl st in 3rd ch of ch-4. (16 sts)

Round 2: Ch 4 (counts as 1tr and ch 1), [skip 1ch, 3tr in next tr, ch 1] 7 times, skip 1ch, 2tr in first ch sp, sl st in 3rd ch of ch-4. (8 groups)

Round 3: Sl st in ch-1 sp, ch 4 (counts as 1tr and ch 1), [1tr, ch 1, 1tr, ch 1, 1tr] in same ch sp, *skip 3tr, [1tr, ch 1] 3 times in next ch sp, 1tr in same ch-sp; rep from * a further 6 times, join with sl st in 3rd ch of ch-4. Break colour A. (8 shell groups)

Round 4: Join colour B to 3rd ch sp of any shell group, ch 2, tr2tog over sp between next [2tr and first ch sp of next shell], *ch 3, sl st in next ch sp of same shell, ch 3, tr3tog over next [ch sp of same shell, sp between next 2tr and first ch sp of next shell]; rep from * a further 6 times, ch 3, sl st in next ch sp, ch 3, sl st in tr2tog at start of round.

Round 5: Ch 5, [1tr, ch 2] 3 times in tr2tog, 1tr in same place, *skip [ch 3, 1 sl st, ch 3], [1tr, ch 2] 4 times in tr3tog, 1tr in same place; rep from * a further 6 times, sl st in 3rd ch of ch-5. Break colour B. (8 daisies)

Round 6: Rejoin colour A to 4th ch sp of any daisy, ch 3 (counts as 1tr), [1trtr between next 2tr with 1dtr in first ch-2 sp of next daisy], ch 6, 1dc in next ch sp, ch 1, 1dc in next ch sp, ch 2, tr3tog over [last ch sp of daisy, sp between 2tr and first ch sp of next daisy, ch 2, 1dc in next ch sp, ch 1, 1dc in next ch sp, ch 6**, [1dtr in last ch sp of daisy, tog with 1trtr between next 2tr and 1dtr in first ch sp of next daisy]; rep from * twice more and then from * to ** once again, sl st tog the trtr and dtr at start of round.

Round 7: Ch 5, 2tr in tr2tog, *ch 3, 1dc in ch-6 sp, ch 3 1tr in ch-1 sp, ch 3, 1dc in tr3tog ch 3, 1tr in ch-1 sp, ch 3, 1dc in ch-6 sp, ch 3**, [2tr, 2ch, 2tr] in 3 sts tog

at corner; rep from * twice more, then from * to ** once again, 1tr in same place as beg of round sl st in 3rd ch of ch-5.

Round 8: Ch 3 (counts as 1tr), *1tr in next tr, [1tr, ch 2, 1tr] in ch-2 corner sp, 1tr in next tr, 3tr in every ch-3 sp, 1tr in next tr; rep from * to end of round, omitting last tr, join with sl st to 3rd ch of ch-3.

Round 9: Ch 3 (counts as 1tr), 1tr in every tr of previous round, working 3tr in every ch-2 corner sp.

Fasten off and weave in ends.

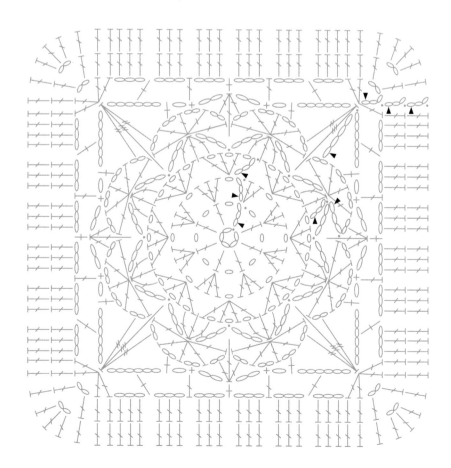

✪✪✪ *Spiralling Lace*   *See page 16*

A=Lavender
B=Nightshade

Foundation ring: Using colour A, ch 5 and join with sl st to form a ring.

Round 1: *Ch 3, 3dc in ring; rep from * a further 3 times, placing a marker in the last dc of the round. Move the marker up as you get to the end of each following round.

Round 2: *Ch 4, 2dc in next ch-3 sp, 1dc in each of the first 2 dc, skip next dc; rep from * a further 3 times.

Round 3: *Ch 4, 2dc in next ch-4 sp, 1dc in each of next 3 dc, skip next dc; rep from * a further 3 times.

Round 4: *Ch 4, 2dc in next ch-4 sp, 1dc in each of next 4 dc, skip next dc; rep from * a further 3 times.

Round 5: *Ch 4, 2dc in next ch-4 sp, 1dc in each of next 5 dc, skip next dc; rep from * a further 3 times.

Round 6: *Ch 4, 2dc in next ch-4 sp, 1dc in each of next 6 dc, skip next dc; rep from * a further 3 times.

Round 7: *Ch 5, 2dc in next ch-4 sp, 1dc in each of next 7 dc, skip next dc; rep from * a further 3 times.

Round 8: *Ch 5, 2dc in next ch-5 sp, 1dc in each of next 8 dc, skip next dc; rep from * a further 3 times.

Round 9: *Ch 5, 2dc in next ch-5 sp, 1dc in each of next 9 dc, skip next dc; rep from * a further 3 times.

Round 10: *Ch 5, 2dc in next ch-5 sp, 1dc in each of next 10 dc, skip next dc; rep from * a further 3 times.

Round 11: *Ch 5, 2dc in next ch-5 sp, 1dc in each of next 11 dc, skip next dc; rep from * a further 3 times.

Round 12: *Ch 8, skip next ch-5 sp and next 2dc, 1dc in each of next 10 dc, skip next dc; rep from * a further 3 times.

Round 13: *Ch 4, [1dc, ch 4, 1dc] in next ch-8 sp, ch 4, skip next 2dc, 1dc in each of the next 7 dc, skip next dc; rep from * a further 3 times.

Round 14: *Ch 4, 1dc in next ch-4 sp, ch 4, [1dc, ch 4, 1dc] in next ch-4 sp (corner made), ch 4, 1dc in next ch-4 sp, ch 4, skip next 2dc, 1dc in each of next 4 dc, skip next dc; rep from * a further 3 times.

Round 15: *4dc in each of next 2 ch-4 sp, [3dc, ch 2, 3dc] in next ch-4 sp (corner made), 4dc in next 2 ch-4 sp,

dc; rep from * a further 3 times.

Round 16: Ch 3 (counts as 1tr), 1tr in every dc of previous Round, working (3tr, ch2, 3tr) in each ch-2 corner sp, changing to colour B when joining with sl st to 3rd ch of ch-3. Break colour A.

Round 17: Ch 1, 1dc in every tr of previous Round, working 3dc in centre tr of each 3tr corner, changing to colour A when joining with sl st to first dc. Break colour B.

Round 18: Ch 1, 1dc in every dc of previous Round, working 3dc in centre dc of each 3dc corner, join with sl st to first dc.

Fasten off and weave in ends.

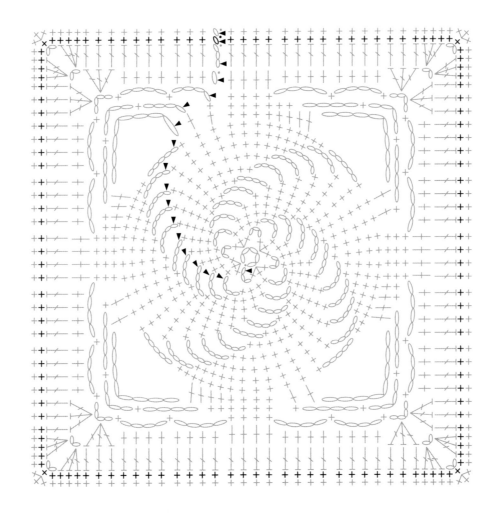

Double Filet Mesh

See page 19

A=Bleached
B=Shell
C=Greengage

Foundation ring: Using colour A, work 6 ch and join with sl st to form a ring.

Round 1: Ch 3 (counts as 1tr), 2tr in ring, ch 2, [3tr in ring, ch 2] 3 times, join with sl st in 3rd ch of ch-3.

Round 2: Sl st in next 2tr and next ch-2 sp, ch 3 (counts as 1tr), [1tr, ch 3, 2tr] in same sp, *[1tr in next tr, ch 1] twice, 1tr in next tr, [2tr, ch 3, 2tr] in next ch-2 sp, 2tr in next tr, 1tr in next tr, 2tr in next tr**, [2tr, ch 3, 2tr] in next ch-2 sp; rep from * to **, join with sl st in 3rd ch of ch-3.

Round 3: Sl st in next tr and next ch-3 sp, ch 3 (counts as 1tr), [1tr, ch 3, 2tr] in same sp, *ch 1, skip next tr, 1tr in next tr, [ch 1, 1tr in next tr] four times, 1tr in next tr, ch 1, skip next tr, [2tr, ch 3, 2tr in next ch-2 sp], 1tr in next tr, 2tr in next tr, 1tr in each of next 5tr, 2tr in next tr, 1tr in next tr**, [2tr, ch 3, 2tr in next ch-2 sp]; rep from * to **, join with sl st in 3rd ch of ch-3. Break colour A.

Round 4: Join colour B to next ch-3 sp, ch 3 (counts as 1tr), [1tr, ch 3, 2tr] in same sp, *[ch 1, 1tr in next tr] eight times, ch 1, skip next tr, [2tr, ch 3, 2tr in next ch-2 sp], 1tr in next tr, 2tr in next tr, 1tr in each of next 11tr, 2tr in next tr, 1tr in next tr**, [2tr, ch 3, 2tr in next ch-2 sp]; rep from * to **, join with sl st in 3rd ch ch-3.

Round 5: Sl st in next tr and next ch-3 sp, ch 3 (counts as 1tr), [1tr, ch 3, 2tr] in same sp, *[ch 1, 1tr in next tr] 11 times, ch 1, skip next tr, [2tr, ch 3, 2tr in next ch-2 sp], 1tr in next tr, 2tr in next tr, 1tr in each of next 17tr, 2tr in next tr, 1tr in next tr**, [2tr, ch 3, 2tr] in next ch-2 sp; rep from * to **, join with sl st in 3rd ch of ch-3. Break colour B.

Round 6: Join colour C to next ch-3 sp, ch 3 (counts as 1tr), [1tr, ch 3, 2tr] in same sp, *[ch 1, 1tr in next tr] 14 times, ch 1, skip next tr, [2tr, ch 3, 2tr in next ch-2 sp], 1tr in next tr, 2tr in next tr, 1tr in each of next 23tr, 2tr in next tr, 1tr in next tr**, [2tr, ch 3, 2tr] in next ch-2 sp; rep from * to **, join with sl st in 3rd ch of ch-3.

Round 7: Sl st in next tr and next ch-3 sp, ch 3 (counts as 1tr), [1tr, ch 3, 2tr] in same sp, *[ch 1, 1tr in next tr] 17 times, ch 1, skip next tr, [2tr, ch 3, 2tr] in next ch-2 sp, 1tr in next tr, 2tr in next tr, 1tr in each of next 29tr, 2tr in next tr, 1tr in next tr**, [2tr, ch 3, 2tr] in next ch-2 sp; rep from * to **, join with sl st in 3rd ch of ch-3.

Fasten off and weave in ends.

Filet Mesh Centre

See page 18

A=Greengage
B=Bleached
C=Shell

Foundation chain: Using colour A, work 12ch.

Row 1: 1tr in 6th ch from hook, [ch 1, skip next ch, 1tr in next ch] 3 times, turn. (4 ch-1 sp)

Row 2: Ch4, (counts as 1tr and ch 1), skip next ch-1 sp, [1tr, ch 1] in each of next 3tr, skip next ch, 1tr in 5th ch of ch-6, turn.

Rows 3-4: Ch 4, (counts as 1tr and ch 1), skip next ch-1 sp, [1tr, ch 1] in each of next 3tr, skip next ch, 1tr in 3rd ch of ch-4, turn.

Round 5: Ch 1, 2dc in first ch-1 sp (half corner made), [1dc in next tr, 1dc in next ch-1 sp] twice, 1dc in next tr, *[2dc, ch 2, 2dc] in next corner sp, 5dc worked across next 2 row-end sts**, [2dc, ch 2, 2dc] in next corner sp, working across opposite side of foundation ch, [1dc in next ch at base of tr, 1dc in next ch-1 sp] twice, 1dc in next ch at base of tr; rep from * to ** once more, 2dc in next corner sp, ch-2, join with sl st to first dc. Break colour A.

Round 6: Join colour B to any ch-2 corner sp, ch 3 (counts as 1tr), [2tr, ch 3, 3tr] in same sp, *ch 4, skip next 4dc, 1tr in next dc, ch 4, skip next 4dc**, [3tr, ch 3, 3tr] in next ch-2 corner sp; rep from * twice more, then from * to ** once again, join with sl st in 3rd ch of ch-3.

Round 7: Sl st in next 2tr and next ch-3 sp, ch 3 (counts as 1tr), [2tr, ch 3, 3tr] in same sp, *ch 4, skip next 4dc, 3tr in next tr, ch 4, skip next 4dc**, [3tr, ch 3, 3tr] in next ch-4 corner sp; rep from * twice more, then from * to ** once again, join with sl st in 3rd ch of ch-3. Break colour B.

Round 8: Join colour C to any ch-3 corner sp, ch 3 (counts as 1tr), [2tr, ch 3, 3tr] in same sp, *ch 2, 1tr in first of ch-4 from previous round, ch 2, 1tr in next tr, ch 2, skip next tr, 1tr in next tr, ch 2, 1tr in 4th ch of ch-4 from previous round, ch 2**, [3tr, ch 3, 3tr] in next ch-2 corner sp; rep from * twice more, then from * to ** once again, join with sl st in 3rd ch of ch-3.

Round 9: Sl st in next 2tr and next ch-3 sp, ch 3 (counts as 1tr), [2tr, ch 3, 3tr] in same sp, *ch 3, 3tr in each of 4tr, ch 3**, [3tr, ch 3, 3tr] in next ch-2 corner sp; rep from * twice more, then from * to ** once again, join with sl st in 3rd ch of ch-3.

Round 10: Ch 3 (counts as 1tr), 1tr in every tr and 3dtr in every ch-3 sp along sides and [1tr, 1dtr, 1tr] in ch-3 corner sps, join with sl st in 3rd ch of ch-3.

Fasten off and weave in ends.

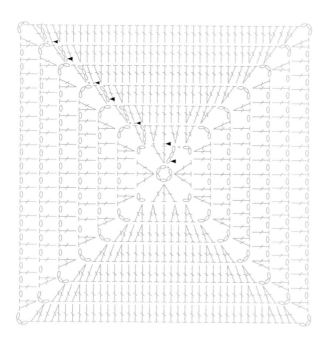

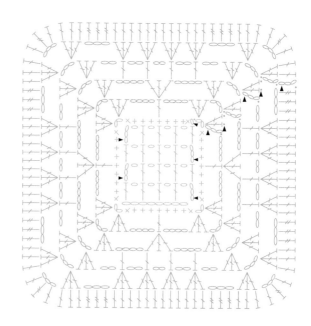

⭐ *Spinner*

See page 20

A=Persimmon
B=Bleached
C=Aqua
D=Winsor

Foundation chain: Using colour A, work 4 ch and join with sl st to form a ring.

Round 1: Ch 3 (counts as 1tr), 15tr in ring, join with sl st in 3rd ch of ch-3.

Round 2: Sl st in space between ch 3 and first tr from previous row, ch 3 (counts as 1tr), 1tr in same sp, 2tr in each remaining space between tr, break colour A and join colour B with sl st in 3rd ch of ch-3.

Round 3: Ch 3 (counts as 1tr), 1tr in same place, 1tr in next tr, [2tr in next tr, 1tr in next tr] 15 times, join with sl st in 3rd ch of ch-3. Break colour B.

Round 4: Join colour C to any tr, ch 4 (counts as 1dtr), [2tr, ch 2, 2tr, 1dtr] in same place, *skip next 2tr, 1htr in next 2tr, 1dc in next 3tr, 1htr in next 2tr, skip next 2tr**, [1dtr, 2tr, ch 2, 2tr, 1dtr] in next tr; rep from * twice more and from * to ** once again, join with sl st to 4th ch of ch-4.

Round 5: Join colour D to any ch-2 corner sp, ch 3 (counts as 1tr), [2dtr, ch 2, 2dtr, 1tr] in same sp, *1tr in every st along side of square**, [1tr, 2dtr, ch 2, 2dtr, 1tr] in next ch-2 corner sp; rep from * twice more and from * to ** once again, join with sl st in 3rd ch of ch-3. Break colour D.

Round 6: Join colour B to any ch-2 corner sp, ch 3 (counts as 1tr), [1tr, ch 2, 2tr] in same sp, *1tr in every st along side of square**, [2tr, ch 2, 2tr] in next ch-2 corner sp; rep from * twice and from * to ** once again, join with sl st in 3rd ch of ch-3. Break colour B.

Round 7: Using colour A, work as Round 6, changing to colour D when joining with sl st to 3rd ch of ch 3. Break colour A.

Round 8: Ch 2 (counts as 1htr), 1htr in every tr to end of round, working [1htr, 1tr, 1htr] in every ch-2 corner sp, join with sl st to 2nd ch of ch-2.

Fasten off and weave in ends.

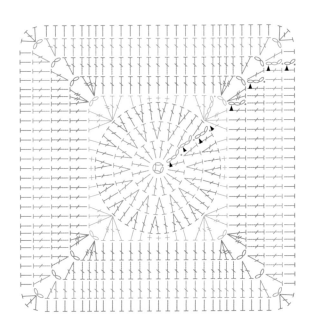

⭐ *Circle in a Square*

See page 23

A=Aqua
B=Winsor
C=Bleached
D=Persimmon

Foundation ring: Using colour A, work 8 ch and join with sl st to form a ring.

Round 1: Ch 3 (counts as 1tr), 15tr in ring, changing to colour B when joining with sl st in 3rd ch of ch-3.

Round 2: Ch 5 (counts as 1tr and ch 2), [1tr in next tr, ch 2] 15 times, join with sl st in 3rd ch of ch-5. Break colour B.

Round 3: Join colour C to any ch-2 sp, ch 3 (counts as 1tr), 2tr in same sp, ch 1, *[3tr, ch 1] in next ch-2 sp; rep from * to end of round, join with sl st in 3rd ch of ch-3. Break colour C.

Round 4: Join colour D to any ch-1 sp, *[ch 3, 1dc in next ch-1 sp] 3 times, ch 6 (corner-sp made), 1dc in next ch-1 sp; rep from * to end of round, join with sl st in base of ch-3.

Round 5: Ch 3 (counts as 1tr), 2tr in first ch-3 sp, 3tr in each of next two ch-3 sps, *[5tr, ch 3, 5tr] in ch-6 corner sp, 3tr in each ch-3 sp to corner; rep from * to end of round, changing to colour C when joining with sl st in 3rd ch of ch-3.

Round 6: Ch 3 (counts as 1tr), 1tr in every tr of previous round, working [1tr, 1dtr, 1tr] in each ch-2 corner sp, changing to colour A when joining with sl st in 3rd ch of ch-3.

Round 7: Ch 3 (counts as 1tr), 1tr in every tr of previous round, working 3tr in each corner dtr, join with sl st in 3rd ch of ch-3. Break colour A.

Round 8: Join colour B to any sp between 2tr, ch 3 (counts as 1tr), *1tr between every 2tr of previous round, working ch 3, between first and third tr of tr3 cluster in each corner, join with sl st in 3rd ch of ch-3.

Fasten off and weave in ends.

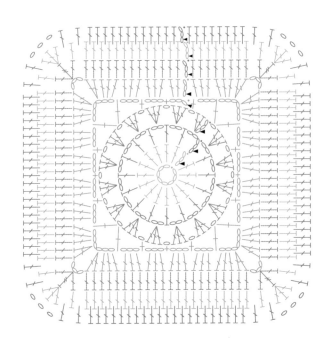

★★ *Squaring the Circle* See page 22

A=Winsor
B=Bleached
C=Persimmon
D=Aqua

Foundation ring: Using colour A, make a magic ring.

Round 1: Ch 1, 8dc in ring, changing to colour B when joining with sl st to first dc.

Round 2: Ch 1, 1dc in same place, [ch 2, 1dc in next st] 7 times, ch 2, join with sl st to first dc. Break colour B.

Round 3: Join colour C to any ch-2 sp, ch 3 (counts as 1tr), 2tr in same sp, [ch 1, 3tr in next ch-2 sp] 7 times, ch 1, join with sl st to 3rd ch of ch-3. Break colour C.

Round 4: Join colour B to any ch-1 sp, ch 3 (counts as 1tr), 1tr in same sp, [ch 1, miss next st, 2tr in next st, ch 1, miss next st, 2tr in ch-1 sp] 7 times, ch 1, miss next st, 2tr in next st, ch 1, miss next st, join with sl st to 3rd ch of ch-3. Break colour B.

Round 5: Join colour A to any ch-1 sp, ch 1, 1dc in same sp, [ch 2, 1dc in next ch-1 sp] 15 times, ch 2, join with sl st to first dc. Break colour A.

Round 6: Join colour D to any ch-2 sp, ch 3 (counts as 1tr), 2tr in same sp, [ch 1, 3tr in ch-2 sp] 15 times, ch 1, join with sl st to 3rd ch of ch-3. Break colour D.

Round 7: Join colour A to any ch-1 sp, ch 1, 1dc in same sp, [ch 3, 1dc in next ch-1 sp] 15 times, ch 2, join with sl st to first dc. Break colour A.

Round 8: Join colour B to any ch-3 sp, ch 1, 4dc in same sp, *[1htr, 3tr] in next ch-3 sp, [1dtr, ch 2, 1dtr] in next dc, [3tr, 1htr], in next ch-3 sp, 4dc in next ch-3 sp**, 4dc in next ch-3 sp; rep from * twice more and from * to ** once again, join with sl st in first dc. Break colour B.

Round 9: Join colour C to any ch-2 corner sp, ch 3 (counts as 1tr), [1dtr, 1tr] in same sp, 1tr in every st, working [1tr, 1dtr, 1tr] in every ch-2 corner sp to end of round, changing to colour A when joining with sl st to 3rd ch of ch-3.

Round 10: Ch 3 (counts as 1tr), *[1tr, 1dtr, 1tr] in next dtr, 1tr in every tr to corner dtr; rep from * to end of round, changing to colour D when joining with sl st to 3rd ch of ch-3.

Round 11: Ch 3 (counts as 1tr), 1tr in next tr, *[1tr, 1dtr, 1tr] in next dtr, 1tr in every tr to corner dtr; rep from * to end of round, join with sl st to 3rd ch of ch-3.
Fasten off and weave in ends.

★★ *Starburst in a Square* See page 21

A=Bleached
B=Aqua
C=Winsor
D=Persimmon

SPECIAL STITCHES

Tr2tog: Work 2tr sts together.
Tr3tog: Work 3tr sts together.

Foundation ring:
Using colour A, make a magic loop.

Round 1: Ch 3 (counts as 1tr), 23tr in centre of loop, join with sl st to 3rd ch of ch-3.

Round 2: Ch 3 (counts as 1tr), 1tr in next 2tr, ch 3, [1tr in next 3tr, ch 3] 7 times, changing to colour B when joining with sl st to 3rd ch of ch-3. Break colour A.

Round 3: Ch 2, tr2tog over next 2tr, [ch 3, 1tr in next 3-ch sp, ch 3, tr3tog over next 3tr] 7 times, ch 3, 1tr in next 3-ch sp, ch 3, join with sl st to 3rd ch of ch-3. Break colour B.

Round 4: Join colour C to any ch-3 sp before a single tr, ch 4 (counts as 1tr and ch 1), [3tr in next ch-3 sp, ch 1] 15 times, 2tr in first ch-sp, join with sl st to 3rd ch of ch-4. Break colour C.

Round 5: Join colour D to any ch-1 sp, ch 4 (counts as 1tr and ch 1), [4tr in next ch-3 sp, ch 1] 15 times, 3tr in first ch-sp, join with sl st to 3rd ch of ch-4. Break colour D.

Round 6: Join colour A to any ch-1 sp, ch 4 (counts as 1tr and ch 1), [5tr in next ch-3 sp, ch 1] 15 times, 4tr in first ch-sp, join with sl st to 3rd ch of ch-4. Break colour A.

Round 7: Join colour B to first tr in any 5tr cluster, ch 1, 1dc in same place, 1dc in next 10tr, 1htr in next 2tr, 1tr in next 2tr, *[1tr, 1dtr, 1tr], in next ch-1 sp, 1tr in next 2tr, 1htr in next 2 tr**, 1dc in next 12tr, 1htr in next 2tr, 1tr in next 2tr; rep from * twice more and from * to ** once again, 1dc in next tr, change to colour D when joining with sl st in first dc. Break colour B.

Round 8: Ch 2 (counts as 1htr), 1htr in every st, working [1htr, 1tr, 1htr] in every dtr corner st to end of round, join with sl st to 2nd ch of ch-2.
Fasten off and weave in ends.

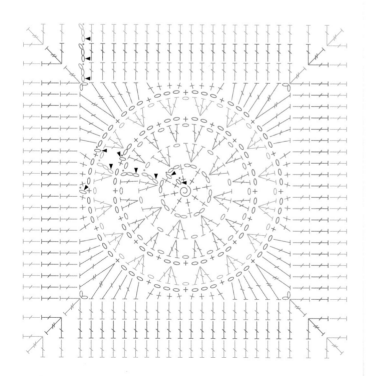

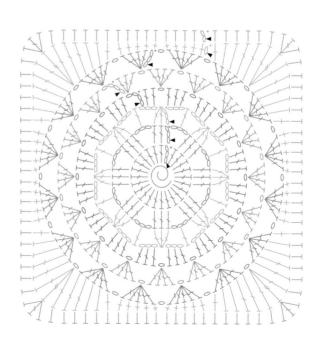

Fretwork Circle
See page 21

A=Dawn Grey
B=Bleached
C=Persimmon

SPECIAL STITCHES

Beg cl: Work two treble sts tog: [yrh draw up a loop in next st, (yrh, pull through 2 loops on hook) twice] twice, yrh and draw through all 3 loops on hook.

Cl: Work three treble sts tog: [yrh draw up a loop in next st, (yrh, pull through 2 loops on hook) twice] three times, yrh and draw through all 4 loops on hook.

Foundation ring: Using colour A, work 6 ch and join with sl st to form a ring.

Round 1: Ch 1, 12dc in ring, join with sl st to first dc.

Round 2: Ch 4 (counts as 1tr and ch 1), [1tr in next dc, ch 1] 11 times, join with sl st to 3rd ch of ch-4. Break colour A.

Round 3: Join colour B to any ch-1 sp, ch 3 (counts as 1tr), beg cl in same sp, ch 3, *cl in next ch-1 sp, ch 3; rep from * a further 10 times, join with a sl st to top of beg cl. Break colour B.

Round 4: Join colour C to any ch-3 sp, ch 1, 4dc in same sp, 4dc in every ch-3 sp to end, join with sl st to first dc. Break colour C.

Round 5: Join colour A to top of any cl, ch 3 (counts as 1tr), [1tr, ch 2, 2tr] in same place*, ch 2, skip next 4dc group, 2dc in sp above next cl, ch 3, skip next 4dc group**, [2tr, ch 2, 2tr] in sp above next cl; rep from * twice more and from * to ** once again, join with sl st to 3rd ch of ch-3.

Round 6: Ch 3 (counts as 1tr), 1tr in next tr, *[2tr, ch 2, 2tr] in ch-2 corner sp, 1tr in next 2tr, ch 2, 1tr in next 2dc, ch 3, 1tr in next 2dc, ch 2**, 1tr in next 2tr; rep from * twice more and from * to ** once again, join with sl st to 3rd ch of ch-3.

Round 7: Ch 3 (counts as 1tr), 1tr in next 3tr, *[2tr, ch 2, 2tr] in ch-2 corner sp, 1tr in next 4tr, ch 2, 1tr in next 2tr, ch 3, 1tr in next 2tr, ch 2**, 1tr in next 4tr; rep from * twice more and from * to ** once again, join with sl st to 3rd ch of ch-3.

Round 8: Ch 3 (counts as 1tr), 1tr in next 5tr, *[2tr, ch 2, 2tr] in ch-2 corner sp, 1tr in next 6tr, ch 2, 1tr in next 2tr, ch 3, 1tr in next 2tr, ch 2**, 1tr in next 6tr; rep from * twice more and from * to ** once again, changing to colour C when joining with sl st in 3rd ch of ch-3.

Round 9: Ch 3 (counts as 1tr), 1tr in every tr and ch from previous round, working 3tr in every ch-2 corner sp, join with sl st to 3rd ch of ch-3.
Fasten off and weave in ends.

Cluster Circle
See page 20

A=Bleached
B=Persimmon
C=Dawn Grey

SPECIAL STITCHES

Beg cl: Work three treble sts tog: [yrh draw up a loop in next st, (yrh, pull through 2 loops on hook) twice] twice, yrh and draw through all 4 loops on hook.

Cl: Work four treble sts tog: [yrh draw up a loop in next st, (yrh, pull through 2 loops on hook) twice] three times, yrh and draw through all 5 loops on hook.

Foundation ring: Using colour A, work 6 ch and join with sl st to form a ring.

Round 1: Ch1, 12tr in ring, join with sl st to first tr.

Round 2: Ch 4 (counts as 1tr and ch1), [1tr in next tr, ch1] 11 times, join with sl st to 3rd ch of ch-4. Break A.

Round 3: Sl st in next ch-1 sp, ch 3 (counts as 1tr), beg cl in same sp, ch 3, *cl in next ch-1 sp, ch 3; rep from * a further 10 times, join with a sl st to top of beg cl. Break colour A.

Round 4: Join colour B to any ch-3 sp, ch 3 (counts as 1tr), beg cl in same sp, *ch 2, 1tr in next cl, ch 2**, cl in next ch-3 sp; rep from * a further 10 times, then from * to ** once, join with a sl st to top of beg cl.

Round 5: Sl st in next ch-2 sp, ch 1, 3tr in same sp, 3tr in every ch-2 sp to end of round, join with sl st in first tr. Break colour B.

Round 6: Join colour A in to top of any cl, ch 3 (counts as 1tr), [1tr, ch 2, 2tr] in same place, *[ch 2, skip next 3tr group, 1tr in sp between next two 3tr groups] 5 times, ch 2**, [2tr, ch 2, 2tr] in sp above next cl; rep from * twice more and from * to ** once again, join with sl st to 3rd ch of ch-3.

Round 7: Ch 3 (counts as 1tr), 1tr in next tr, *[2tr, ch 2, 2tr] in ch-2 corner sp, 1tr in next 2tr, ch 2, 1tr in next tr, [ch 2, 1tr in next tr] 3 times, ch 2, 1tr in next tr, ch 2**, 1tr in next 2tr; rep from * twice more and from * to ** once again, changing to colour C when joining with sl st in 3rd ch of ch-3. Break colour A.

Round 8: Ch 3 (counts as 1tr), 1tr in next 3tr, *[2tr, ch 2, 2tr] in ch-2 corner sp, 1tr in next 4tr, ch 2, 1tr in next tr, [ch 2, 1tr in next tr] 3 times, ch 2, 1 tr in next tr, ch 2**, 1tr in next 4tr; rep from * twice more and from * to ** once again, join with sl st to 3rd ch of ch-3.

Round 9: Ch 3 (counts as 1tr), 1tr in every tr and ch from previous round, working 3tr in every ch-2 corner sp, join with sl st to 3rd ch of ch-3.
Fasten off and weave in ends.

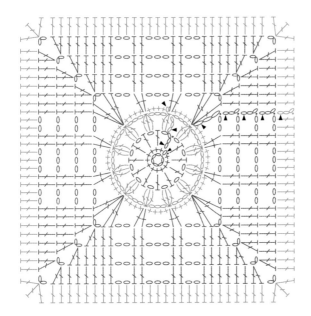

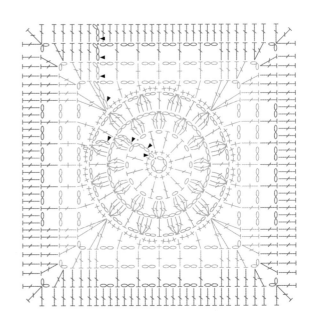

Starflower Circle

See page 20

A=Persimmon
B=Bleached
C=Dawn Grey

SPECIAL STITCHES

Dtr2tog (work two treble sts tog):
[Yrh (twice) draw up a loop in next st, (yrh, pull through 2 loops on hook) twice] twice, yrh and draw through all 3 loops on hook.

Foundation chain: Using colour A, ch 4 and join with a sl st to form a ring.

Round 1: Ch 4, 1dtr into the ring (counts as dtr2tog), ch 3, [dtr2tog, ch 3] 7 times into the ring, join with sl st in 4th ch of ch 4. Break A.

Round 2: Join colour B to any 3ch-sp, ch 1, 1dc in same sp, *[ch 5, 1dc] in each of next seven 3ch-sps, ch 5, join with sl st in first dc.

Round 3: Sl st in first 3 ch sts of next 5ch-sp ch 4 (counts as 1dtr and ch 1), *[dtr2tog, ch 1] 5 times in next 5ch-sp **, 1tr in next 5ch-sp, ch 1; rep from * twice and then from * to ** once, change to colour C when joining with sl st in 3rd ch of ch-4.

Round 4: Ch 4 (counts as 1dtr), 1dtr in same st, ch 1, *[1tr, ch 1] in each of next four 1ch-sp**, [2dtr, ch 2, 2dtr] in next dtr; rep from * twice more and from * to ** once again, 2dtr in same sp as first half corner, ch 2, join with sl st in 3rd ch of ch-3.

Round 5: Sl st in next dtr and next 1ch-sp, ch 3 (counts as 1tr), *[1tr in next tr, 1tr in next ch-1 sp] 4 times, 1tr in each of next 2dtr, [2dtr, ch 2, 2dtr] in ch-2 corner sp, 1tr in each of next 2dtr**, 1tr in next 1ch-sp; rep from * twice more and from * to ** once again, change to colour B when joining with sl st in 3rd ch of ch-3.

Round 6: Ch 2 (counts as 1htr), 1htr in every tr and [2tr, ch 2, 2tr] in every ch-2 corner sp to end of round, change to colour A when joining with sl st in 2nd ch of ch-2.

Round 7: Ch 3 (counts as 1tr), 1tr in every htr and [2dtr, ch 2, 2dtr] in every ch-2 corner sp to end of round, change to colour B when joining with sl st to 3rd of ch-3.

Round 8: Ch 1 (does not count as st), 1dc in every tr and [2htr, ch 2, 2htr] in every ch-2 corner sp to end of round, change to colour C when joining with sl st to first dc.

Round 9: Ch 2 (counts as 1htr), 1htr in every dc and 3tr in every ch-2 corner sp to end of round, join with sl st in 2nd ch of ch-2.

Fasten off and weave in ends.

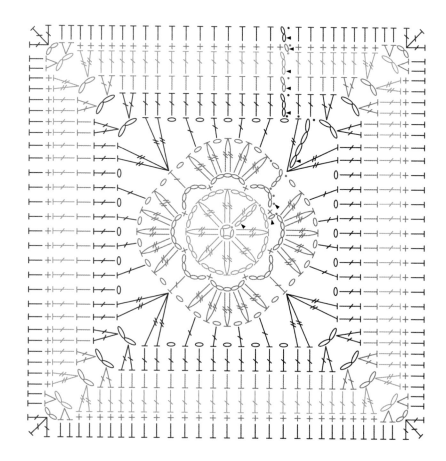

⭐⭐ *Framed Circle*

See page 20

A=Winsor
B=Dawn Grey
C=Bleached
D=Aqua

SPECIAL STITCHES
BPtr: Work a tr in the back post of designated stitch.

Foundation chain: Using colour A, work 4 ch and join with sl st to form a ring.
Round 1: Ch 3 (counts as 1tr), 11tr in the ring, changing to colour B when joining with sl st to 3rd ch of ch-3. Break colour A.
Round 2: Ch 3 (counts as 1tr), 1tr in same place, 2tr in every tr to end of round, changing to colour C when joining with sl st to 3rd ch of ch-3. Break colour B.
Round 3: Ch 3 (counts as 1tr), 1tr in same place, [1tr in next tr, 2tr in next tr] 11 times, changing to colour A when joining with sl st to 3rd ch of ch-3. Break colour C.
Round 4: Ch 1, 1dc in same place, [ch 3, skip 2 tr, 1dc in next tr] 11 times, ch 3, changing to colour D when joining with sl st to first dc. Break colour A.
Round 5: Sl st in next ch-3 sp, [1dc, 1htr, 1tr, ch 3, 1tr, 1htr, 1dc] in same ch-3 sp, *[1dc, 1htr, 2tr, 1htr, 1dc] in next 2 ch-3 sp**, *[1dc, 1htr, 1tr, ch 3, 1tr, 1htr, 1dc] in next ch-3 sp; rep from * twice more, then from * to ** once again, join with sl st to first dc. Break colour D.

Round 6: Join colour C to any ch-3 corner sp, ch 1, 1dc in same sp, *ch 2, [1BPtr around dc from Round 4, ch 3] twice, 1BPtr around next dc from Round 4, ch 2**, [1dc, 1htr, 1tr, 1htr, 1dc] in ch-3 sp from Round 5; rep from * to ** once more, [1dc, 1htr, 1tr, 1htr] in ch-3 sp from Round 5, join with sl st to first dc.
Round 7: Ch 3 (counts as 1tr), 2tr in ch-2 sp, 1tr in next tr, [3tr in ch-3 sp, 1tr in next tr] twice, 2tr in ch-2 sp, 1tr in next 2sts, [1tr, 1dtr, 1tr) in next st**, 1tr in next 2sts; rep from * twice and then from * to ** once more, 1tr in next st, changing to colour B when joining with sl st to 3rd ch of ch-3. Break colour C.

Round 8: Ch 3 (counts as 1tr), 1tr in every tr, working [1tr, 1dtr, 1tr] in every corner dtr, changing to colour A when joining with sl st to 3rd ch of ch-3. Break colour B.
Round 9: Ch 3 (counts as 1tr), 1tr in every tr, working [1tr, 1dtr, 1tr] in every corner dtr, changing to colour D when joining with sl st to 3rd ch of ch-3. Break colour A.
Round 10: Ch 3 (counts as 1tr), 1tr in every tr, working [1tr, 1dtr, 1tr] in every corner dtr, join with sl st to 3rd ch of ch-3.
Fasten off and weave in ends.

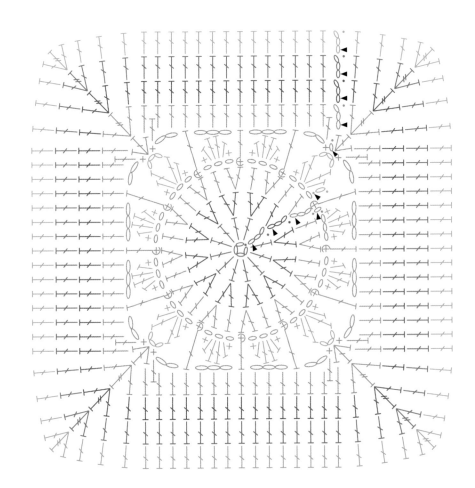

⊛⊛ Flower in a Web
See page 21

A=Aqua
B=Bleached
C=Winsor
D=Dawn Grey

SPECIAL STITCHES

Beg cl: Work two treble sts tog: [yrh draw up a loop in next st, (yrh, pull through 2 loops on hook) twice] twice, yrh and draw through all 3 loops on hook.
Cl: Work three treble sts tog: [yrh draw up a loop in next st, (yrh, pull through 2 loops on hook) twice] three times, yrh and draw through all 4 loops on hook.

Foundation ring: Using colour A, work 4 ch and join with sl st to form a ring.
Round 1: Ch 3, (counts as 1tr), 2tr in ring, ch 3, [3tr in ring, ch 3] 3 times, ch 3, join with sl st to 3rd ch of ch-3. Break colour A.
Round 2: Join colour B to any ch-3 sp, ch 3 (counts as 1tr), [1tr, ch 2, 2tr, ch 2, 2tr] in same sp, *[2tr, ch 2, 2tr, ch 2, 2tr] in next ch-3 sp; rep from * twice more, join with sl st to 3rd ch of ch-3. Break colour B.
Round 3: Join colour C to 2nd tr of any 3tr cluster from Round 1, ch 5 (counts as 1tr and ch 2), *[1dc in ch-2 sp, ch 2] twice**, 1tr in 2nd tr of next 3tr cluster from Round 1, ch 2; rep from * twice more and from * to ** once again.
Round 4: Ch 7 (counts as 1tr and ch 4), *1dc in next dc, 3dc in next ch-2 sp, 1dc in next dc, ch 4**, 1tr in next tr, ch 4; rep from * twice more and then from * to ** once again, changing to

colour D when joining with a sl st to 3rd ch of ch-7. Break colour C.
Round 5: Ch 3, (counts as 1tr), 1dtr, 1tr in same place, *5tr in ch-4 sp, 1tr in next 5 sts, 5tr in ch-4 sp**, [1tr, 1dtr, 1tr] in corner tr; rep from * twice more and then from * to ** once again, join with sl st to 3rd ch of ch-3. Break colour D.
Round 6: Join colour B to any tr 2 sts to the left of a dtr from Round 5. Ch 3 (counts as 1tr), 1tr in next 2 sts, *[ch 3, skip 3 sts, 1tr in next 3 sts] to 1 st before next dtr, ch 3, skip 1 st, 1tr in corner dtr, ch 3, skip 1 st**, 1tr in next 3 sts; rep from * twice and from * to ** once more, join with sl st to 3rd ch of ch-3.
Round 7: Ch 3 (counts as 1tr), 1tr in next 2 sts, ch 3, [1tr in next 3 sts, ch 3] to corner st, 5tr in corner st, ch 3; rep from * to end of round, changing to colour A when joining with a sl st to 3rd ch of ch-3. Break colour B.
Round 8: Ch 3 (counts as 1tr), 1tr in next 2 sts, ch 3, [1tr in next 3 sts, ch 3] to 5tr corner group, 1tr in next 2tr, [1tr, ch 3, 1tr] in next tr, 1tr in next 2tr, ch 3; rep from * to end of round, changing to colour C when joining with a sl st to 3rd ch of ch-3. Break colour A.
Round 9: Ch 1, 1dc in same place, 1dc in every tr and 3dc in every ch-3 sp from previous round, join with sl st to first dc.
Fasten off and weave in ends.

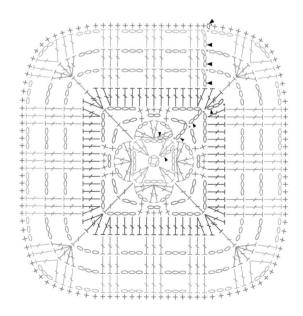

⊛⊛ Snowflake in a Square
See page 23

A=Bleached
B=Aqua
C=Winsor
D=Persimmon

SPECIAL STITCHES

Beg cl: Work three treble sts tog: [yrh draw up a loop in next st, (yrh, pull through 2 loops on hook) twice] three times, yrh and draw through all 4 loops on hook.
Cl: Work four treble sts tog: [yrh draw up a loop in next st, (yrh, pull through 2 loops on hook) twice] four times, yrh and draw through all 5 loops on hook.

Foundation ring: Using colour A, work 8 ch and join with sl st to form a ring.
Round 1: Ch 3 (counts as 1tr), 2tr in ring, ch 7, [3tr, ch 7] 7 times in ring, join with sl st to 3rd ch of ch-3.
Round 2: Sl st in next 2tr and next ch-7 sp, ch 3 (counts as 1tr), beg cl in first ch-7 sp, [ch 9, cl in next ch-7 sp] 7 times, ch 9, join with sl st in top of beg cl.
Round 3: Ch 1, *[2dc, ch 5, 2dc] in next ch-9 sp, ch 7 [cl, ch 5, cl], in next ch-9 sp, ch 7; rep from * a further 3 times, join with sl st in first dc. Break colour A.
Round 4: Join colour B to ch-5 sp, between 2 groups of 2dc, ch 1, 2dc in

same loop, *ch 5, 2dc in next ch-7 sp, ch 5, [cl, ch 5, cl] in next ch-5 sp, ch 5, 2dc in ch-7 sp, ch 5**, 2dc in next ch-5 sp; rep from * twice more and from * to ** once again, join with sl st in first dc.
Round 5: Ch 2 (counts as 1htr), 1htr in next dc, 3dc in next ch-5 sp, 1htr in next 2dc, 3dc in next ch-5 sp, *1dc in top of next cl, [1dc, 1htr, 1tr, 1htr, 1dc] in next ch-5 corner sp, 1dc in next cl**, [3dc in next ch-5 sp, 1htr in next 2dc] 3 times, 3dc in next ch-5 sp; rep from * twice more and from * to ** once again, 3dc in next ch-5sp, 1htr in next 2dc, 3dc in next ch-5 sp, changing to colour C when joining with sl st to 2nd ch of ch-2. Break colour B.
Round 6: Ch 2 (counts as 1htr), 1htr in every st from previous round, working 5htr in centre st of each corner group, change to colour D when joining with sl st to 2nd of ch-2. Break colour C.
Round 7: Ch 1, 1dc in same place, 1dc in every st from previous round, working 3dc in centre st of each corner group, join with sl st to first dc.
Fasten off and weave in ends.

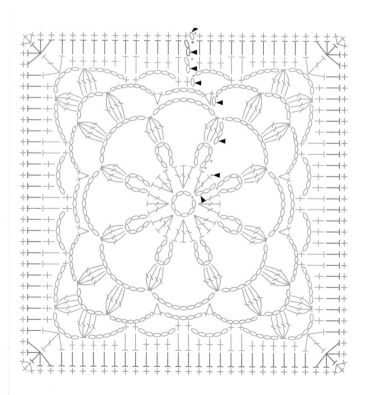

★★ *Star in a Square*

See page 21

A=Persimmon
B=Winsor
C=Aqua

Foundation ring: Using colour A, work 4 ch and join with sl st to form a ring.

Round 1: Ch 1, 8dc in ring, join with sl st to first dc.

Round 2: *Ch 6, 1dc in 3rd and 4th ch from hook, 1htr in 5th and 6th ch from hook, sl st in next dc (spike made); rep from * a further 7 times, join with sl st in first ch of ch-6. Break colour A.

Round 3: Join colour B to the tip of any spike, ch 5 (counts as 1tr and ch 2), 1tr in same place (corner made), ch 4, sl st in top of next spike, ch 4, *[1tr, ch 2, 1tr] in tip of next spike (corner made), ch 4, sl st in tip of next spike, ch 4; rep from * twice, join with sl st to 3rd ch of ch-5.

Round 4: Sl st in ch-2 corner space, ch 3 (counts as 1tr), [2tr, ch 2, 3tr] in same ch-2 sp, 4tr in each of next 2 ch-4 sp, *[3tr, ch 2, 3tr] in next ch 2 corner sp, 4tr in each of next 2 ch-4 sp; rep from * twice more, join with sl st to 3rd ch of ch-3.

Round 5: Ch 3 (counts as 1tr), 1tr in every tr of previous round, working [3tr, ch 2, 3tr] in every ch-2 corner sp, changing to colour B when joining with sl st to 3rd ch of ch-3. Break colour A.

Round 6: Ch 3 (counts as 1tr), 1tr in every tr of previous round, working [3tr, ch 2, 3tr] in every ch-2 corner sp, changing to colour C when joining with sl st to 3rd ch of ch-3. Break colour B.

Round 7: Ch 3 (counts as 1tr), 1tr in every tr of previous round, working [3tr, ch 2, 3tr] in every ch-2 corner sp, changing to colour C when joining with sl st to 3rd ch of ch-3. Break colour B.

Round 8: Ch 2 (counts as 1htr), 1htr in every tr of previous round, working 3htr in every ch-2 corner sp, join with sl st to 2nd ch of ch-2.

Fasten off and weave in ends.

★ *Diamond in a Square*

See page 23

A=Winsor
B=Aqua
C=Bleached
D=Persimmon

Foundation ring: Using colour A, work 4 ch and join with sl st to form a ring.

Round 1: Ch 6 (counts as 1tr and 3 ch), [3tr in ring, ch 3] 3 times, 2tr in ring, join with sl st in 3rd ch of ch-6.

Round 2: Sl st in next ch-3 sp, ch 3 (counts as 1tr), [2tr, ch 2, 3tr] in same sp, *1tr in each of next 3tr, [3tr, ch 3, 3tr] in next ch-3 sp; rep from * twice more, 1tr in each of next 3tr, join with sl st in 3rd ch of ch-3. Break colour A.

Round 3: Join colour B to any ch-2 sp, *ch 6, skip 4tr, 1dtr in next tr, ch 6, skip 4tr, sl st in next ch-2 sp; rep from * a further 3 times, join with sl st to in first ch.

Round 4: Ch 1, *7dc in next ch-6 sp, [1htr, ch 2, 1htr] in next dtr (corner made), 7dc in next ch-6 sp, 1dc in ch-2 sp from Round 2; rep from * a further 3 times, join with sl st in first dc.

Round 5: Ch 2 (counts as 1htr), 1htr in next 6dc, 1tr in next htr, * [2tr, ch 2, 2tr] in next ch-2 corner sp, 1tr in next htr, 1htr in next 7dc, 1tr in next dc**, 1htr in next 7dc; rep from * twice more and from * to ** once again, join with sl st to 2nd ch of ch-2. Break colour B.

Round 6: Join colour C to a centre tr along one side of the square, ch 3 (counts as 1tr), *1tr in each of next 7htr, 1htr, in next 3tr, [2tr, ch 2, 2tr] in next ch-2 corner sp, 1htr in each of next 3tr, 1tr in next tr; rep from * a further 3 times, 1tr in each of next 7htr, changing to colour D when joining with sl st to 3rd ch of ch-3. Break colour C.

Round 7: Ch 3 (counts as 1tr), 1tr in every st from previous round, working 3tr in each ch-2 corner sp, changing to colour A when joining with sl st to 3rd ch of ch-3. Break colour D.

Round 8: Ch 3 (counts as 1tr), 1tr in every st from previous round, working 3tr in 2nd tr of 3tr corner group to end of round, join with sl st to 3rd ch of ch-3.

Fasten off and weave in ends.

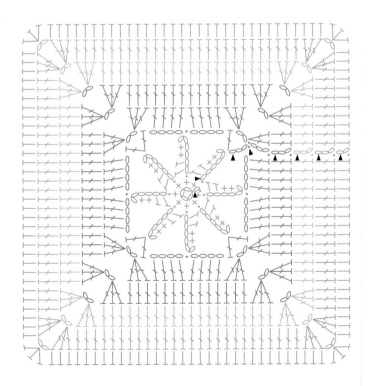

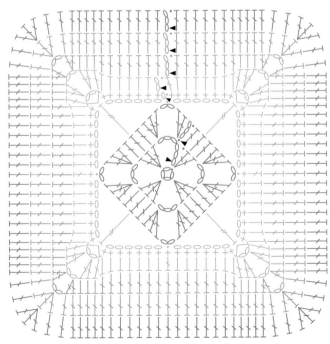

Edwardian Fancy

See page 22

A=Dawn Grey
B=Winsor
C=Bleached

Foundation chain: Using colour A, work 4 ch and join with sl st to form a ring.

Round 1: Ch 3 (counts as 1tr), 11tr in ring, changing to colour B when joining with sl st to 3rd ch of ch-3. Break colour A.

Round 2: Ch 5 (counts as 1tr and ch 2), [1tr in next tr, ch 2] 11 times, changing to colour C when joining with sl st to 3rd ch of ch-5. Break colour B.

Round 3: Sl st in next ch-2 sp, ch 1, 3dc in same sp, *3dc in next ch-2 sp; rep from * to end of round, join with sl st to first dc.

Round 4: Sl st in next 2dc, ch 1, 1dc in same place (2nd of 2dc), 1dc in next dc, [2dc in next dc, 1dc in next 2dc] 11 times, 2dc in next dc, join with sl st in first dc.

Round 5: Ch 1, [1dc, 1tr] in same place, ch 1, [1tr, 1dc] in next dc, *sl st in each of next 2dc, [1dc, 1tr] in next dc, ch 1, [1tr, 1dc] in next dc; rep from * a further 10 times, sl st in each of next 2dc, join with sl st in first dc. Break colour C.

Round 6: Join colour D to any ch-1 sp, ch 1, 1dc in same sp, ch 5, [1dc in next ch-1 sp, ch 5] 11 times, join with sl st in first dc.

Round 7: Sl st in next ch-5 sp, ch 1, [1dc, 1htr, 2tr, ch 2, 2tr, 1htr, 1dc] in same sp (corner made), *1dc in next dc, [4dc in next ch-5 sp, 1dc in next dc] twice**, [1dc, 1htr, 2tr, ch 2, 2tr, 1htr, 1dc] in next ch-5 sp (corner made); rep from * twice more and from * to ** once again, join with sl st in first dc.

Round 8: Ch 3 (counts as 1tr), 1tr in every st of previous round, working 3tr in each ch-2 corner sp, join with sl st in 3rd ch of ch-3. Break colour D.

Round 9: Join colour B to 2nd tr of any 3tr corner group, ch 3 (counts as 1tr), [1tr, ch 1, 2tr] in same place, *1tr in next tr, ch 1, skip next tr, [1tr in next tr, ch 1, skip 1tr] 9 times, 1tr in next tr**, [2tr, ch 1, 2tr] in next tr; rep from * twice and from * to ** once again, changing to colour A when joining with sl st to 3rd ch of ch-3. Break colour B.

Round 10: Ch 3 (counts as 1tr), 1tr in every st and ch-1 sp of previous round, working 3tr in each ch-1 corner sp, changing to colour B when joining with sl st to 3rd ch of ch-3. Break colour A.

Round 11: Ch 1, 1dc in same place, 1dc in every tr from previous round, working 3dc in 2nd tr of each 3tr corner group. Join with sl st to first dc.

Fasten off and weave in ends.

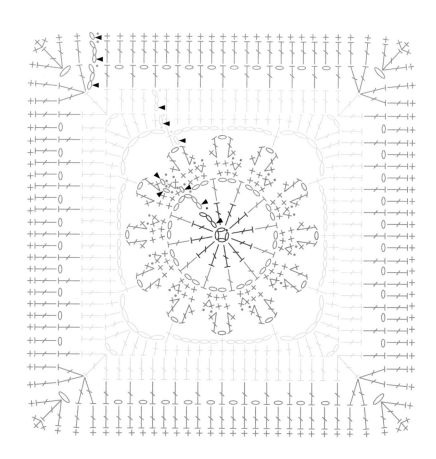

Octagon Tile

See page 23

A=Dawn Grey
B=Persimmon
C=Bleached
D=Windsor

SPECIAL STITCHES

Tr2tog (work two treble sts tog):
[Yrh draw up a loop in next st, (yrh, pull through 2 loops on hook) twice] twice, yrh and draw through all 3 loops on hook.

Foundation ring: Using colour A, ch 8 and join with sl st in first ch to form a ring.

Round 1: Ch 3, (counts as 1tr), 1tr into ring, [ch 1, 2tr into ring] 7 times, ch 1, change to colour B when joining with sl st in 3rd ch of ch-3. (16 sts and 8 ch-sps)

Round 2: Ch 3 (counts as 1tr), 1tr in next st, [(1tr, ch 2, 1tr) in 1ch-sp, 1tr in each of next 2 sts] 7 times, [1tr, ch 2, 1tr] in next 1ch-sp, change to colour B when joining with sl st in 3rd ch of ch-3. (32 sts and 8 ch-sps)

Round 3: Ch 1, 1dc in same place, [1dc in each st to 2ch-sp, 3dc in 2ch-sp] 8 times, 1dc in next st, change to colour D when joining with sl st into first dc. (56 sts)

Round 4: Ch 1, 1dc in same place, 1dc in each of next 3 sts, [3dc in next st, 1dc in next 6 sts] 7 times, 3dc in next dc, 1dc in each of next 2 sts, change to colour A when joining with sl st in first dc. (72 sts)

Round 5: Ch 1, 1dc in same place,
1dc in each of next 5 sts, 1htr in next st, 1tr in each of next 2 sts, *2dtr in next st, ch 2, 2dtr in next st, 1tr in each of next 2 sts, 1htr in next st**, 1dc in each of next 10 sts, 1htr in next st, 1tr in each of next 2 sts; rep from * twice more and from * to ** once again, 1dc in each of next 4 sts, change to colour D when joining with sl st in first dc. (80 sts and 4 ch-sps)

Round 6: Ch 3 (counts as first tr), *1tr in each st to corner, [1tr, 1dtr, 1tr] in 2ch-corner sp; rep from * 3 times, 1tr in each st to end of round, change to colour B when joining with sl st in first tr. (92 sts)

Round 7: Ch 3 (counts as 1tr), 1tr in every st from previous round, working 3tr in centre st of each corner group, change to colour C when joining with sl st to 2nd of ch-2.

Round 8: Ch 1, 1dc in same place, 1dc in each st from previous round, working 3dc in centre st of each corner group, change to colour A when joining with sl st in first dc.

Round 9: Ch 2 (counts as 1htr), 1htr in every st from previous round, working 3htr in centre st of each corner group, join with sl st in 2nd ch of ch-2.

Fasten off and weave in ends.

Octagon Framed Flower

See page 22

A=Bleached
B=Persimmon
C=Dawn Grey
D=Windsor

SPECIAL STITCHES

Cl: Work 1tr in each of next 3 sts, leaving last 2 loops of each st on hook, (7 loops on hook), yrh, pull through all loops on hook, ch 1 to close the cluster. (The ch 1 counts as the top of the stitch).

Foundation ring: Using colour A, work 6 ch and join with sl st to form a ring.

Round 1: Ch 1, 16dc in ring, change to colour B when joining with sl st to first dc. Break colour A.

Round 2: Ch 3 (counts as 1tr), 2tr in same sp, *ch 3, skip next dc, 3tr in next st; rep from * a further 6 times, ch 3, join with a sl st to 3rd ch of ch-3.

Round 3: Ch 3, *cl over next 3 sts, ch 3, sl st in ch-3 sp**, ch 3: rep from * a further 6 times, then from * to ** once again, changing to colour A when joining with a sl st in last ch-3 sp. Break colour B.

Round 4: Ch 4 (counts as 1dtr), 2tr in same sp, *1dc in top of cl, [2tr, 1dtr, 2tr] in next ch-3 sp of Round 2; rep from * a further 6 times, 1dc in top of next cl, 2tr in ch-3 sp of Round 2, change to colour C when joining with sl st to to 4th ch of ch-4. Break colour
A.

Round 5: Ch 3 (counts as 1tr), 2tr in same place, 1tr in every st to next dtr, 3tr in next dtr; rep from * a further 6 times, 1tr in each st to end of round, changing to colour D when joining with sl st to 3rd ch of ch-3. Break colour C.

Round 6: Sl st in next tr, ch 1, 1dc in same st, 1dc in next st, *1htr in next st, 1tr in next st, 1dtr in next st, [1dtr, ch 3, 1dtr] in next st, 1dtr in next st, 1tr in next st, 1htr in next st**, 1dc in next 9 sts; rep from * twice more and then from * to ** once again, 1dc in next 7 sts, join with sl st to first dc.

Round 7: Ch 3, 1tr in every st from previous round, working 5tr in ch-3 corner spaces and changing to colour A when joining with sl st to 3rd ch of ch-3. Break colour D.

Round 8: Ch 3, 1tr in every st from previous round, working 3tr in centre tr of 5tr corner group and changing to colour C when joining with sl st to 3rd ch of ch-3. Break colour A.

Round 9: Ch 2, 1htr in every st from previous round, working 3htr in centre tr of 3tr corner group, join with sl st to 2nd of ch-2.

Fasten off and weave in ends.

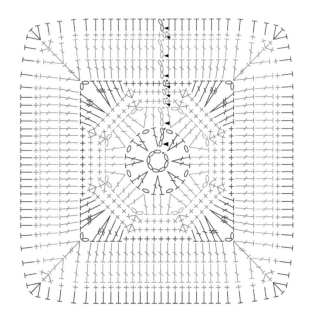

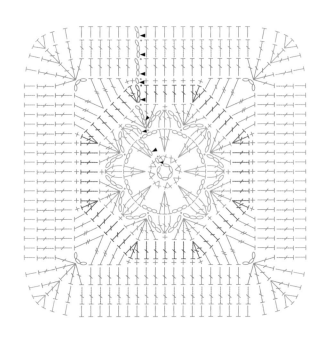

⊛⊛ Diamonds

See page 22

A=Winsor
B=Bleached
C=Persimmon
D=Dawn Grey

Foundation ring: Using colour A, work 6 ch and join with sl st to form a ring.

Round 1: Ch 4 (counts as 1dtr), [4tr in the ring, 1dtr in the ring] 3 times, 4tr in the ring, changing to colour B when joining with sl st to 4th ch of ch 4. Break colour A.

Round 2: Ch 1, 1dc in same place, *skip next st, [2tr, 1dtr] in next st, ch 1, [1dtr, 2tr] in next st, skip next st**, 1dc in next st; rep from * twice and from * to ** once more, change to colour C when joining with sl st to first dc. Break colour B.

Round 3: Ch 4 (counts as 1dtr), 3dtr in same st, *1dc in ch-1 sp, [4dtr, ch 1, 4dtr] in next dc; rep from * twice more, 1dc in ch-1 sp, 4dtr in dc at beg of round, ch 1, changing to colour D when joining with sl st to 4th ch of ch 4. Break colour C.

Round 4: Ch 2 (counts as 1htr), *1tr in next 2 sts, 1dtr in next st, [2dtr, ch 2, 2dtr] in next st, 1dtr in next st, 1tr in next 2 sts, 1htr in next st, 1dc in ch-1 sp**, 1htr in next st; rep from * twice more and from * to ** once again,

change to colour A when joining with sl st to first dc. Break colour D.

Round 5: Ch 3 (counts as 1tr), 1tr in every st, working [2tr, ch 2, 2tr] in each ch-2 corner sp, changing to colour B when joining with sl st to 3rd of ch-3. Break colour A.

Round 6: Ch 2 (counts as 1htr), 1htr in every st, working 5htr in each ch-2 corner sp, changing to colour C when joining with sl st to 2nd of ch-2. Break colour B.

Round 7: Ch 4 (counts as 1tr and ch 1), skip next st, [1tr in next st, ch 1, skip next st] 4 times, *3tr in next st, ch 1, skip next st, [1tr in next st, ch 1, skip next st] 10 times; rep from * twice more, 3tr in next st, ch 1, skip next st, [1tr in next st, ch 1, skip next st] 5 times, changing to colour D when joining with sl st to 3rd ch of ch-3. Break colour C.

Round 8: Ch 3 (counts as 1tr), [1tr in every st and ch-1 sp, working 3tr in 2nd st of 3tr corner cluster, join with sl st to 3rd of ch-3.

Fasten off and weave in ends.

⊛⊛ Mitered Curve

See page 23

A=Persimmon
B=Bleached
C=Windsor
D=Dawn Grey

SPECIAL STITCHES
Picot: Ch 3, sl st in first ch.

Foundation ring: Using colour A, make a Magic Ring.

Row 1: Ch 1, 3dc in ring, turn. (3 sts)
Row 2: Ch 1, 1dc in first st, 2dc in next st, 1dc in next st, turn. (4 sts)
Row 3: Ch 1, 1dc in first st, 2dc in next 2 sts, 1dc in next st, turn. (6 sts)
Row 4: Ch 1, 2dc in first st, 1dc in next 4 sts, 2dc in next st, turn. (8 sts)
Row 5: Ch 3 (counts as 1tr), 1tr in first st, 1tr in next 6 sts, 2tr in last st, turn. (10 sts)
Row 6: Ch 3 (counts as 1tr), 1tr in first st, 1tr in next st, 2tr in next st, 1tr in next 4 sts, 2tr in next st, 1tr in next st, changing to colour B at the end of 2nd tr when working 2tr in 3rd ch of ch-3, turn. (14 sts)
Row 7: Ch 1, 1dc in every st to the end, turn.
Row 8: Ch 1, 1dc in first st, skip next st, [2tr, 1dtr, picot, 1dtr, 2tr] in next st, skip 1 st, 1dc in next st, skip next st, [2tr, 2dtr, picot] in next st, [2dtr, 2tr] in next st, skip 1 st, 1dc in next st, skip next st, [2tr, 1dtr, picot, 1dtr, 2tr] in next st, skip next st, changing to colour C when working 1dc in last st, turn.
Row 9: Ch 3 (counts as 1tr), 2tr in first st, 1dc in picot, [(2dtr, 2tr, 2dtr) in next

dc, 1dc in picot] twice, changing to colour D when working 3rd of 3tr in last dc, turn. (21 sts)
Row 10: Ch 1, 1dc in first st, 1dc in next 2 sts, 1htr in next 3 sts, 1tr in next 2 sts, 1dtr in next 2 sts, [2trtr, ch 2, 2trtr] in next st, 1dtr in next 2 sts, 1tr in next 2 sts, 1htr in next 3 sts, 1dc in next 2 sts, changing to colour B when working last dc in 3rd ch of ch-3, turn. (24 sts)
Row 11: Ch 1, 1dc in every st to ch-2 sp, [2dc, 1htr, 2dc] in ch-2 sp (corner made), 1dc in every st to end, changing to A when working last dc, turn. (29 sts)
Row 12: Ch 3 (counts as 1tr), skip first st, 1tr in every st to htr, [1tr, 1dtr, 1tr] in htr, 1tr in every st to end of row, turn. (31 sts)
Row 13: Ch 3 (counts as 1tr), skip first st, 1tr in every tr to dtr, [1tr, 1dtr, 1tr] in dtr, 1tr in every tr to end of row, 1tr in 3rd ch of ch-3, turn. (33 sts)
Row 14: As Row 13.
Row 15: As Row 13, changing to colour C when working last tr in 3rd ch of ch-3.
Row 16: As Row 13, changing to colour D when working last tr in 3rd ch of ch-3.
Rows 17-18: As Row 13.
Fasten off and weave in ends.

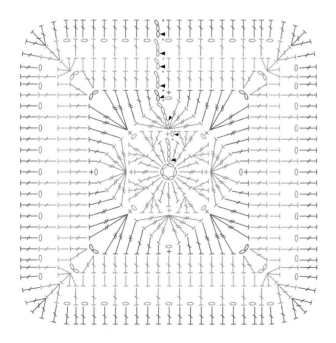

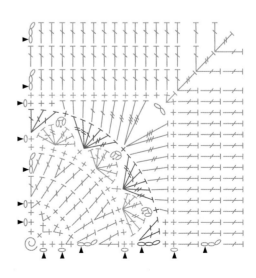

⭐⭐ *Hexagon in a Square*

See page 22

A=Persimmon
B=Bleached
C=Aqua
D=Windsor

Foundation ring: Using colour A, work 4 ch and join with sl st to form a ring.

Round 1: Ch 3 (counts as 1tr), 1tr in the ring, [ch 1, 2tr in ring] 5 times, ch 1, join with sl st to 3rd ch of ch-3. Break colour A.

Round 2: Join colour B to any ch-1 sp with a sl st, ch 3 (counts as 1tr), [1tr, ch 1, 2tr] in same sp, [2tr, ch 1, 2tr] in every ch-1 sp, join with sl st to 3rd ch of ch-3. Break colour B.

Round 3: Join colour C to any ch-1 sp with a sl st, ch 3 (counts as 1tr), 6tr in same sp, 7tr in every ch-1 sp, join with sl st to 3rd ch of ch-3. Break colour C.

Round 4: Join colour D to first tr of any shell, ch 1, 1dc in same place, 1dc in next 6tr, *1tr in sp between two shells from Round 2, 1dc in next 7tr; rep from * to end, changing to colour B when joining with sl st to first dc. Break colour D.

Round 5: Ch 1, 1dc in same place, 1dc in next 6dc, *[1tr, ch 2, 1tr] in next st**, 1dc in next 11dc; rep from * twice more and from * to ** once again, 1dc in next 4dc, join with sl st to first dc.

Round 6: Ch 1, 1dc in same place, 1dc in next 3dc, 1htr in next 4dc, *[2tr, ch 3, 2tr] in next ch-2 sp, 1htr in next 4dc**, 1dc in next 5dc, 1htr in next 4dc; rep from * twice more and from * to ** once again, 1dc in next dc, join with sl st to first dc.

Round 7: Ch 3 (counts as 1tr), 1tr in next 9 sts, *[2tr, ch 3, 2tr] in next ch-3 sp**, 1tr in next 17 sts; rep from * twice more and from * to ** once again, 1tr in next 7 sts, changing to colour C when joining with sl st to 3rd ch of ch-3. Break colour B.

Round 8: Ch 3 (counts as 1tr), 1tr in next 13 sts, *[2tr, ch 3, 2tr] in next ch-3 sp**, 1tr in next 21 sts; rep from * twice more and from * to ** once again, 1tr in next 11 sts, changing to colour D when joining with sl st to 3rd ch of ch-3. Break colour C.

Round 9: Ch 3 (counts as 1tr), 1tr in next 17 sts, *[2tr, ch 2, 2tr] in next ch-3 sp**, 1tr in next 25 sts; rep from * twice more and from * to ** once again, 1tr in next 15 sts, changing to colour A when joining with sl st to 3rd ch of ch-3. Break colour D.

Round 10: Ch 1, 1dc in next 21 sts, *3dc in ch-2 sp**, 1dc in next 29 sts; rep from * twice more and from * to ** once again, 1dc in next 19 sts, join with sl st to first dc.

Fasten off and weave in ends.

⭐⭐ *Circle in a Hexagon*

See page 20

A=Winsor
B=Aqua
C=Bleached
D=Persimmon

Foundation ring: Using colour A, ch 8 and join with sl st in first ch to form a ring.

Round 1: Ch 3 (counts as 1tr), 23tr into the ring, change to yarn B when joining with sl st in 3rd ch of ch-3. Break colour A.

Round 2: Ch 3 (counts as 1tr, 1tr in each of next 2tr, ch 5, skip next tr, *1tr in each of next 3tr, ch 5, skip next tr; rep from * a further 4 times, join with sl st in 3rd ch of ch-3.

Round 3: Ch 1, 1dc in same place, 1dc in each of next 2tr, *[2dc, ch 2, 2dc] in next ch-5 sp; rep from * 5 more times, change to colour C when joining with sl st in first dc.

Round 4: Ch 3 (counts as 1tr), 1tr in each of next 4dc, 3tr in 2ch-sp, *1tr in each of next 7dc, 3tr in next 2ch-sp; rep from * a further 4 times, 1tr in each of next 2dc, join with sl st in 3rd ch of ch-3.

Round 5: Ch 3 (counts as 1tr), 1tr in each of next 3tr, ch 5, skip next 5tr, *1tr in each of next 5tr, ch 5, skip next 5tr; rep from * 4 more times, change to colour D when joining with sl st in 3rd ch of ch-3.

Round 6: Ch 1, 1dc in same place, 1dc in each of next 4tr, *[2dc in next ch-5 sp, working over 5ch-sp, 1dc in in centre tr from 3tr group in Round 3, 2dc in same ch-5 sp], (2htr, ch 2, 2htr) in next tr, 1dc in each of next 4tr, rep between [ ] once, 1dc in each of next 4tr, (2htr, ch 2, 2htr) in next tr, rep between [ ] once more*, 1dc in each of next 5tr; rep from * to * once more, 1dc in next dc, join with sl st in first dc. Break colour D.

Round 7: Join colour C to any ch-2 corner sp, ch 1, *[2dc, ch 1, 2dc] in ch-2 corner sp, 1dc in every dc to next ch-2 corner sp; rep from * a further 3 times, change to colour B when joining with sl st in first dc.

Round 8: Ch 3 (counts as 1tr), 1tr in every st and 3tr in every 1ch-sp to end of round, change to colour A when joining with sl st in 3rd ch of ch-3.

Round 9: Ch 3 (counts as 1tr), 1tr in every st and 3tr in centre tr of every 3tr corner cluster to end of round, change to colour D when joining with sl st in 3rd ch of ch-3.

Round 10: Ch 1, 1dc in every st and [1dc, 1htr, 1dc] in centre tr of every 3tr corner cluster to end of round, join with sl st in first dc.

Fasten off and weave in ends.

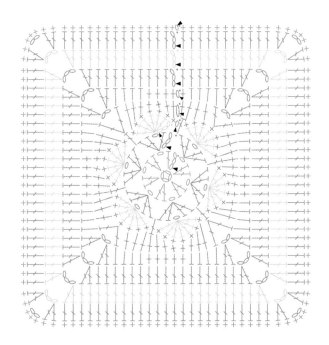

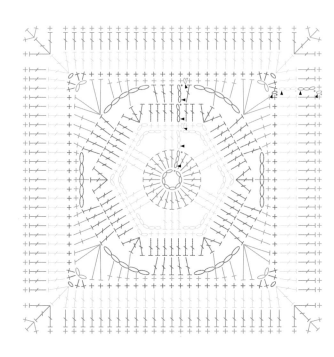

Double Diamonds

See page 21

A=Bleached
B=Dawn Grey
C=Persimmon

SPECIAL STITCHES

PS (Puff Stitch): Yrh, insert hook into designated stitch, [yrh, pull up a loop to the height of a htr] 3 times, yrh and pull through all 7 loops on hook.

Foundation ring: Using colour A, ch 6 and join with sl st in first ch to form a ring.

Round 1: Ch 4 (counts as 1dtr), [5tr into the ring, 1dtr into the ring] 3 times, 5tr into the ring, change to colour B when joining with sl st in 4th ch of ch-4.

Round 2: Ch 1, 1dc in same place, *skip 2tr, [3tr, ch 3, 3tr] in next st, skip 2 sts**, 1dc in next tr; rep from * twice more, then from * to ** once more, join with sl st in first dc. Fasten off colour B.

Round 3: Join colour A to any 3ch-sp, ch 4 (counts as 1dtr), [1dtr, 3tr, ch 2, 3tr, 2dtr] in same 3ch-sp, skip 3 sts, sl st in next dc, *[2dtr, 3tr, ch 2, 3tr, 2dtr] in same 3ch-sp, skip 3 sts, sl st in next dc**; rep from * once again and then from * to ** once more, 1dtr in first ch-3 corner sp, join with sl st in 4th ch of ch-4. Fasten off colour A.

Round 4: Join colour C to any 2ch-sp, ch 1, 3dc in 2ch-sp, 1dc in each of next 5 sts, 1dc in dc from Round 2, 1dc in each of next 5 sts; rep from * 3 more times, change to colour A when joining with sl st in first dc.

Round 5: Ch 1, 1dc in same place, *3dc in next dc, 1dc in each of next 3 sts, 1htr in each of next 2 sts, 1tr in each of next 3dc, 1htr in each of next 2 sts**, 1dc in each of next 3 sts; rep from * twice more and from * to ** once more, 1dc into each of next 2dc, join with sl st to first dc, Fasten off colour A.

Round 6: Join colour C to 2nd dc of 3dc corner cluster, ch 4 (counts as 1htr and ch 2), 1htr in same place, *[ch 1, skip 1 st, PS in next st] 7 times, ch 1**, skip 1 st, [1htr, ch 2, 1htr] in next st; rep from * twice more and then from * to ** once more, join with sl st in 2nd ch of ch-4. Fasten off colour C.

Round 7: Join colour A in 2ch-sp, ch 4 (counts as 1htr and ch 2), 1htr in same place, 1dc in htr, [1dc over ch-sp and into corresponding st from Round 5, 1dc in PS] 7 times, 1dc over ch-sp and into corresponding st from Round 5**, 1htr in htr, ch 2, 1htr in htr; rep from * twice more and from * to **

once more, join with sl st in 2nd ch of ch-4. Fasten off colour A.

Round 8: Join colour B to any dc, ch 3 (counts as 1tr), 1tr in every dc and htr from previous round and [2dtr, ch 2, 2dtr] in every ch-2 corner sp to end of round, change to colour A when joining with sl st in 3rd ch of ch-3.

Round 9: Ch 2 (counts as 1htr), 1htr in every htr and tr around and [2tr, ch 2, 2tr] in every ch-2 corner sp to end of round, change to colour C when joining with sl st in 2nd ch of ch-2.

Round 10: Ch 2 (counts as 1htr), 1htr in every htr and tr around and 3tr in every ch-2 corner sp to end of round, join with sl st in 2nd ch of ch-2.

Fasten off and weave in ends.

Lacy Cross

A=Greengage

See page 25

Foundation ring: Using colour A, ch 6 and join with sl st in first ch to form a ring.

Round 1: Ch 3 (counts as 1tr throughout), 15tr into ring, join with sl st in 3rd ch of ch-3.

Round 2: Ch 3, 2tr in same place, ch 2, skip 1tr, 1tr in next tr, ch 2, skip 1tr, *3tr in next tr, ch 2, skip 1tr, 1tr in next tr, ch 2, skip 1tr; rep from * twice more, join with sl st in 3rd ch of ch-3.

Round 3: Ch 3, 5tr in next tr, *1tr in next tr, [ch 2, 1tr in next tr] twice, 5tr in next tr; rep from * twice more, [1tr in next tr, ch 2] twice, join with sl st in 3rd ch of ch-3.

Round 4: Ch 3, 1tr in each of next 2tr, 5tr in next tr, *1tr in each of next 3tr, ch 2, 1tr in next tr, ch 2, 1tr in each of next 3tr, 5tr in next tr; rep from * twice more, 1tr in each of next 3tr, ch 2, 1tr in next

tr, ch 2, join with sl st in 3rd ch of ch-3.

Round 5: Ch 3, 1tr in each of next 4tr, 5tr in next tr, *1tr in each of next 5tr, ch 2, 1tr in next tr, ch 2, 1tr in to each of next 5tr, 5tr in next tr; rep from * twice more, 1tr in each of next 5tr, ch 2, 1tr in next tr, ch 2, join with sl st in 3rd ch of ch-3.

Round 6: Ch 3, 1tr in each of next 6tr, 5tr in next tr, *1tr in each of next 7tr, ch 2, 1tr in next tr, ch 2, 1tr in each of next 7tr, 5tr in next tr; rep from * twice more, 1tr in each of next 7tr, ch 2, 1tr in next tr, ch 2, join with sl st in 3rd ch of ch-3.

Round 7: Ch 3, 1tr in each tr and 2tr in each ch-2 sp of previous round, working [2tr, ch 1, 2tr] in centere of each 5tr corner group, join with sl st in 3rd ch of ch-3.

Fasten off and weave in ends.

Criss Cross

A=Oyster

See page 27

Foundation ring: Using colour A, ch 6 and join with sl st in first ch to form a ring.

Round 1: Ch 3 (counts as 1tr), 3tr in ring, ch 3, [4tr in ring, ch3] 3 times, join with sl st in 3rd ch of ch-3.

Round 2: Ch 5 (counts as 1tr, 2ch), *skip 2tr, 1tr in next tr, [2tr, ch 3, 2tr] in next ch-3 sp**, 1tr in next tr, ch 2; rep from * twice more and then from * to ** once again, join with sl st in 3rd ch of ch-5.

Round 3: Ch 5 (counts as 1tr, 2ch), *1tr in each of next 3tr, [2tr, ch 3, 2tr] in next ch-3 sp**, 1tr in each of next 3tr, ch 2; rep from * twice more and then from * to ** once again, 1tr in each of next 2tr, join with sl st in 3rd ch of ch-5.

Round 4: Ch 5 (counts as 1tr, 2ch), *1tr in each of next 5tr, [2tr, ch 3, 2tr in next tr] in next ch-3 sp**, 1tr in each of next 5tr, ch 2; rep from * twice more

and from * to ** once again, 1tr in each of next 4tr, join with sl st in 3rd ch of ch-5.

Round 5: Ch5 (counts as 1tr, ch 2), *1tr in each of next 7tr, [2tr, ch 3, 2tr in next tr] in next ch-3 sp**, 1tr in each of next 7tr, ch 2; rep from * twice more and from * to ** once again, 1tr in each of next 6tr, join with sl st in 3rd ch of ch-5.

Round 6: Ch 5 (counts as 1tr, ch 2), *1tr in each of next 9tr, [2tr, ch 3, 2tr in next tr] in next ch-3 sp**, 1tr in each of next 9tr, ch 2; rep from * twice more and from * to ** once again, 1tr in each of next 8tr, join with sl st in 3rd ch of ch-5.

Round 7: Ch 1, 1dc in same place, 1dc in each tr and 2dc in each ch-2 sp of previous round, working [2dc, ch 1, 2dc] in each ch-3 corner sp, join with sl st to first dc.

Fasten off and weave in ends.

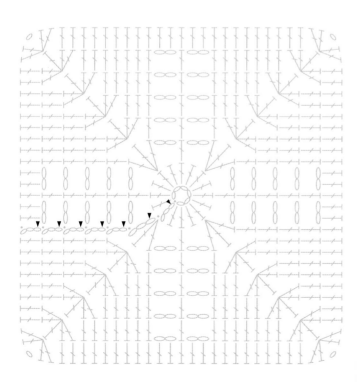

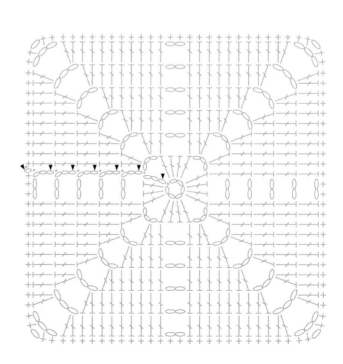

Sunray Cross

See page 24

A=Greengage

Popcorn Cross

See page 26

A=Oyster

Foundation ring: Using colour A, ch 6 and join with sl st in first ch to form a ring.

Round 1: Ch 4 (counts as 1dtr), 1dtr into ring, ch 2, [2dtr into ring, ch 2] 7 times, join with sl st in 4th ch of ch-4.

Round 2: Ch 3 (counts as 1tr), 2tr in next dtr, ch 2, [1tr in next dtr, 2tr in next dtr, ch 2] 7 times, join with sl st in 3rd ch of ch-3.

Round 3: Ch 3 (counts as 1tr), 3tr in next tr, 1tr in next tr, ch 2, *1tr in next tr, 3tr in next tr, 1tr in next tr, ch 2; rep from * a further 6 times, join with sl st in 3rd ch of ch-3.

Round 4: Ch 3 (counts as 1tr), 2htr in next tr, 1dc in each of next 3tr, 2dc in next ch-2 sp, 1dc in each of next 3tr, 2htr in next tr, 1tr in next tr, *ch 3 (corner sp made), 1tr in next tr, 2htr in next tr, 1dc in each of next 3tr, 2dc in next ch-2 sp, 1dc in each of next 3tr, 2htr in next tr, 1tr in next tr; rep from *

twice, ch 3 (corner sp made), join with sl st in 3rd ch of ch-3.

Round 5: Ch 3 (counts as 1tr), 2tr in same place, *1htr in each of next 5 sts, skip 1 st, ch 2, 1tr in each of next 5 sts, 3tr in next st, ch 3**, 3tr in next st; rep from * twice more and from * to ** once again, join with sl st in 3rd ch of ch-3.

Round 6: Ch 3 (counts as 1tr), 1tr in each of next 7 sts, *2tr in next ch-2 sp, 1tr in each of next 8 sts, 5tr in next ch-3 corner sp**, 1tr in each of next 8 sts; rep from * twice more and from * to ** once again, join with sl st in 3rd ch of ch-3.

Round 7: Ch 2 (counts as 1htr), 1htr in each tr of previous round, working 3htr in centre st of each 5tr group, join with sl st in 2nd ch of ch-2.

Fasten off and weave in ends.

SPECIAL STITCHES

Beg PC (Beginning Popcorn): Ch 3, work 4tr in same place, remove hook from working loop and insert under both loops of first tr in the group. Pick up the working loop with the hook and draw it through to fold the group of sts together and close it at the top.

PC (Popcorn): Work 5tr in same place, remove hook from working loop and insert under both loops of first tr in the group. Pick up the working loop with the hook and draw it through to fold the group of sts together and close it at the top.

Foundation ring: Using colour A, ch 8 and join with sl st in first ch to form a ring.

Round 1: Beg PC into ring, [ch 5, PC in ring] 3 times, ch 5, join with sl st in top of beg PC.

Round 2: Ch 3 (counts as 1tr), *[2tr, ch 2, PC, ch 2, 2tr] in next ch-5 sp**, 1tr in next PC; rep from * twice more and from * to ** once again, join with sl st in 3rd ch of ch-3.

Round 3: Ch 3 (counts as 1tr), 1tr in each of next 2 sts, *2tr in next ch-2 sp, ch 2, PC in next PC, ch 2, 2tr in

next ch-2 sp**, 1tr in each of next 5tr; rep from * twice more and from * to ** once again, 1tr in each of last 2 sts, join with sl st in 3rd ch of ch-3.

Round 4: Ch 3 (counts as 1tr), 1tr in each of next 4tr, *2tr in next ch-2 sp, ch 2, PC in next PC, ch 2, 2tr in next ch-2 sp**, 1tr in each of next 9tr; rep from * twice more and from * to **once again, 1tr in each of last 4tr, join with sl st in 3rd ch of ch-3.

Round 5: Ch 3 (counts as 1tr), 1tr in each of next 6tr, *2tr in next ch-2 sp, ch 2, PC in next PC, ch 2, 2tr in next ch-2 sp**, 1tr in each of next 13tr; rep from * twice more and from * to ** once again, 1tr in each of last 6tr, join with sl st in 3rd ch of ch-3.

Round 6: Ch 3 (counts as 1tr), 1tr in each of next 8tr, *2tr in next ch-2 sp, ch 2, PC in next PC, ch 2, 2tr in next ch-2 sp**, 1tr in each of next 17tr; rep from * twice more and from * to ** once again, 1tr in each of last 8tr, join with sl st in 3rd ch of ch-3.

Round 7: Ch 1, 1dc in every st of previous round, working 3dc in each ch-2 sp and [1htr, 1tr, 1htr] in top of each PC, join with sl st to first dc.

Fasten off and weave in ends.

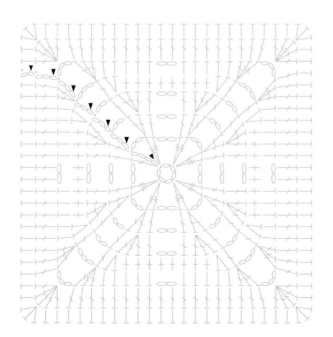

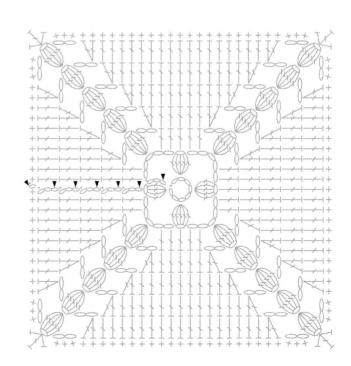

 **Anemone**   *See page 27*

A=Blood Orange
B=Garnet
C=Ecru
D=Oyster

Foundation ring: Using colour A, ch 4 and join sl st in first ch to form a ring.

Round 1: Ch 3 (counts as 1tr), 3tr into ring, ch 1, *4tr into ring, ch 1; rep from * twice more, join with sl st in 3rd ch of ch-3. Break colour A.

Round 2: Join colour B to any ch-1 sp, ch 3 (counts as 1tr), [3tr, ch 1, 4tr] in next ch-1 sp (corner made), ch 1, *[4tr, ch 1, 4tr] in next ch-1 sp, ch 1; rep from * twice more, change to colour C when joining with sl st in 3rd ch of ch-3. Break colour B.

Round 3: Ch 1, 1dc in same place, 1dc in each tr and ch-1 sp from previous round, join with sl st to first dc.

Round 4: Join colour D to any corner dc, ch 3 (counts as 1tr), [2tr, ch 1, 3tr] in same dc, ch 1, *skip 4dc, [2tr, ch 1, 2tr] in next dc, ch 1, skip 4dc**, [4tr, ch 1, 4tr] in next dc, ch1; rep from * twice more and from * to ** once again, join with sl st in 3rd ch of ch-3. Break colour D.

Round 5: Join colour A to first tr of any corner group, ch 3 (counts as 1tr), 1tr in every tr and ch-1 sp along the edges of previous round and [2tr, ch1, 2tr] in each ch-1 corner sp, join with sl st in 3rd ch of ch-3.

Rounds 6-8: Ch 3 (counts as 1tr), 1tr in every tr of previous round and [2tr, ch 1, 2tr] in each ch-1 corner sp, join with sl st in 3rd ch of ch-3.

Fasten off and weave in ends.

 Seville   *See page 25*

A=Blood Orange
B=Oyster
C=Garnet

Foundation ring: Using colour A, ch 8 and join with sl st in first ch to form a ring.

Round 1: Ch 3 (counts as 1tr), 2tr in the ring, ch 7, [3tr in ring, ch 7] 7 times, change to colour B when joining with sl st in 3rd ch of ch-3.

Round 2: Sl st in next 2tr and ch-7 sp, ch 3 (counts as 1tr), [2tr, ch 2, 3tr] in same sp, *ch 7, skip next ch-7 sp, [3tr, ch 2, 3tr] in next ch-7 sp; rep from * twice more, ch 7, skip next ch-7 sp, join with sl st in 3rd ch of ch-3.

Round 3: Ch 3 (counts as 1tr), 1tr in each of next 2tr, *[2tr, ch 2, 2tr] in ch-2 corner sp, 1tr in each of next 3tr, ch 7**, 1tr in each of next 3tr; rep from * twice more and from * to ** once more, join with sl st in 3rd ch of ch-3.

Round 4: Ch 3 (counts as 1tr), 1tr in each of next 4tr, *[2tr, ch 2, 3tr] in ch-2 corner sp, 1tr in each of next 5tr, ch 4, 1dc in skipped ch-7 sp from Round 1 enclosing ch made on Rounds 2 and 3, ch 4**, 1tr in each of next 5tr; rep from * twice more and from * to ** once more, join with sl st in 3rd ch of ch-3.

Round 5: Ch 1, 1dc in same place, 1dc in each of next 6tr, *3dc in next ch-2 corner sp, 1dc in each of next 7tr, 1dc in next ch-4 sp, ch 3, 1dc in next ch-4 sp**, 1dc in each of next 7tr; rep from * twice more and from * to ** once again, change to colour C when joining with sl st in first dc.

Round 6: Ch 4 (counts as 1tr and ch 1), *[skip 1dc, 1tr in next dc, ch 1] 3 times, 5tr in centre st of next 3dc corner group, ch 1, [skip 1 dc, 1tr in next dc, ch 1] 3 times, skip next dc, 1 tr in each of next 2dc, 2tr in next ch-3 sp**, 1tr in each of next 2dc; rep from * twice more and from * to ** once again, 1tr in next dc, join with sl st in 3rd ch of ch-4.

Round 7: Ch 4 (counts as 1tr and ch 1), *[1tr in next tr, ch 1] 3 times, 1tr in each of next 2tr, 3tr in centre st of 5tr corner group, 1tr in each of next 2tr, ch 1, [1tr in next tr, ch1] 3 times**, 1tr in each of next 6tr; rep from * twice more and from * to ** once again, 1tr in each of next 5tr, join with sl st in 3rd ch of ch-4.

Fasten off and weave in ends.

Italian Cross

See page 24

A=Blackcurrant
B=Oyster
C=Garnet

SPECIAL STITCHES

htr3tog (beg pf): Work three half treble sts tog: [yrh, draw up a loop in next st] 3 times, yrh and draw through all 7 loops on hook.

htr4tog (pf): Work four half treble sts tog: [yrh, draw up a loop in next st] 4 times, yrh and draw through all 5 loops on hook.

Foundation ring: Using colour A, ch 4 and join with sl st in first ch to form a ring.

Round 1: Ch 3 (counts as 1tr), 11tr into the ring, change to colour B when joining with sl st in 3rd ch of ch-3. Break colour A.

Round 2: Ch 2 (counts as 1htr), beg pf in same place, *[ch 1, pf in next st]

twice, ch 5**, pf in next st; rep from * twice more and from * to ** once again, join with sl st in top of beg pf.

Round 3: Sl st in next 1ch-sp, ch 2 (counts as 1htr), beg pf in same sp, *ch 1, pf in next sp, ch 2, 5tr in next 5ch-sp, ch 2**, pf in next 1ch-sp; rep from * twice more and from * to ** once again, join with sl st in top of beg pf.

Round 4: Sl st in next 1ch-sp, ch 2 (counts as 1htr), beg pf in same sp, *ch 3, skip 2ch, [1tr in next tr, ch 1] twice, [1tr, (ch 1, 1tr) twice] in next tr, [ch 1, 1tr in next tr] twice, ch 3, skip 2ch**, pf in next 1ch-sp; rep from * twice more and from * to ** once again, join with sl st to top of beg pf. Break colour B.

Round 5: Join colour C to first tr of

any 7tr corner group, ch 4 (counts as 1tr and ch 1), *[1tr in next tr, ch 1] twice, [1tr, (ch 1, 1tr) twice] in next tr, [ch 1, 1tr in next tr] 3 times, 3tr in next 3ch-sp, ch 1, 3tr in next 3ch-sp**, 1tr in next tr, ch 1; rep from * twice more and from * to ** once again, change to colour A when joining with sl st in 3rd ch of ch-4.

Round 6: Ch 4 (counts as 1tr and ch 1), *[1tr in next tr, ch 1] 3 times, [1tr, (ch 1, 1tr) twice] in next tr, [ch 1, 1tr in next tr] 4 times, 1tr in each of next 3tr, 1tr in 1ch-sp, 1tr in each of next 3tr**, 1tr in next tr, ch 1; rep from * twice more and from * to ** once again, change to colour C when joining with sl st in 3rd ch of ch-4.

Round 7: Ch 4 (counts as 1tr and ch

1), *[1tr in next tr, ch 1] 4 times, [1tr, (ch 1, 1tr) twice] in next tr, [ch 1, 1tr in next tr] 5 times**, 1tr in each of next 8tr, ch 1; rep from * twice more and from * to ** once again, 1tr in each of next 7tr, join with sl st in 3rd ch of ch-4.

Round 8: Ch 4 (counts as 1tr and ch 1), *[1tr in next tr, ch 1] 5 times, [1tr, (ch 1, 1tr) twice] in next tr, [ch 1, 1tr in next tr] 6 times**, 1tr in each of next 8tr, ch 1; rep from * twice more and from * to ** once again, 1tr in each of next 7tr, join with sl st in 3rd ch of ch-4.

Fasten off and weave in ends.

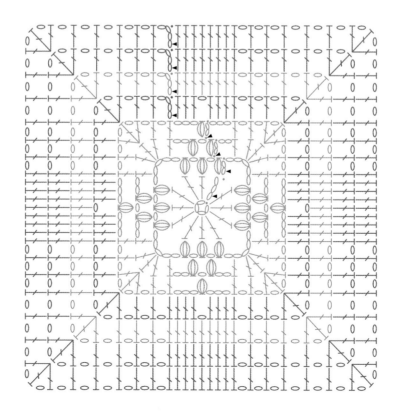

✦ ✦ *Looped Cross*

See page 26

A=Oyster
B=Greengage
C=Ecru
D=Dark Forest

Chain section: Using colour A, ch 4 and join with sl st in first ch to form a ring, ch 16, *1dc into the ring, ch 15; rep from * twice more, join with a sl st in first ch. Fasten off.

Centre motif: Using colour B, ch 4 and join with sl st in first ch to form a ring, ch 3, (counts as 1tr), 2tr into the ring, ch 3, *3tr into the ring, ch 3; rep from * twice more, join with sl st in 3rd ch of ch-3. Fasten off. Hold the centre motif in front of the chain section and pull each 15ch-loop through a corresponding 3ch-sp from the centre motif.

Round 1: Join colour B to any 15ch-sp, ch 1, [1dc, ch 3, 1dc] in same 15ch-sp, ch 8, *[1dc, ch 3, 1dc] in next 15ch-sp, ch 8; rep from * twice more, join with sl st in first dc.

Round 2: Ch 3 (counts as 1tr), *[1tr, ch 3, 1tr] in next 3ch-sp, 1tr in next dc, 8tr in 8ch-sp, 1tr in next dc; rep from * to end of round, omitting last tr, join with sl st in 3rd ch of ch-3.

Round 3: Ch 1, 1dc in same place, 1dc in next tr, *[(1dc, ch 1) twice, 1dc] in next 3ch-sp**, 1dc in each tr to corner; rep from * twice more and from * to ** again, 1dc in every tr to end of round, change to colour C when joining with sl st in first dc.

Round 4: Ch 1, 1dc in same place, 1dc in in each of next 2dc, *1dc in next 1ch-sp, [1dc, ch 1, 1dc] in next dc, 1dc in next 1ch-sp**, 1dc in each of next 14 dc; rep from * twice more and from * to ** again, 1dc in every dc to end of round, change to colour D when joining with sl st in first dc.

Round 5: Ch 1, 1dc in every dc to corner, [1dc, ch 1, 1dc] in 1ch-corner sp; rep from * a further 3 times, 1dc in every dc to end of round, join with sl st in first dc.
Fasten off and weave in ends.

✦ ✦ *Interlocking Cross*

See page 25

A=Dark Forest
B=Ecru
C=Greengage
D=Oyster

Foundation ring: Using colour A, ch 4 and join with sl st in first ch to form a ring.

Round 1: Ch 1, [3dc into ring, ch 10] 4 times, change to colour B when joining with sl st in first dc.

Round 2: Ch 2 (counts as 1htr), 1htr in same st, 1htr in next dc, 2htr in next dc, ch 12, *2htr in next dc, 1htr in in next dc, 2htr in next dc, ch 12; rep from * twice more, change to colour C when joining with sl st in 2nd ch of ch-2.

Round 3: Ch 3 (counts as 1tr), 1tr in same st, 1tr in each of next 3htr, 2tr in next htr, ch 12, *2tr in next dc, 1tr in each of next 3htr, 2tr in next htr, ch 12; rep from * twice more, change to colour D when joining with sl st in 3rd ch of ch-3.

Round 4: Ch 3 (counts as 1tr), 1tr in same st, 1tr in each of next 5tr, 2tr in next tr, ch 12, *2tr in next tr, 1tr in each of next 5tr, 2tr in next tr, ch 12; rep from * twice more, change to colour B when joining with sl st in 3rd ch of ch-3. Drop loop from hook. Form the corner chain links by slipping the loop from Round 1 over the loop from Round 2, slip Round 2 loop over Round 3 loop, and Round 3 loop over Round 4 loop. Insert hook back into dropped loop and continue with following round.

Round 5: Ch 3 (counts as 1tr), 1tr in same st, 1tr in each of next 7tr, 2tr in next tr, 5tr in 12ch-loop from Round 4, *2tr in next tr, 1tr in each of next 5tr, 2tr in next tr, 5tr in 12ch-loop from Round 4; rep from * twice more, join with sl st in 3rd ch of ch-3.
Fasten off and weave in ends.

Centre motif

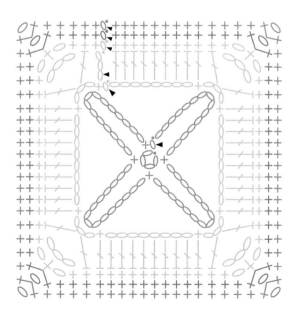

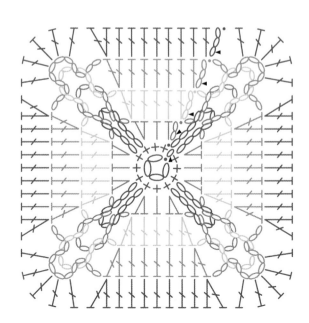

Crossroads

See page 27

 Embossed Cross

See page 24

A=Greengage

A=Oyster
B=Ecru
C=Greengage
D=Dark Forest

SPECIAL STITCHES

tr2tog (work 2 treble sts tog): Work two tr sts to the last "yrh, pull through," yrh once again and draw through all three loops on the hook.

tr3tog (work 3 treble sts tog): Work three tr sts to the last "yrh, pull through," yrh once again and draw through all four loops on the hook.

Foundation ring: Using colour A, ch 4 and join with sl st in first ch to form a ring.

Round 1: Ch 3 (counts as 1tr), tr2tog into the ring, ch 1, tr3tog into the ring, ch 3, *tr3tog into ring, ch 1, tr3tog into ring, ch 3; rep from * twice more, join with sl st in top of first cluster.

Round 2: Sl st to next 1ch-sp, [ch 3, tr2tog, ch 1, tr3tog] in same sp, *ch 3, [(1tr, ch 3) twice in next 3ch-sp**, [tr3tog, ch 1, tr3tog] in next 1ch-sp; rep from * twice more and from * to **

once again, join with sl st in top of first cluster.

Round 3: Sl st to next 1ch-sp, [ch 3, tr2tog, ch 1, tr3tog] in same sp, ch 1, *1tr in next 3ch-sp, ch 3 [(1tr, ch 3) twice in 3ch-corner sp, 1tr in next 3ch-sp, ch 1**, [(tr3tog, ch 1) twice] in next 1ch-sp; rep from * twice more and from * to ** once again, join with sl st to top of first cluster.

Round 4: Sl st to next 1ch-sp, [ch 3, tr2tog, ch 1, tr3tog] in same sp, *ch 3, skip next 1ch-sp, 1tr in next 3ch-sp, ch 3 [(1tr, ch 3) twice in 3ch-corner sp, 1tr in next 3ch-sp, ch 3, skip next 1ch-sp**, [tr3tog, ch 1, tr3tog] twice in next 1ch-sp; rep from * twice more and from * to ** once again, join with sl st to top of first cluster.

Fasten off and weave in ends.

SPECIAL STITCHES

tr5tog (cluster): Work five treble sts tog: [Yrh, draw up a loop in next st, (yrh, pull through 2 loops on hook) twice] 5 times, yrh and draw through all 6 loops on hook.

Spiked tr: Yarn round hook, insert hook into stitch one round below the next stitch and pull loop through up to the level of current round, [yarn round hook and pull through two loops on hook] twice.

Foundation ring: Using colour A, ch 6 and join with sl st in first ch to form a ring.

Round 1: Ch 3 (counts as 1tr), 15tr into the ring, change to colour B when joining with sl st in 3rd ch of ch-3.

Round 2: Ch 1, 1dc in same place, *tr5tog in next dc, 1dc in each of next 3tr; rep from * to end of round, omitting last dc and joining with a sl st in first dc. Break colour B.

Round 3: Join colour A to top of any cluster from previous round, ch 3 (counts as 1tr), 4tr in same stitch, 1spiked tr in row below in each of next 3 sts, *5tr in top of corner cluster, 1spiked tr in row below in each of next 3 sts; rep from * twice more, change

to colour C when joining with sl st in 3rd ch of ch-3.

Round 4: Ch 1, 1dc in same place, *1dc in next st, tr5tog in next st, 1dc in each of next 6 sts; rep from * to end of round, omitting last dc and joining with a sl st in first dc. Break colour C.

Round 5: Join colour A to top of any cluster from previous round, ch 3 (counts as 1tr), 4tr in same stitch, 1spiked tr in row below in each of next 7 sts, *5tr in corner cluster, 1spiked tr in row below in each of next 7 sts; rep from * twice more, change to colour D when joining with sl st in 3rd ch of ch-3.

Round 6: Ch 1, 1dc in same place, *1dc in next st, tr5tog in next st, 1dc in each of next 10 sts; rep from * to end of round, omitting last dc and joining with a sl st in first dc. Break colour D.

Round 7: Join colour A to top of any cluster from previous round, ch 3 (counts as 1tr), 4tr in same stitch, 1spiked tr in row below in each of next 11 sts, *5tr in corner cluster, 1spiked tr in row below in each of next 11 sts; rep from * twice more, join with sl st in 3rd ch of ch-3.

Fasten off and weave in ends.

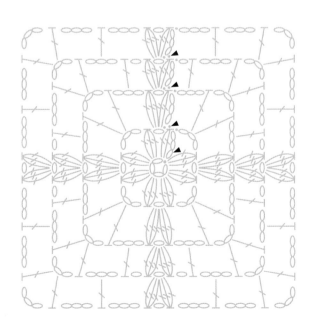

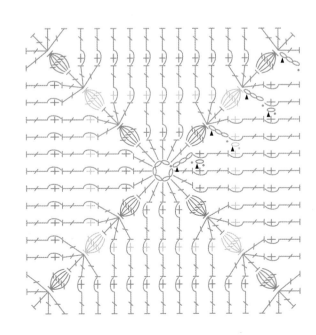

Catherine Wheel

See page 26

A=Garnet
B=Oyster
C=Ecru
D=Greengage

Foundation ring: Using colour A, ch 6 and join with sl st in first ch to form a ring.

Round 1: Ch 3 (counts as 1tr), work 19tr in ring, changing to colour B when joining with sl st to 3rd ch of ch-3. (20 tr)

Round 2: Ch 4 (counts as 1tr, ch 1), [1tr in next tr, ch 1] 19 times, changing to colour C when joining with sl st in 3rd ch of ch-3. (20 tr)

Round 3: Sl st in next ch-sp, ch 3 (counts as 1tr), 2tr in same sp, [3tr in next ch-sp] 3 times, ch 5, *skip next ch-sp, [3tr in next ch-sp] 4 times, ch 5; rep from * twice more and change to colour A when joining with sl st in 3rd ch of ch-3.

Round 4: Ch 3 (counts as 1tr), 1tr in every tr of previous round, working [3tr, ch 2, 3tr] in each ch-5 corner sp, and change to colour C when joining with sl st to 3rd ch of ch-3.

Round 5: Join yarn C to next ch-2 corner sp, ch 3 (counts as 1tr), [2tr, ch 3, 3tr] in same sp, *[ch 2, skip 2tr, 1tr in next tr] 3 times, [1tr in next tr, ch 2, skip 2tr] 3 times**, [3tr, ch 2, 3tr] in

next ch-2 corner sp; rep from * twice more and from * to ** once again, and change to colour B when joining with sl st in 3rd ch of ch-3.

Round 6: Ch 3 (counts as 1tr), 1tr in each of next 2tr, *[3tr, ch 2, 3tr] in same sp, 1tr in each of next 3tr, [ch 2, 1tr in next tr] 3 times, [1tr in next tr, ch 2] 3 times**, 1tr in each of next 3tr; rep from * twice more and from * to ** once again, join with sl st in 3rd ch of ch-3.

Round 7: Ch 3 (counts as 1tr), 1tr in each of next 2tr *[3tr, ch 2, 3tr] in same sp, 1tr in each of next 6tr, [ch 2, 1tr in next tr] 3 times, [1tr in next tr, ch 2] 3 times**, 1tr in each of next 6tr; rep from * twice more and from * to ** once again, and change to colour D when joining with sl st in 3rd ch of ch-3.

Round 8: Ch 1, 1dc in each tr of previous round, working 2dc in each ch2-sp along sides of the square and 3dc in each ch-2 corner sp, join with sl st in first dc.

Fasten off and weave in ends.

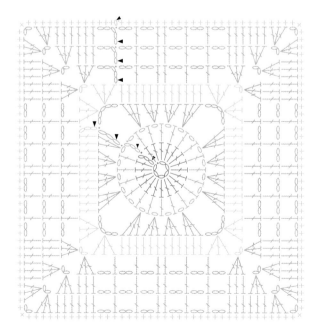

Gothic Square

See page 25

A=Ecru
B=Oyster
C=Garnet
D=Greengage

SPECIAL STITCHES

Beg cl (Beginning cluster): Ch 3, [Yarn round hook, insert hook, yarn round hook, draw a loop through, yarn round hook, draw through 2 loops] twice in same stitch or space, yarn round hook and draw through all 3 loops on hook.

Cl (Cluster): [Yarn round hook, insert hook, yarn round hook, draw a loop through, yarn round hook, draw through 2 loops] three times in same stitch or space, yarn round hook and draw through all 4 loops on hook.

Foundation ring: Using colour A, ch 4 and join with sl st in first ch to form a ring.

Round 1: Ch 4, (counts as 1tr, ch 1), [1tr into ring, ch 1] 11 times, change to colour B when joining with sl st in 3rd ch of ch-4. (12 spaced tr)

Round 2: Ch 3 (counts as 1tr), beg cl in same sp, [ch 3, cl in ch-1 sp] 11 times, ch 3, join with sl st to top of beg cl.

Round 3: Sl st in top of beg cl and centre st of next ch-3 sp, ch 1, 1dc in same sp, [ch 5, 1dc in next ch-3 sp] 11 times, ch 5, join with sl st to first dc. Break colour B.

Round 4: Join colour C to centre st of any ch-5 sp, ch 3 (counts as 1tr), 4tr in same sp, *ch 1, 1dc in next ch-5 sp, ch 5, 1dc in next ch-5 sp, ch 1**, [5tr, ch 3, 5tr] in next ch-5 sp; rep from * twice more and from * to ** once again, 5tr in next ch-5 sp, ch 3, join with sl st in 3rd ch of ch-3. Break colour C.

Round 5: Join colour D to any ch-3

sp, ch 3 (counts as 1tr), [1tr, ch 2, 2tr] in same sp, *1tr in each of next 4tr, ch 5, 1dc in next ch-5 sp, ch 4, skip next tr, 1tr in each of next 4tr**, [2tr, ch 2, 2tr in next ch-3 sp; from * twice more and from * to ** once again, 5tr in next ch-5 sp, ch 3, join with sl st in 3rd ch of ch-3.

Round 6: Ch 3 (counts as 1tr), [1tr, ch 2, 1tr] in same sp, *1tr in each of next 4tr, [ch 4, 1dc in next ch-5 sp] twice, ch 4, skip next tr, 1tr in each of next 4tr**, [2tr, ch 2, 2tr in next ch-3 sp]; from * twice more and from * to ** once again, 5tr in next ch-5 sp, ch 3, change to colour A when joining with sl st in 3rd ch of ch-3.

Round 7: Ch 3 (counts as 1tr), [1tr, ch 2, 1tr] in same sp, *1tr in each of next 4tr, [ch 4, 1dc in next ch-5 sp] 3 times, ch 4, skip next tr, 1tr in each of next 4tr**, [2tr, ch 2, 2tr] in next ch-3 sp; from * twice more and from * to ** once again, 5tr in next ch-5 sp, ch 3, change to colour B when joining with sl st in 3rd ch of ch-3.

Round 8: Ch 2 (counts as 1htr), 1htr in next tr, *3htr in next ch-2 corner sp, 1htr in each of next 6tr, 4htr in each of next ch-4 sp**, 1htr in each of next 6tr; rep from * twice more and from * to ** once again, 1htr in each of next 4tr, change to colour C when joining with sl st to 2nd of ch-2.

Round 9: Ch 1, 1dc in every st from previous round, working 3dc in centre st of every 3htr cluster, to end of round, join with sl st to first dc.

Fasten off and weave in ends.

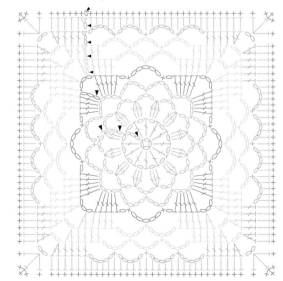

Treble Cross

See page 26

A=Greengage
B=Ecru
C=Oyster
D=Blackcurrant

SPECIAL STITCHES

tr2tog (work two treble sts tog):
[Yrh draw up a loop in next st, (yrh, pull through 2 loops on hook) twice] twice, yrh and draw through all 3 loops on hook.

Foundation ring: Using colour A, ch 8 and join with sl st in first ch to form a ring.

Round 1: Ch 1, 16dc into the ring, join with sl st in first dc.

Round 2: Ch 1, 1dc in same place, [ch 7, skip 3dc, 1dc in next dc] 3 times, ch 7, skip 3dc, join with sl st in first dc.

Round 3: Sl st to 3rd ch of next 7ch-sp, ch 3 (counts as 1tr), 1tr in same place, *ch 3, 2tr in same sp, ch 3,

tr2tog inserting hook into same sp for first leg and into next 7ch-sp for second leg, ch 3, 2tr in next sp; rep from * a further 3 times, omitting 2tr at end of last rep, join with sl st in 3rd ch of ch 3. Break colour A.

Round 4: Join colour B to next 3ch-corner sp, ch 3 (counts as 1tr), 1tr in same place, *ch 3, 2tr in same 3ch-sp, ch 3, skip 2tr, 3tr in next 3ch-sp, 1tr in top of cluster, 3tr in next 3ch-sp, ch 3, skip 2tr, 2tr in next 3ch-sp; rep from * a further 3 times, omitting 2tr at end of last rep, join with sl st in 3rd ch of ch 3. Break colour B.

Round 5: Join colour C to next 3ch-corner sp, ch 3 (counts as 1tr), 2tr in same sp, *ch 3, 3tr in same 3ch-sp, ch 2, 2tr in next 3ch-sp, ch 2, skip 1tr,

1tr in each of next 5tr, ch 2, 2tr in next 3ch-sp, ch 2, 3tr in next 3ch-sp; rep from * a further 3 times, omitting 3tr at end of last rep, change to colour D when joining with sl st in 3rd ch of ch 3. Break colour C.

Round 6: Ch 3 (counts as 1tr), 1 tr in each of next 2tr, *[3tr, ch 3, 3tr] in next 3ch-sp, 1tr in each of next 3tr, ch 2, 2tr in each of 2tr, ch 2, skip 1tr, 1tr in each of next 3tr, ch 2, 1tr in each of next 2tr, ch 2, 1tr in each of next 3tr; rep from * a further 3 times, omitting 3tr at end of last rep, change to colour C when joining with sl st in 3rd ch of ch 3. Break colour D.

Round 7: Ch 3 (counts as 1tr), 1tr in each of next 5tr, *[3tr, ch 3, 3tr] in next 3ch-sp, 1tr in each of next 6tr, ch

2, 1tr in each of next 2tr, ch 2, skip 1tr, 1tr in next tr, skip 1tr, ch 2, 1tr in each of next 2tr, ch 2, 1tr in each of next 6tr; rep from * a further 3 times, omitting 6tr at end of last rep, change to colour B when joining with sl st in 3rd ch of ch 3. Break colour C.

Round 8: Ch 3 (counts as 1tr), 1tr in every tr of previous round, working 2tr in every 2ch-sp and [3tr, ch 3, 3tr] in next 3ch-sp to end of round, change to colour A when joining with sl st in 3rd ch of ch-3. Break colour B.

Round 9: Ch 1, 1dc in every tr of previous round, working 3dc in every 3ch-corner sp, join with sl st in first dc.
Fasten off and weave in ends.

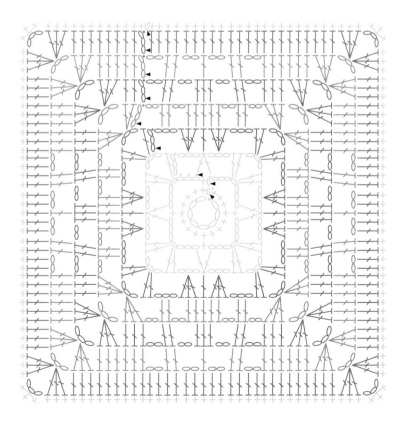

Compass Cross

See page 26

A=Garnet

Foundation ring: Using colour A, ch 6 and join with sl st in first ch to form a ring.

Round 1: Ch 3 (counts as 1tr), 4tr into the ring, ch 8, [5tr, ch 8] 3 times into the ring, join with sl st in 3rd ch of ch-3.

Round 2: Sl st in next 4tr and in 8ch-sp, ch 3, [2tr, ch 3, 3tr] in same sp, ch 5, *[3tr, ch 3, 3tr] in next 8ch-sp, ch 5; rep from * twice more, join with sl st in 3rd ch of ch-3.

Round 3: Ch 3, 1tr in each of next 2tr, *[3tr, ch 3, 3tr] in next 3ch-sp, 1tr in each of next 3tr, ch 2, 1dc in 3rd ch of next 5ch-sp, ch 2**, 1tr in each of next 3tr; rep from * twice more and from * to ** once again, join with sl st in 3rd ch of ch-3.

Round 4: Ch 3, 1tr in each of next 5tr, *[3tr, ch 3, 3tr] in next 3ch-sp, 1tr in each of next 6tr, 5ch-sp, skip next two 2ch-sps**, 1tr in each of next 6tr; rep

from * twice more and from * to ** once again, join with sl st in 3rd ch of ch-3.

Round 5: Ch 3, 1tr in each of next 8tr, *[3tr, ch 3, 3tr] in next 3ch-sp, 1tr in each of next 9tr, ch 2, 1dc in 3rd ch of next 5ch-sp, ch 2**, 1tr in each of next 9tr; rep from * twice more and from * to ** once again, join with sl st in 3rd ch of ch-3.

Round 6: Ch 3, 1tr in each of next 11tr, *[3tr, ch 3, 3tr] in next 3ch-sp, 1tr in each of next 12tr, 5ch-sp, skip next two 2ch-sps**, 1tr in each of next 12tr; rep from * twice more and from * to ** once again, join with sl st in 3rd ch of ch-3.

Round 7: Ch 2 (counts as 1htr), work 1htr in every tr, [2ch, 1dc, ch 2] in each in 5ch-sp , and 3htr in every 3ch-corner sp around, join with sl st in 2nd ch of ch-2.

Fasten off and weave in ends.

Double Popcorn Cross

See page 25

A=Persimmon

SPECIAL STITCHES

PC (Popcorn): Work 5htr into designated stitch, remove hook from last loop, place hook from front to back in top of the first of the last 5 htr, pick up dropped loop, draw through loop on hook to complete the stitch.

Foundation ring: Using colour A, ch 6 and join with sl st in first ch to form a ring.

Round 1: Ch 3 (counts as 1tr), 1tr into the ring, [ch 3, 3tr into the ring] 3 times, ch 3, 1tr into the ring, join with sl st in 3rd ch of ch-3.

Round 2: Ch 3 (counts as 1tr), *1pc in next st, 5tr in next ch-3 sp, 1pc in next tr**, 1tr in next tr; rep from * twice more and from * to ** once again, join with sl st in 3rd ch of ch-3.

Round 3: Ch 5 (counts as 1tr and ch 2), *skip next pc, 1pc in next tr, 1tr in next tr, 3tr in next tr, 1tr in next tr, 1pc in next tr, ch 2, skip next pc**, 1tr in next tr, ch 2; rep from * twice more and from * to ** once again, join with sl st in 3rd ch of ch-5.

Round 4: Sl st in next 2ch-sp, ch 5 (counts as 1tr and ch 2), *skip next pc, 1pc in next tr, 1tr in next tr, 3tr in next tr, 1tr in next tr, 1pc in next tr, ch 2, skip next pc**, [1tr in next 2ch-sp, ch 2] twice; rep from * twice more and from * to ** once again, 1tr in next 2ch-sp, ch 2, join with sl st in 3rd ch of ch-5.

Round 5: Sl st in next 2ch-sp, ch 5 (counts as 1tr and ch 2), *skip next pc, 1pc in next tr, 1tr in next tr, 3tr in next tr, 1tr in next tr, 1pc in next tr, ch 2, skip next pc**, [1tr in next 2ch-sp, ch

2] 3 times; rep from * twice more and from * to ** once again, [1tr in next 2ch-sp, ch 2] twice, join with sl st in 3rd ch of ch-5.

Round 6: Sl st in next 2ch-sp, ch 5 (counts as 1tr and ch 2), *skip next pc, 1pc in next tr, 1tr in next tr, 3tr in next tr, 1tr in next tr, 1pc in next tr, ch 2, skip next pc**, [1tr in next 2ch-sp, ch 2] 4 times; rep from * twice more and from * to ** once again, [1tr in next 2ch-sp, ch 2] 3 times, join with sl st in 3rd ch of ch-5.

Round 7: Sl st in next 2ch-sp, ch 5 (counts as 1tr and ch 2), *skip next pc, 1pc in next tr, 1tr in next tr, 3tr in next tr, 1tr in next tr, 1pc in next tr, ch 2, skip next pc**, [1tr in next 2ch-sp, ch 2] 5 times; rep from * twice more and from * to ** once again, [1tr in next 2ch-sp, ch 2] 4 times, join with sl st in 3rd ch of ch-5.

Round 8: Sl st in next 2ch-sp, ch 5 (counts as 1tr and ch 2), *skip next pc, 1pc in next tr, 1tr in next tr, 3tr in next tr, 1tr in next tr, 1pc in next tr, ch 2, skip next pc**, [1tr in next 2ch-sp, ch 2] 6 times; rep from * twice more and from * to ** once again, [1tr in next 2ch-sp, ch 2] 5 times, join with sl st in 3rd ch of ch-5.

Round 9: Ch 3 (counts as 1tr), *2tr in next 2ch-sp, 1tr in next pc, 1tr in each of next 2tr, 3tr in next tr, 1tr in each of next 2tr, 1tr in next pc, [2tr in next 2ch-sp, 1tr in next st] 6 times; rep from * a further 3 times, omitting last tr on final repeat, join with sl st in 3rd ch of ch-3.

Fasten off and weave in ends.

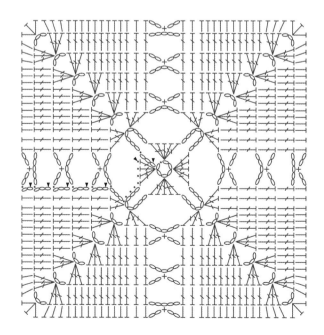

Wisteria

See page 24

A=Oyster
B=Garnet
C=Ecru
D=Blood Orange

SPECIAL STITCHES

Beg cl (Beginning cluster): Work two treble crochet stitches together: [yarn round hook, pull through a loop in next st, yarn round hook, pull through 2 loops on the hook] twice, yarn round hook and pull through all 3 loops on hook.

Cl (Cluster): Work three treble crochet stitches together: [yarn round hook, pull through a loop in next st, yarn round hook, pull through 2 loops on the hook] three times, yarn round hook and pull through all 4 loops on hook.

Foundation ring: Using colour A, ch 4 and join with sl st in first ch to form a ring.

Round 1: Ch 3 (counts as 1tr), beg cl in ring, ch 5, *cl in ring, ch 2**, *cl in ring, ch 5; rep from * twice more and from * to ** once again, join with sl st in 3rd ch of ch-3. Break colour A.

Round 2: Join colour B to any ch-5 corner sp, ch 3 (counts as 1tr), [beg cl, ch 2, cl] in same sp, *ch2, 3tr in next ch-2 sp, ch2**, [cl, ch2, cl] in next ch-5 sp; rep from * twice more and from * to ** once again, join with sl st in 3rd ch of ch-3.

Round 3: Sl st in next ch-2 corner sp, ch 3 (counts as 1tr), [beg cl, ch 2, cl] in same sp, *ch 2, 2tr in next ch-2 sp, 1tr in each of next 3tr, 2tr in next ch-2 sp, ch 2**, [cl, ch 2, cl] in next ch-2 sp; rep from * twice more and from * to ** once again, join with sl st in 3rd ch of ch-3. Break colour B.

Round 4: Join colour C in next ch-2 corner sp, ch 3 (counts as 1tr), [beg cl, ch 2, cl] in same sp, *ch 2, 2tr in next ch-2 sp, 1tr in each of next 7tr, 2tr in next ch-2 sp, ch 2**, [cl, ch 2, cl] in next ch-2 sp; rep from * twice more and from * to ** once again, join with sl st in 3rd ch of ch-3. Break colour C.

Round 5: Join colour D in next ch-2 corner sp, ch 3 (counts as 1tr), [beg cl, ch 2, cl] in same sp, *ch 2, 2tr in next ch-2 sp, 1tr in each of next 11tr, 2tr in next ch-2 sp, ch2**, [cl, ch 2, cl] in next ch-2 sp; rep from * twice more and from * to ** once again, join with sl st in 3rd ch of ch-3.

Round 6: Sl st in top of cl and next ch-2 corner sp, ch 3 (counts as 1tr), [beg cl, ch 2, cl] in same sp, *ch 2, 2tr in next ch-2 sp, 1tr in each of next 15tr, 2tr in next ch-2 sp, ch 2**, [cl, ch 2, cl] in next ch-2sp; rep from * twice more and from * to ** once again, join with sl st in 3rd ch of ch-3.

Round 7: Ch 1, 1dc in same place, 1dc in every tr and cluster top of previous round, working 2dc in each ch-2 sp and [2dc, ch 1, 2dc] in each ch-2 corner sp, join with sl st to first dc.

Fasten off and weave in ends.

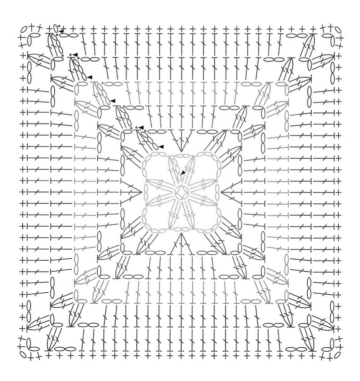

✪ ✪ *Danish Diamond*

See page 27

A=Greengage
B=Ecru
C=Persimmon
D=Oyster
E=Blood Orange

Foundation ring: Using colour A, ch 10 and join with sl st to form a ring.

Round 1: Ch 1, 20dc into ring, join with sl st to first dc. (20 dc)

Round 2: Ch 1, 1dc, ch 8, *skip 4dc, 1dc in next dc, ch 8; rep from * twice more, join with sl st in first dc.

Round 3: Ch 1, 1dc in same place, [9dc in next 8ch-sp, 1dc in next dc] 3 times, 9dc in next 8ch-sp, join with sl st in first dc. Break colour A.

Round 4: Join yarn B to 5th of 9dc corner group, ch 1, 2dc in same place, [1dc in each of next 9dc, 2dc in next dc] 3 times, 1dc in each of next 9dc, change to yarn C when joining with sl st in first dc.

Round 5: Ch 1, 2dc in same place, [1dc in each of next 10dc, 2dc in next dc] 3 times, 1dc in each of next 10dc, change to yarn D when joining with sl st in first dc.

Round 6: Ch 4 (counts as 1tr and ch 1], 1tr in same place, *ch 1, [1tr in next dc, ch 1, skip 1dc] 5 times, 1tr in next dc, ch1**, [1tr, ch 1, 1tr] in next dc; rep from * twice and from * to ** once again, join with sl st in 3rd ch of ch-4.

Round 7: Sl st in next 1ch-sp, 3dc in same place, 1dc in next tr, *[1dc in 1ch-sp, 1dc in next tr] 7 times, 3dc in next 1ch-corner-sp, 1dc in next tr; rep from * twice more, [1dc in 1ch-sp, 1dc in next tr] 6 times, change to yarn E when joining with sl st in first dc. Break colour D.

Round 8: Ch 3 (counts as 1tr), 1tr in every st to end of the round working 3tr in centre dc of every 3dc corner cluster, change to yarn C when joining with sl st in 3rd ch of ch-3.

Round 9: Ch 3 (counts as 1tr), 1tr in every st to end of round working [1tr, ch 2, 1tr] in centre tr of every 3tr corner cluster, change to yarn D when joining with sl st in 3rd ch of ch-3.

Round 10: Ch 3 (counts as 1tr), 1tr in every st to the end of the round working [1tr, ch 2, 1tr] in each 2ch-corner-sp, change to yarn B when joining with sl st in 3rd ch of ch-3.

Round 11: Ch 1, 1dc in every st to end of round working [1dc, ch 2, 1dc] in each 2ch-corner-sp, change to yarn A when joining to first dc.

Round 12: Ch 2 (counts as 1htr), 1htr in every st to end of round working [1htr, ch 2, 1htr] in each 2ch-corner-sp, join with sl st in 2nd of ch-2.

Fasten off and weave in ends.

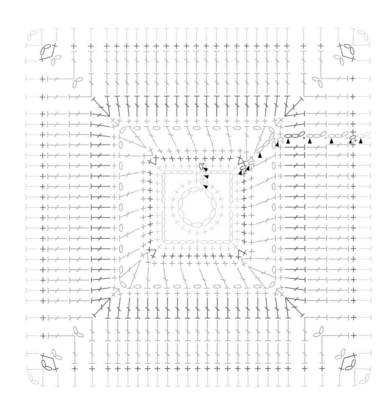

Tricolour Square

See page 27

A=Persimmon
B=Oyster
C=Garnet
D=Ecru

SPECIAL STITCHES

Beg cl (Beginning cluster): Work 5 treble sts together [yarn round hook twice, draw up a loop in next st, (yarn round hook, pull through 2 loops on hook) over next 5 sts, yarn round hook and draw through all 6 loops on hook.

Cl (Cluster): Work 6 treble sts together [yarn round hook twice, draw up a loop in next st, (yarn round hook, pull through 2 loops on hook) over next 6 sts, yarn round hook and draw through all 7 loops on hook.

Foundation ring: Using colour A, ch 8 and and join with sl st in first ch to form a ring.
Round 1: Ch 4, (counts as 1dtr), 5dtr, [ch 3, 6dtr in ring] 3 times, ch 3, join wth sl st in 4th ch of ch-4.
Round 2: Ch 4, (counts as 1dtr), beg cl in each of next 5dtr, *ch 5, sl st in 2nd ch of ch-3, ch 5**, Cl over next 6dtr; rep from * twice more and from * to ** once again, join with sl st in 4th ch of ch-4. Break colour A.
Round 3: Join colour B to top of any cl, *[3dtr, ch 1, 3dtr, ch 2, 3dtr, ch 1, 3dtr] in next ch-3 sp of Round 1, sl st in top of next cl; rep from * 3 times, join with sl st to top of first cl. Break colour B.

Round 4: Join colour C to sl st at top of cl, ch 4 (counts as 1dtr), 5dtr in same place, *[6dtr, ch 2, 6dtr] in next ch-2 sp**, 6dtr in sl st at top of next cl; rep from * twice more and from * to ** once again, join with sl st in 4th ch of ch-4. Break colour C.
Round 5: Join colour A to last sl st of previous round, ch1, 1dc in each of next 6dtr, 1tr in ch-1 sp between groups of dtr worked on Round 3, *1dc in each of next 6dtr, 3dc in ch-2 corner sp**, [1dc in each of next 6dtr, 1tr in ch-1 sp between groups of dtr worked on Round 3] twice; rep from * twice more and from * to ** once again, 1dc in each of next 6tr, 1tr in ch-1 sp between groups of dtr worked on Round 3, change to colour D when joining with sl st to first dc. Break colour A.
Round 6: Ch 3 (counts as 1tr), 1tr in every st from previous round, working 3tr in centre st of each 3dc corner group, change to colour B when joining with sl st to first dc. Break colour D.
Round 7: C h3 (counts as 1tr), 1tr in every st from previous round, working 3tr in centre st of each 3tr corner group, join with sl st in 3rd ch of ch-3.
Fasten off and weave in ends.

St. Petersburg

See page 24

A=Blood Orange
B=Oyster
C=Ecru
D=Greengage
E=Persimmon

SPECIAL STITCHES

FRtr (Front Raised treble crochet): Yarn round hook, insert hook from front to back around the post of designated stitch, yarn round hook, pull up a loop, [yarn round hook, pull through two loops on the hook] twice more.

BRtr (Back Raised treble crochet): Yarn round hook, insert hook from back to front around the post of designated stitch, yarn round hook, pull up a loop, [yarn round hook, pull through two loops on the hook] twice more.

Foundation ring: Using colour A, ch 8 and join with sl st in first ch to form a ring.
Round 1: Ch 3 (counts as 1tr), 2tr into ring, ch 3, [3tr into ring, ch 3] 3 times, join with sl st in 3rd ch of ch-3. Break colour A.
Round 2: Join colour B to any ch-3 corner sp, ch 3 (counts as 1tr), 2tr in same sp, *1FRtr round each of next 3tr**, [3tr, ch 3, 3tr] in next ch-3 corner sp; rep from * twice more and from * to ** once again, [3tr, ch 3] in next ch-3 corner sp, join with sl st in 3rd ch of ch-3. Break colour B.
Round 3: Join colour C to any ch-3 corner sp, ch 6 (counts as 1tr, ch 3), 3tr in same sp, *1BRtr around each of next 3tr, 1FRtr around each of next 3 sts, 1BRtr around each of next 3tr**, [3tr, ch 3, 3tr] in next ch-3 corner sp;

rep from * twice more and from * to ** once again, 2tr in next ch-3 corner sp, join with sl st in 3rd ch of ch-3, Break colour C.
Round 4: Join colour D to any ch-3 corner sp, ch 3 (counts as 1tr,) 2tr in same sp, *[1FRtr around each of next 3 sts, 1BRtr round each of next 3 sts] twice, 1FRtr around each of next 3 sts**, [3tr, ch 3, 3tr] in next ch-3 corner sp; rep from * twice more and from * to ** once again, [3tr, ch3] in next ch-3 corner sp, join with sl st in 3rd ch of ch-3. Break colour D.
Round 5: Join colour E to any ch-3 corner sp, ch 1, *[2dc, ch 2, 2dc] in each of next 15 sts, 1dc in each of next 3tr; rep from * a further 3 times, join with sl st to first dc. Break colour E.
Round 6: Join colour A to any ch-2corner sp, ch 2, (counts as 1htr), 2htr in same sp, *1htr in each of next 5dc, 1tr in each of next 15htr, 1htr in each of next 5dc**, 3htr in next ch-2 corner sp; rep from * twice more and from * to ** once again, join with sl st in 2nd ch of ch 2. Break colour A.
Round 7: Join colour B to any htr, ch 3 (counts as 1tr), 1tr in every st of previous round, working 3tr in centre htr of each 3htr corner cluster, join with sl st in 3rd ch of ch-3.
Fasten off and weave in ends.

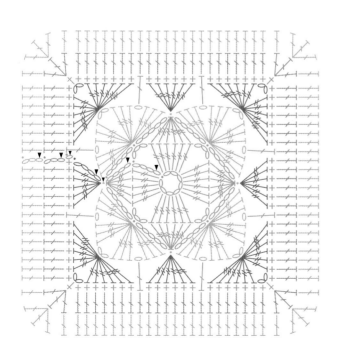

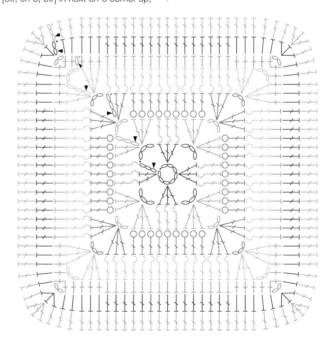

Quartet

See page 30

A=Cobalt
B=Nightshade
C=Blood Orange
D=Oyster

 Intarsia Steps

See page 28

A=Cobalt
B=Nightshade
C=Blood Orange
D=Oyster

Foundation chain: Using colour A, work 29 ch.

The centre of the block is worked entirely from the chart.

Each square on the chart represents one stitch, but does not show any turning chain. Charts are read from bottom to top and the first row will count as a RS row and be read from right to left. The following row is a WS row and therefore read from left to right. This is illustrated by start-of-row indicators.

Change colours at the last stage of the preceding stitch. When you are changing colour on a WS row you will need to take the old colour forward and take the new one to the back, looping the old yarn around the new one so that you prevent a hole from occurring. Fasten off.

Border

Round 1: Join colour C to LH row edge of Row 17 with a sl st, ch 1, 1dc in same place, *work 12dc evenly along this row-end edge to corner, [1dc, 1htr, 1dc] in corner, 1dc in each of next 25 ch, [1dc, 1htr, 1dc] in corner**, work 12dc evenly along RH lower row-end edge, changing to colour B at end of Row 17; rep from * to ** once more working 25dc across the top sts, 12dc evenly along upper LH edge, changing to colour A when joining with sl st in first dc.

Round 2: Ch 2 (counts as 1htr), 1htr in every dc and [1htr, 1tr, 1htr] in every corner htr from previous round, change to colour D when joining with sl st in 2nd ch of ch-2.

Round 3: Ch 2 (counts as 1htr), 1htr in every dc and [1htr, 1tr, 1htr] in every htr from previous round, join with sl st in 2nd ch of ch-2.

Fasten off and weave in ends.

Foundation chain: Using colour A, work 29 ch.

The centre of the block is worked entirely from the chart.

Each square on the chart represents one stitch, but does not show any turning chain. Charts are read from bottom to top and the first row will count as a RS row and be read from right to left. The following row is a WS row and therefore read from left to right. This is illustrated by start-of-row indicators.

Change colours at the last stage of the preceding stitch. When you are changing colour on a WS row you will need to take the old colour forward and take the new one to the back, looping the old yarn around the new one so that you prevent a hole from occurring. Fasten off.

Border

Round 1: Join colour C to any ch along Foundation edge with a sl st, ch 1, 1dc in same place, 1dc in every ch to corner, *[1dc, 1htr, 1dc] in corner, work 21dc evenly along row-end edge to corner, [1dc, 1htr, 1dc] in corner**, 1dc in each of next 26 sts, rep from * to ** once more, 1dc in every ch to end of round, join with sl st in first dc.

Round 2: Ch 2 (counts as 1htr), 1htr in every dc and [1htr, 1tr, 1htr] in every htr from previous round, changing to colour D when joining with sl st in 2nd ch of ch-2.

Round 3: Ch 2 (counts as 1htr), 1htr in every htr and [1htr, 1tr, 1htr] in every tr from previous round, join with sl st in 2nd ch of ch-2.

Fasten off and weave in ends.

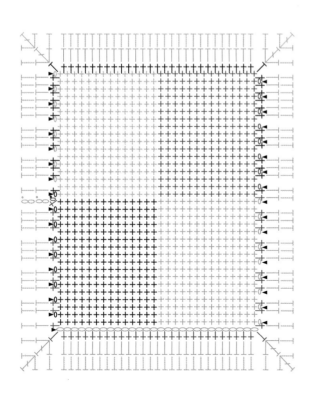

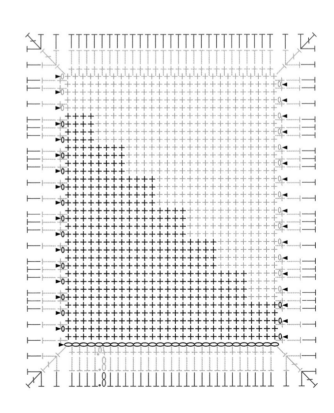

Zig Zag

See page 31

A=Cobalt
B=Nightshade
C=Blood Orange
D=Oyster

Foundation chain: Using colour A, work 29ch.

The centre of the block is worked entirely from the chart.

Each square on the chart represents one stitch, but does not show any turning chain. Charts are read from bottom to top and the first row will count as a RS row and be read from right to left. The following row is a WS row and therefore read from left to right. This is illustrated by start-of-row indicators.

Change colours at the last stage of the preceding stitch. When you are changing colour on a WS row you will need to take the old colour forward and take the new one to the back, looping the old yarn around the new one so that you prevent a hole from occurring. Fasten off.

Border

Round 1: Join colour D to any ch along Foundation edge with a sl st, ch 1, 1dc in same place, 1dc in every ch to corner, *[1dc, 1htr, 1dc] in corner, work 25dc evenly along row-end edge to corner, [1dc, 1htr, 1dc] in corner**, 1dc in each of next 26 sts; rep from * to ** once more, 1dc in every ch to end of round, change to colour B when joining with sl st in first dc.

Round 2: Ch 1, 1dc in every dc and [1dc, 1tr, 1dc] in every corner htr from previous round, join with sl st in first dc.

Fasten off and weave in ends.

Random Patches

See page 28

A=Cobalt
B=Sky
C=Nightshade
D=Bleached
E=Blood Orange
F=Oyster

Foundation chain: Using colour A, work 29 ch.

The centre of the block is worked entirely from the chart.

Each square on the chart represents one stitch, but does not show any turning chain. Charts are read from bottom to top and the first row will count as a RS row and be read from right to left. The following row is a WS row and therefore read from left to right. This is illustrated by start-of-row indicators.

Change colours at the last stage of the preceding stitch. When you are changing colour on a WS row you will need to take the old colour forward and take the new one to the back, looping the old yarn around the new one so that you prevent a hole from occurring. Fasten off.

Border

Round 1: Join colour D to any ch along Foundation edge with a sl st, ch 1, 1dc in same place, 1dc in every ch to corner, *[1dc, 1htr, 1dc] in corner, work 22dc evenly along row-end edge to corner, [1dc, 1htr, 1dc] in corner**, 1dc in each of next 26 sts; rep from * to ** once more, 1dc in every ch to end of round, change to colour F when joining with sl st in first dc.

Round 2: Ch 2 (counts as 1htr), 1htr in every dc and [1htr, 1tr, 1htr] in every htr from previous round, join with sl st in 2nd ch of ch-2.

Fasten off and weave in ends.

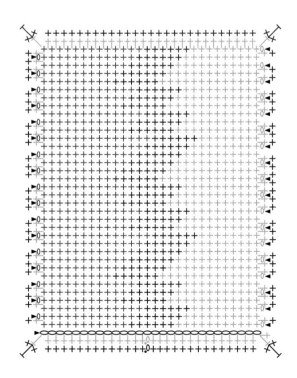

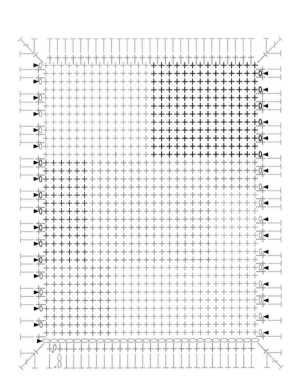

Seminole

See page 28

A=Blood Orange
B=Sky
C=Nightshade
D=Cobalt
E=Bleached
F=Oyster
G=Cadmium

Foundation chain: Using colour A, work 29 ch.

The centre of the block is worked entirely from the chart.

Each square on the chart represents one stitch, but does not show any turning chain. Charts are read from bottom to top and the first row will count as a RS row and be read from right to left. The following row is a WS row and therefore read from left to right. This is illustrated by start-of-row indicators.

Change colours at the last stage of the preceding stitch. When you are changing colour on a WS row you will need to take the old colour forward and take the new one to the back, looping the old yarn around the new one so that you prevent a hole from occurring. Fasten off.

Border

Round 1: Join colour F to the 14th ch (last one worked in colour A), of Foundation chain with a sl st, ch 1, 1dc in same place, 1dc in every ch to corner, *[1dc, 1htr, 1dc] in corner, work 25dc evenly along row-end edge to corner, [1dc, 1htr, 1dc] in corner**, 1dc in each of next 12 sts, change to colour C when working dc in last ch in colour A, (do not break colour F), continue to work 1dc in every st to corner; rep from * to ** once more, 1dc in every ch to end of round, join with sl st in first dc.

Round 2: Ch 2 (counts as 1htr), 1htr in every dc previously worked in colour F and [1htr, 1tr, 1htr] in every htr from previous round, continue as set to end of round, changing to colour F when you reach the first dc in colour C from previous round, join with sl st in 2nd ch of ch-2.

Fasten off and weave in ends.

Interlocking Stripes

See page 31

A=Nightshade
B=Oyster
C=Cobalt
D=Bleached
E=Sky
F=Winsor
G=Cadmium
H=Blood Orange

Foundation chain: Using colour A, work 29 ch.

The centre of the block is worked entirely from the chart.

Each square on the chart represents one stitch, but does not show any turning chain. Charts are read from bottom to top and the first row will count as a RS row and be read from right to left. The following row is a WS row and therefore read from left to right. This is illustrated by start-of-row indicators.

Change colours at the last stage of the preceding stitch. When you are changing colour on a WS row you will need to take the old colour forward and take the new one to the back, looping the old yarn around the new one so that you prevent a hole from occurring. Fasten off.

Border

Round 1: Join colour D to any ch along Foundation edge with a sl st, ch 1, 1dc in same place, 1dc in every ch to corner, *[1dc, 1htr, 1dc] in corner, work 25dc evenly along row-end edge to corner, [1dc, 1htr, 1dc] in corner**, 1dc in each of next 26 sts; rep from * to ** once more, 1dc in every ch to end of round, change to colour C when joining with sl st in first dc.

Round 2: Ch 2 (counts as 1htr), 1htr in every dc and [1htr, 1tr, 1htr] in every htr from previous round, join with sl st in 2nd ch of ch-2.

Fasten off and weave in ends.

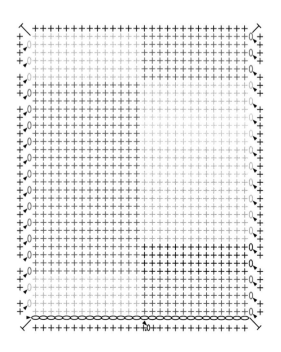

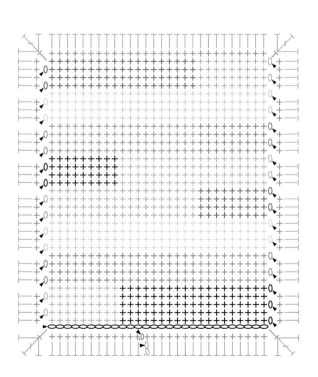

Jaquard Stripes

See page 29

A=Blood Orange
B=Oyster
C=Cobalt
D=Nightshade

Foundation chain: Using colour A, work 29 ch.

The centre of the block is worked by repeating Rows 1–2 of the chart, 14 times.

Remember that RS rows (odd numbers) are worked from right to left and WS rows (even numbers) are worked from left to right. Fasten off.

Border

Round 1: Join colour C to any ch along Foundation edge with a sl st, ch 1, 1dc in same place, 1dc in every ch to corner, *[1dc, 1htr, 1dc] in corner, work 21dc evenly along row-end edge to corner, [1dc, 1htr, 1dc] in corner**,

1dc in each of next 26 sts; rep from * to ** once more, 1dc in every ch to end of round, change to colour D when joining with sl st in first dc.

Round 2: Ch 2 (counts as 1htr), 1htr in every dc and [1htr, 1tr, 1htr] in every htr from previous round, change to colour B when joining with sl st in 2nd ch of ch-2.

Round 3: Ch 1, 1dc in every htr and [1dc, 1htr, 1dc] in every tr from previous round, join with sl st in first dc.

Fasten off and weave in ends.

Jaquard Checks

See page 31

A=Nightshade
B=Oyster
C=Blood Orange

Foundation chain: Using colour A, work 29 ch.

The centre of the block is worked entirely from the chart working Rows 2–9 a total of 3 times, then repeat Rows 2–5 once more.

Each square on the chart represents one stitch, but does not show any turning chain. Charts are read from bottom to top and the first row will count as a RS row and be read from right to left. The following row is a WS row and therefore read from left to right. This is illustrated by start-of-row indicators.

Change colours at the last stage of the preceding stitch. When you are changing colour on a WS row you will need to take the old colour forward and take the new one to the back, looping the old yarn around the new one so that you prevent a hole from occurring. Fasten off.

Border

Round 1: Join colour C to any ch along Foundation edge with a sl st. Ch 1, 1dc in same place, 1dc in every ch to corner, *[1dc, 1htr, 1dc] in corner, work 21dc evenly along row-end edge to corner, [1dc, 1htr, 1dc] in corner**, 1dc in each of next 26 sts; rep from * to ** once more, 1dc in every ch to end of round, change to colour A when joining with sl st in first dc.

Round 2: Ch 2 (counts as 1htr), 1htr in every dc and [1htr, 1tr, 1htr] in every htr from previous round, change to colour B when joining with sl st in 2nd ch of ch-2.

Round 3: Ch 1, 1dc in every htr and [1dc, 1htr, 1dc] in every tr from previous round, join with sl st in first dc.

Fasten off and weave in ends.

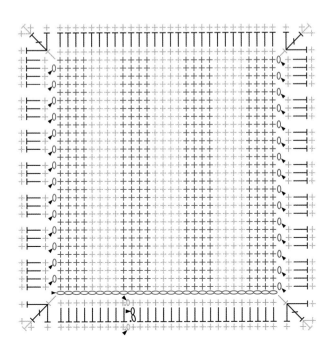

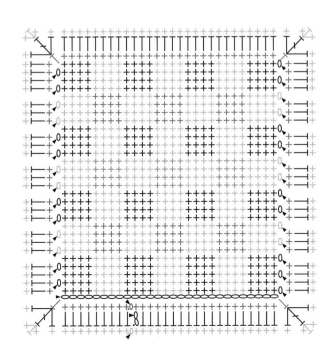

⬤⬤ Darts

See page 30

A=Nightshade
B=Bleached
C=Cobalt
D=Blood Orange
E=Oyster

Foundation chain: Using colour A, ch 21, do not break A, but join in B for a further ch. (22ch)
The centre of the block is worked entirely from the chart working Rows 1–24 once.
Each square on the chart represents one stitch. Charts are read from bottom to top and the first row will count as a RS row and be read from right to left. The following row is a WS row and therefore read from left to right. This is illustrated by start-of-row indicators.
Change colours at the last stage of the preceding stitch. When you are changing colour on a WS row you will need to take the old colour forward and take the new one to the back, looping the old yarn around the new one so that you prevent a hole from occurring. Fasten off.

Border
Round 1: Join colour E to any ch along Foundation edge with a sl st. Ch 1, 1dc in same place, 1dc in every ch to corner, [1dc, 1htr, 1dc] in corner, work 16dc evenly along row-end edge to corner, *[1dc, 1htr, 1dc] in corner, 1dc in each of next 20 sts, [1dc, 1htr, 1dc] in corner**, work 16dc evenly along next row-end edge; rep from * to **, work 1dc in every ch to end of round, join with sl st in first dc.
Round 2: Ch 2 (counts as 1htr), 1htr in every dc and [3htr] in every htr from previous round, change to colour C when joining with sl st in 2nd ch of ch-2.
Round 3: As Round 2 in C.
Round 4: As Round 2 in E.
Round 5: As Round 2 in D.
Round 6: As Round 2 in A.
Fasten off and weave in ends.

⬤⬤ Half and Half

See page 29

A=Blood Orange
B=Sky
C=Nightshade

Foundation chain: Using colour A, make 2ch.
Foundation row (WS): 3dc in 2nd ch from hook, turn. (3 dc)
Row 1: Ch 1, 2dc in first dc, 1dc in next dc, 2dc in last dc, turn. (5 dc)
Rows 2–4: Ch 1, 2dc in first dc, 1dc in each dc to last dc, 2dc in last dc, turn. (2 sts increased)
Row 5: Ch 1, 1dc in every dc to end, turn.
Rep Rows 2–5 a further 5 times, changing to colour B in the last dc of the final Row 5 repeat. (41 dc)
Break colour A.
Next row: Ch 1, 1dc in every dc to end, turn.

Next 3 rows: Ch 1, skip first dc, 1dc in each dc to last 2dc, skip 1dc, 1dc in last dc, turn. (2 sts decreased)
Rep last 4 rows a further 5 times. (5 dc)
Next row: Ch 1, skip first dc, 1dc in each of next 2dc, skip 1dc, 1dc in last dc, turn. (3 dc)
Next row: Ch 1, dc3tog over next 3dc. Fasten off.
Border
Round 1: Join colour C to any corner with a sl st, ch 1, *[1dc, 1htr, 1dc] in corner, 25dc evenly along row-end edge to corner; rep from * 3 more times, join with sl st in first dc.
Fasten off and weave in ends.

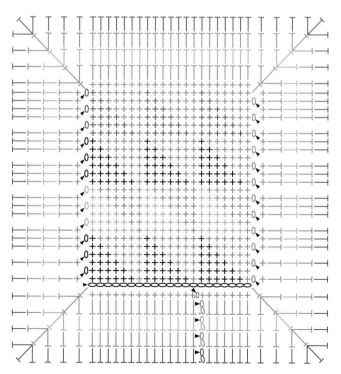

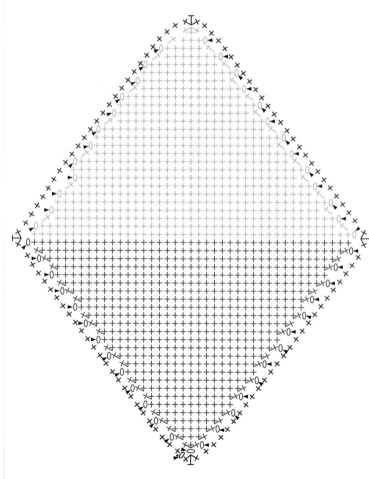

Trio

See page 29

A=Nightshade
B=Cobalt
C=Sky
D=Bleached

Foundation chain: Using colour A, work 29 ch.

The centre of the block is worked entirely from the chart.

Each square on the chart represents one stitch, but does not show any turning chain. Charts are read from bottom to top and the first row will count as a RS row and be read from right to left. The following row is a WS row and therefore read from left to right. This is illustrated by start-of-row indicators.

Change colours at the last stage of the preceding stitch. When you are changing colour on a WS row you will need to take the old colour forward and take the new one to the back, looping the old yarn around the new one so that you prevent a hole from occurring. Fasten off.

Border

Round 1: Join colour C to any ch along Foundation edge with a sl st, ch 1, 1dc in same place, 1dc in every ch to corner, *[1dc, 1htr, 1dc] in corner, work 26dc evenly along row-end edge to corner, [1dc, 1htr, 1dc] in corner**, 1dc in each of next 26dc; rep from * to **, 1dc in every ch to end of round, change to colour D when joining with sl st in first dc.

Round 2: Ch 1, 1dc in every dc and [1dc, 1htr, 1dc] in every htr from previous round, change to colour B when joining with sl st in first dc.

Round 3: Ch 2 (counts as 1htr), 1htr in every dc and [1htr, 1tr, 1htr] in every htr from previous round, join with sl st in 2nd ch of ch-2.

Fasten off and weave in ends.

Hourglass

See page 28

A=Nightshade
B=Cobalt
C=Blood Orange
D=Bleached

Foundation chain: Using colour A, work 29 ch.

The centre of the block is worked entirely from the chart.

Each square on the chart represents one stitch, but does not show any turning chain. Charts are read from bottom to top and the first row will count as a RS row and be read from right to left. The following row is a WS row and therefore read from left to right. This is illustrated by start-of-row indicators.

Change colours at the last stage of the preceding stitch. When you are changing colour on a WS row you will need to take the old colour forward and take the new one to the back, looping the old yarn around the new one so that you prevent a hole from occurring. Fasten off.

Border

Round 1: Join colour D to any ch along Foundation edge with a sl st, ch 1, 1dc in same place, 1dc in every ch to corner, *[1dc, 1htr, 1dc] in corner, work 26dc evenly along row-end edge to corner, [1dc, 1htr, 1dc] in corner**, 1dc in each of next 26dc, rep from * to **, 1dc in every ch to end of round, change to colour A when joining with sl st in first dc.

Round 2: Ch 2 (counts as 1htr), 1htr in every dc and [1htr, 1tr, 1htr] in every htr from previous round, join with sl st in 2nd ch of ch-2.

Fasten off and weave in ends.

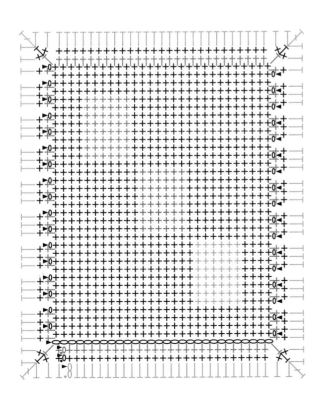

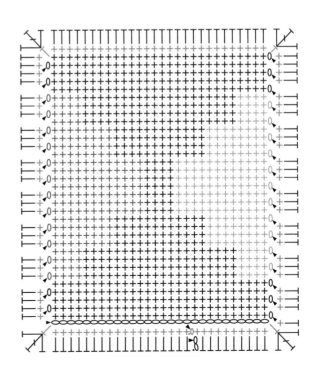

Flying Carpet

See page 30

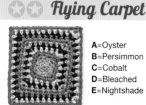

A=Oyster
B=Persimmon
C=Cobalt
D=Bleached
E=Nightshade

Foundation ring: Using colour A, make a Magic Ring.
Round 1: Ch 1, 8dc into the ring, join with sl st in first dc. (8 dc)
Round 2: Ch 1, *[1dc, ch 2, 1dc] in next dc, 1dc in next dc; rep from * a further 3 times, change to colour B when joining with sl st in first dc. (12 sts, 4 ch-sp)
Round 3: Sl st into corner ch-sp, ch 1, [1dc, ch 2, 1dc] in same sp, *ch 1, skip next st, 1dc in next st, ch 1**, skip next st, [1dc, ch 2, 1dc] in corner ch-2 sp; rep from * twice more and from * to ** once again, change to colour C when joining with sl st in first st. (12 sts, 12 ch-sp)
Round 4: As Round 3, change to colour D when joining with sl st in first st. (16 sts, 16 ch-sp)
Round 5: As Round 3, change to colour E when joining with sl st in first st. (20 sts, 20 ch-sp)

Round 6: As Round 3, change to colour A when joining with sl st in first st. (24 sts, 24 ch-sp)
Round 7: As Round 3, change to colour C when joining with sl st in first st. (28 sts, 28 ch-sp)
Round 8: As Round 3, change to colour B when joining with sl st in first st. (32 sts, 32 ch-sp)
Round 9: As Round 3, change to colour E when joining with sl st in first st. (36 sts, 36 ch-sp)
Round 10: As Round 3, change to colour D when joining with sl st in first st. (40 sts, 40 ch-sp)
Round 11: As Round 3, change to colour C when joining with sl st in first st. (44 sts, 24 ch-sp)
Round 12: As Round 3, join with sl st in first st. (48 sts, 48 ch-sp).
Fasten off and weave in ends.

Bold Block

See page 31

A=Cobalt
B=Oyster
C=Persimmon

SPECIAL STITCH

Cl (Cluster): Work 3tr sts leaving the last loop of each st on the hook each time, yrh and pull through all 4 loops on hook.

Foundation ring: Using colour A, make a Magic Ring.
Round 1: Ch 4 (counts as 1dtr), *5tr in ring**, 1dtr in ring; rep from * twice more and from * to ** once again, changing to colour B when joining with sl st in 4th ch of ch-4.
Round 2: Ch 5 (counts as 1tr, ch 2), 1tr in same place, *[ch 1, skip 1 st, Cl in next st] twice, ch 1, skip next st**, [1tr, ch 2, 1tr] in corner dtr; rep from * twice more and from * to ** once again, join with sl st in 3rd ch of ch-5. Break colour B.
Round 3: Join colour A to any ch-2 corner sp, ch 1, *[1dc, 1htr, 1dc] in ch-2 sp, [1dc in next st, 1dc over ch-sp and into corresponding st from Round 1] 3 times, 1dc in next st; rep from * a further 3 times, join with sl st in

first dc. Break colour A.
Round 4: Join colour C to any corner htr, ch 1, *[1dc, 1htr, 1dc] in htr, 1dc in every st to next htr; rep from * a further 3 times, join with sl st in first dc. Break colour C.
Round 5: Join colour B to any corner htr, ch 5 (counts as 1tr, ch 2), 1tr in same st, *[ch 1, skip 1 st, Cl in next st] 5 times, ch 1, skip 1 st**, [1tr, ch 2, 1tr] in corner htr; rep from * twice more and from * to ** once again, join with sl st in 3rd ch of ch-5. Break colour B.
Round 6: Join colour C to any ch-2 corner sp, ch 1, *[1dc, 1htr, 1dc] in ch-2 sp, [1dc in next st, 1dc over ch-sp and into corresponding st from Round 4] 6 times, 1dc in next st; rep from * 3 more times, join with sl st in first dc. Break colour C.
Round 7: Join colour A to any corner htr, ch 1, *[1dc, 1htr, 1dc] in htr, 1dc in every st to next htr; rep from * a further 3 times, join with sl st in first dc.
Fasten off and weave in ends.

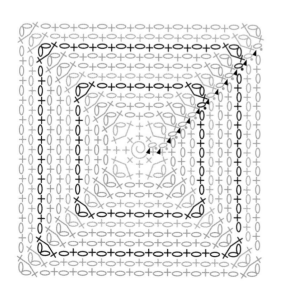

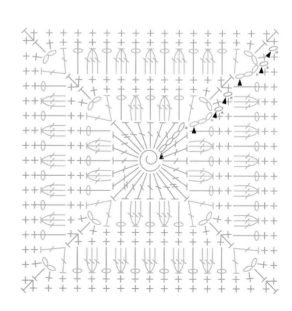

Florentine Tile

See page 28

A=Nightshade
B=Cobalt
C=Persimmon

Foundation ring: Using colour A, ch 6 and join with sl st in first ch to form a ring.

Round 1: Ch 1, 16dc into ring, join with sl st in first dc. (16 dc)

Round 2: Ch 6 (counts as 1tr and ch 3), 1tr in same st, *ch 1, skip next dc, 1tr in next dc, ch 1, skip next dc**, [1tr, ch 3, 1tr] in next dc (corner made); rep from * twice more and from * to ** once again, change to colour B when joining in 3rd ch of ch-6 with a sl st.

Round 3: Join colour B to any ch-3 corner-sp, ch 1, 5dc in same sp, *[1dc in next tr, working behind next ch-1 sp, 1tr in next skipped st 2 rounds below] twice, 1dc in next tr**, 5dc in next ch-3 corner sp; rep from * twice more and from * to ** one again, change to colour B when joining with sl st in first dc. Break colour A.

Round 4: Ch 4 (counts as 1tr and ch 1), skip next st, *[1tr, ch 3, 1tr] in next st**, [ch 1, skip next st, 1tr in next st] 4 times, ch 1, skip next st; rep from * twice more and from * to ** once again, [ch 1, skip next st, 1tr in next st] 3 times, ch 1, skip last st. join with sl st in 3rd ch of ch-4. Break colour B.

Round 5: Join colour C to any ch-3 corner sp, ch 1, 5dc in same sp, *[1dc in next st, working behind next ch-1 sp, 1tr in next skipped st 2

rounds below] 5 times, 1dc in next tr**, 5dc in next ch-3 corner sp; rep from * twice more and from * to ** once again, join with sl st in first dc.

Round 6: Ch 4 (counts as 1tr and ch 1), skip next st, *[1tr, ch 3, 1tr] in next st**, [ch 1, skip next dc, 1tr in next dc] 7 times, ch 1, skip next st; rep from * twice more and from * to ** once again, [ch 1, skip next dc, 1tr in next dc 6 times, ch 1, skip next st, join with sl st in 3rd ch of ch-4. Break colour C.

Round 7: Join colour B to any ch-3 corner sp, ch 1, 5dc in same sp, *[1dc in next st, working behind next ch-1 sp, 1tr in next skipped st 2 rounds below] 8 times, 1dc in next tr**, 5dc in next ch-3 corner sp; rep from * twice more and from * to ** one again, join with sl st in first dc.

Round 8: Join colour A to 3rd dc of any 5dc corner cluster, ch 3 (counts as 1tr), 1tr in same st (half corner made), *[ch 1, skip next st, 1tr in next st] 10 times, ch 1**, skip next st, [2tr, ch 3, 2tr] in next st (corner made); rep from * twice more and from * to ** once again, skip next st, 2tr in same st as first half corner, ch 3, join with a sl st in 3rd ch of ch-3.
Fasten off and weave in ends.

Stacking Squares

See page 31

A=Sky
B=Bleached
C=Nightshade
D=Oyster
E=Persimmon

SPECIAL STITCHES

BPtr (Back Post treble crochet):
Yarn round hook, insert hook from front to back around post of designated stitch, yarn round hook, pull a loop through, then [yarn round hook, pull through 2 loops on the hook] twice more.

Foundation ring: Using colour A, ch 4 and join with sl st in first ch to form a ring.

Round 1: Ch 3 (counts as 1tr), 2tr into ring, ch 2, [3tr into ring, ch 2] 3 times, join with sl st in 3rd ch of ch-3. Break colour A. (4 groups of 3tr, 4 ch-sp)

Round 2: Join colour B to any ch-3 sp, ch 3 (counts as 1tr), 1tr in same ch-sp, *BPtr around each st to corner ch-sp, [2tr**, ch 2, 2tr] in ch-2 sp; rep from * twice more and from * to ** once again, join with sl st in 3rd ch of ch-3. Break colour B. (24 tr, 4 ch-sp)

Round 3: As Round 2 in colour C. (44 tr, 4 ch-sp)

Round 4: As Round 2 in colour D. (60 tr, 4 ch-sp)

Round 5: As Round 2 in colour E. (76 tr, 4 ch-sp)

Fasten off and weave in ends.

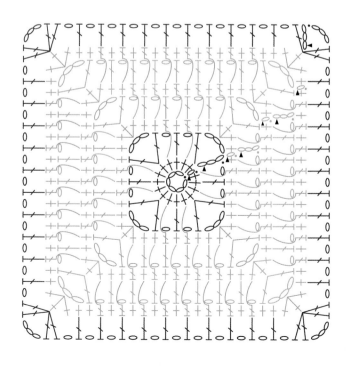

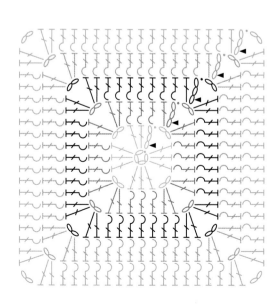

Rose of Sharon

See page 30

A=Oyster
B=Cobalt
C=Persimmon

Tudcan Tile

See page 30

A=Persimmon
B=Nightshade
C=Cobalt

SPECIAL STITCHES

Beg PC (Beginning popcorn): Ch 3 (counts as 1tr), 4tr in same st or space, remove hook from loop, insert hook in 3rd ch of beg ch-3, pick up the dropped loop and pull a loop through.

PC (Popcorn): 4tr in same st or space, remove hook from loop, insert hook into first of 5tr just made, pick up the dropped loop and pull a loop through.

Exdc (Extended dc): Yarn round hook, insert hook into designated st or space, yarn round hook, pull yarn through sts so that it is level with the round being worked, yarn round hook, draw through 2 loops on hook.

Extr (Extended tr): Yarn round hook, insert hook into designated st or space, yarn round hook, pull yarn through sts so that it is level with the round being worked, [yarn round hook, draw through 2 loops on hook] twice.

Foundation chain: Using colour A, ch 4 and join with sl st in first ch to form a ring.

Round 1: Ch 3 (counts as 1tr), 11tr into the ring, join with sl st in 3rd ch of ch-3.

Round 2: Beg PC in first st, ch 2, [PC, ch 2] in every tr to end of round, change to colour B when joining with sl st in 3rd ch of ch-3. Do not break colour A.

Round 3: Sl st in first PC, ch 1, 1dc in first st, *1dc in next ch-2 sp, 1Exdc in

base of next PC, 1dc in same ch-2 sp, 1dc in next PC; rep from * to end of round, omitting last dc and joining with sl st in first dc.

Round 4: Ch 1, working blo for this round, 1dc in every st to end, changing to colour A when joining with sl st in first dc.

Round 5: Beg PC in first dc, ch 3, skip next 2dc, *PC in next dc, ch 3, skip next 2dc; rep from * to end of round, changing to colour B when joining with sl st in first dc. Break colour A.

Round 6: Ch 1, 1dc in first st, *1dc in next ch-3 sp, 1Extr in each of next 2dc two rounds below, 1dc in same ch-3 sp, 1dc in next PC; rep from * omitting last dc and joining with sl st in first dc. Break colour B.

Round 7: Join colour C between any 2 Extr, ch 3, 2tr in same sp (half corner made), *[ch 2, skip next 3dc, 2tr between next 2Extr] 3 times, ch 2, skip next 3dc**, [3tr, ch 3, 3tr] between next 2Extr (corner made); rep from * twice more and from * to ** once again, 3tr in same sp as first half corner, ch 3, join with sl st in 3rd ch of ch 3.

Round 8: Ch 1, *1dc in each of next 3tr, [2dc in next ch-2 sp, 1dc in each of next 2tr] 3 times, 2dc in next ch-2 sp, 1dc in each of next 3tr, [1dc, ch 3, 1dc] in next ch-3 sp corner; rep from * a further 3 times, join with sl st in first dc.

Fasten off and weave in ends.

Foundation ring: Using colour A, ch 4 and join with sl st in first ch to form a ring.

Round 1: Ch 5 (counts as 1dtr and ch 1), [1dtr, ch 1] 11 times into the ring, change to colour B when joining to 4th ch of ch-5 with sl st.

Round 2: Ch 3 (counts as 1tr), [1tr, ch 3, 2tr] in same place (corner made), *[ch 1, 1tr] in each of next 2dtr ch 1**, [2tr, ch 3, 2tr] in next dtr, (corner made); rep from * twice more and from * to ** once again, ch 1, change to colour C when joining in 3rd ch of ch-3 with sl st.

Round 3: Sl st in next ch-3 corner sp, ch 2 (counts as 1htr), [1htr, ch 3, 2htr] in same sp, *1htr in each of next 2tr, work over next ch-1 sp in Round 2 and 1dtr in next ch-1 sp in Round 1, 1dc in each of next 2tr, work over next ch-1 sp in Round 2 and 1dtr in next ch-1 sp in Round 1, 1htr in each of

next 2tr**, [2htr, ch 3, 2htr] in next ch-3 sp; rep from * twice more and from * to ** once again, change to colour B when joining in 2nd ch of ch-2 with sl st.

Round 4: Sl st to next ch-3 corner sp, ch 1, *[1dc, ch 2, 1dc] in ch-2 corner sp, 1tr in each of next 12 sts; rep from * 3 times, change to colour C when joining in first dc with sl st.

Round 5: Sl st in next ch-3 corner sp, ch 1, *[1dc, ch 2, 1dc] in ch-2 corner sp, 1dc in each of next 14 sts; rep from * 3 a further times, join with sl st in first dc.

Round 6: Sl st in next ch-3 corner sp, ch 3, [1tr, ch 2, 2tr] in same sp, *[ch 1, skip next dc, 1tr in each of next 2dc] 5 times, ch 1**, [2tr, ch 2, 2tr] in next ch-2 corner sp; rep from * twice more and from * to ** once again, join in 3rd ch of ch-3 with sl st.

Fasten off and weave in ends.

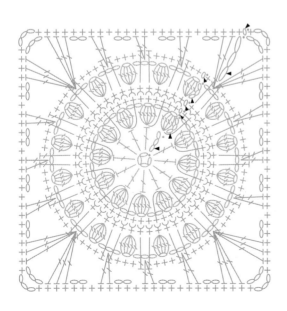

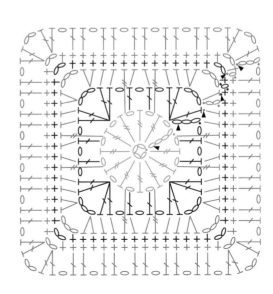

Spiky Square

See page 29

A=Persimmon
B=Bleached
C=Oyster
D=Sky

SPECIAL STITCHES

BPdtr (back post double treble):
Yarn round hook, insert hook from back to front around the post of designated stitch, yarn round hook, pull up a loop, then [yarn round hook, pull through two loops on the hook] twice more.

Foundation ring: Using colour A, ch 4 and join with sl st in first ch to form a ring.

Round 1: Ch 3 (counts as 1tr), 2tr into ring, ch 2, [3tr into ring, ch 2] 3 times, join with sl st in 3rd ch of ch-3. Break colour A. (12 sts, 4ch-sp)

Round 2: Join colour B to any ch-3 corner sp, ch 3 (counts as 1tr), 1tr in same sp, *1tr in next 3 tr**, [2tr, ch 2, 2tr] in ch-2 sp; rep from * twice more and from * to ** once again, [2tr, ch 2] in corner sp, join with sl st in 3rd ch of ch-3. Break colour B. (28 sts, 4ch-sp)

Round 3: Join colour C to any ch-3 corner sp, ch 3 (counts as 1tr), 1tr in same sp, ch 2, 2tr in same sp, *1tr in next st, ch 1, skip next st, 1tr in next st, BPdtr around middle tr of 3tr from Round 1, 1tr in next st, ch 1, skip next st, 1tr in next st**, [2tr, ch 2, 2tr] in

ch-2 sp; rep from * twice more and from * to ** once again, 2tr in ch-2 sp, join with htr in 3rd ch of ch-3. Break colour C. (36 sts, 4ch-sp)

Round 4: Join colour A to any ch-3 corner sp, ch 3 (counts as 1tr), 1tr in same sp, ch 2, 2tr in same sp, *1tr in next st, ch 1, skip next st, 1tr in next st, BPdtr around middle 2nd tr of Round 2, 1tr in next st, ch 1, skip next st, skip next st, 1tr in next st, BPdtr around middle 6th tr of Round 2, 1tr in next st, ch 1, skip next st, 1tr in next st**, [2tr, ch 2, 2tr] in ch-2 sp; rep from * twice more and from * to ** once again, 2tr in ch-2 sp, join with htr in 3rd ch of ch-3. Break colour A. (48 sts, 4ch-sp)

Round 5: Join colour D to any ch-3 corner sp, ch 3 (counts as 1tr), 1tr in same sp, ch 2, 2tr in same sp *1tr in next 3 sts, BPdtr around second tr from Round 3, 1tr in next 3 sts, BPdtr around BPdtr from Round 3, 1tr in next 3 sts, BPdtr around eighth tr from Round 3, 1tr in next 3 sts**, [2tr, ch 2, 2tr] in ch-2 sp; rep from * twice more and from * to ** once again, 2tr in ch-2 sp, ch 2, join with sl st in 3rd ch of ch-3. (76 sts, 4 ch-sp)

Fasten off and weave in ends.

Dip Stitch Cross

See page 29

A=Bleached
B=Sky
C=Nightshade
D=Persimmon

SPECIAL STITCHES

Spike dc: Insert hook into stitch one round below the next stitch and pull loop through up to the level of current round, yarn round hook and pull through both loops on hook.

Foundation ring: Using colour A, ch 6 and join with sl st in first ch to form a ring.

Round 1: Ch 3 (counts as 1tr), 15tr into the ring, join with sl st in 3rd ch of ch-3.

Round 2: Ch 1, 3dc in first tr, 1dc in each of next 3tr, *3dc in next tr, 1dc in each of next 3tr; rep from * twice more, change to colour B when joining with sl st in first dc.

Round 3: Ch 1, *1dc in next dc, 3dc in corner dc, 1dc in each of next 4dc; rep from * a further 3 times, change to colour B when joining with sl st in first dc.

Round 4: Ch 1, *1dc in each of next 2dc, 3dc in corner dc, 1dc in each of

next 5dc; rep from * a further 3 times, change to colour C when joining with sl st in first dc.

Round 5: Ch 1, *Spike dc in row below next dc, 1dc in each of next 2dc, 3 Spike dc in next st 2 rows below, 1dc in next 2dc, Spike dc in row below next dc, Spike dc 2 rows below next dc, Spike dc 3 rows below next dc, Spike dc 2 rows below next dc; rep from * a further 3 times, join with sl st in first dc.

Round 6: Ch 1, 1dc in each dc around and 3dc in each corner dc, change to colour D when joining with sl st in first dc.

Round 7: Ch 2 (counts as 1htr), 1htr in each of dc around and 3 htr in corner dc, change to colour C when joining with sl st in 2nd ch of ch-2.

Round 8: Ch 1, 1dc in each of htr around and 3dc in corner htr, join with sl st in first dc.

Fasten off and weave in ends.

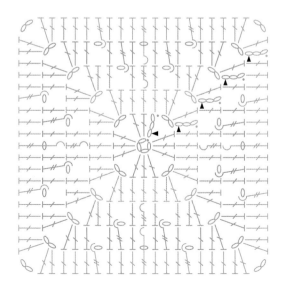

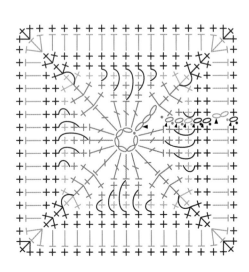

Eight-petal Flower

See page 32

A=Bleached
B=Bubbles
C=Greengage

Foundation ring: Using A, ch 8 and join with sl st in first ch to form a ring.

Round 1: Ch 1, 16dc into the ring, join with a sl st in first dc.

Round 2: Ch 8 (counts as 1tr and ch 5), [skip next dc, 1tr in next dc, ch 5] 7 times, skip last dc, join with sl st in 3rd ch of ch 8. Break colour A.

Round 3: Join colour B to any 5ch-sp, [1dc, 1htr, 1tr, 2dtr, ch 1, 2dtr, 1tr, 1htr, 1dc] in each 5ch-sp, join with sl st in first dc. Break colour B.

Round 4: Join colour C to any 1ch-sp, ch 1, 1dc in same sp, [ch 7, 1dc in next 1ch-sp, ch 9, 1dc in next 1ch-sp] 4 times, replacing last dc with sl st in first dc.

Round 5: Sl st in first 7ch-sp, ch 1, *7dc in 7ch-sp, [6dc, ch 3, 6dc] in next 9ch-sp; rep from * a further 3 times, join with sl st in first dc.

Round 6: Ch 1, 1dc in same place, 1dc in each of next 12dc, *[1dc, ch 3, 1dc] in next ch-3 sp, 1dc in each of next 19dc; rep from * twice more, [1dc, ch 3, 1dc] in last 3ch-sp, 1dc in each of last 6dc, join with sl st to first dc.

Round 7: Ch 4 (counts as 1tr and ch 1), [skip next dc, 1tr in foll dc, ch 1] 6 times, *skip next dc, [1tr, ch 3, 1tr] in next 3ch-sp, ch 1, [skip next dc, 1tr in foll dc, ch 1] 10 times; rep from * twice more, skip next dc, [1tr, ch 3, 1tr] in next 3ch-sp, ch 1, [skip next dc, 1tr in foll dc, ch 1] 3 times, change to colour A when joining with sl st in 3rd ch of ch 4.

Round 8: Ch 3 (counts as 1tr), 1tr in every tr and 1ch-sp from previous round, working [1tr, ch 3, 1tr] in every 3ch corner-sp, change to colour B when joining with sl st in 3rd ch of ch 3.

Round 9: Ch 2 (counts as 1htr), 1htr in every tr from previous round, working 3htr in every 3ch corner-sp, join with sl st in 3rd ch of ch-3.

Fasten off and weave in ends.

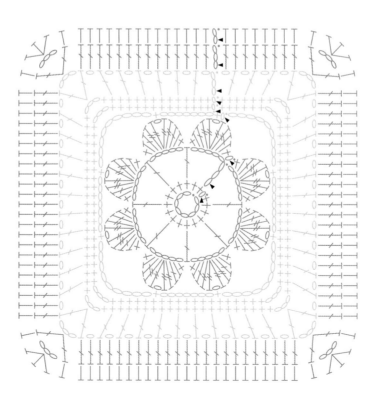

Framed Flower

See page 35

A=Bubbles
B=Bleached
C=Greengage

Foundation chain: Using colour A, ch 7.

Round 1: [1tr and ch 3] 3 times in 7th ch from hook, join with sl st in 3rd ch of ch-7.

Round 2: Ch 1, 1dc in same place, *[1tr, 5dtr, 1tr] in next 3ch-sp (petal made)**, 1dc in next tr; rep from * twice more and from * to ** once again, change to colour B, when joining with sl st in first dc.

Round 3: Ch 1, 1dc in same place, *1tr in next tr, 2tr in each of next 2dtr, 3tr in next dtr, 2tr in each of next 2dtr, 1tr in next tr**, 1dc in next dc; rep from * twice more and from * to ** once again, join with sl st in first dc. Break colour B.

Round 4: Join colour C in 4th tr of any petal, ch 1, 1dc in same place, *ch 5, skip next 5 sts, 1dc in next tr, ch 5**, 1dc in 4th tr of next petal; rep from * twice more and from * to ** once again, join with sl st in first dc.

Round 5: Sl st in next 5ch-sp, ch 3 (counts as 1tr), [3tr, ch 3, 4tr] in same 5ch-sp, *ch 1, 7tr in next 5ch-sp, ch 1**, [4tr, ch 3, 4tr] in next 5ch-sp; rep from * twice more and from * to ** once again, join with sl st in 3rd ch of ch-3. Break colour C.

Round 6: Join colour A in any 3ch-corner-sp, ch 2 (counts as 1htr), [1htr, ch 2, 2htr in same sp, *1htr in each of next 4tr, skip 1ch-sp, 1dc in each of next 7htr, skip 1ch-sp, 1htr in each of next 4tr**, [2htr, ch 2, 2htr] in next 3ch-corner-sp; rep from * twice more and from * to ** once again, join with sl st in 2nd ch of ch-2. Break colour A.

Round 7: Join colour B in any 2ch-corner-sp, ch 3 (counts as 1tr), [1tr, ch 2, 2tr] in same sp, *1tr in each htr and dc along side of square**, [2tr, ch 2, 2tr] in next 2ch-corner-sp; rep from * twice more and from * to ** once again, change to colour C when joining with sl st in 3rd ch of ch-3. Break colour B.

Round 8: Ch 3 (counts as 1tr), 1tr in every tr of previous round and work [2tr, ch 2, 2tr] in each 2ch-corner-sp to end of round, change to colour B when joining with sl st in 3rd ch of ch-3. Break colour C.

Round 9: Ch 3 (counts as 1tr), 1tr in every tr of previous round and work 3tr in each 2ch-corner-sp to end of round, join with sl st in 3rd ch of ch-3.
Fasten off and weave in ends.

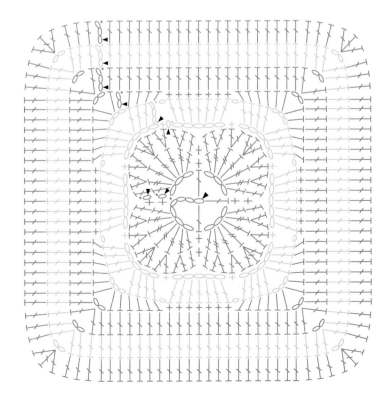

✪ ✪ Cartwheel Flower

See page 32

A=Bleached
B=Greengage
C=Bubbles

SPECIAL STITCHES

Beg PS (Beginning Puff stitch): Ch 2, [Yarn round hook, insert hook into next stitch, draw a loop through] twice, yarn round hook and draw through all 5 loops on hook.

PS (Puff stitch): [Yarn round hook, insert hook into next stitch, draw a loop through] three times, yarn round hook and draw through all 7 loops on hook.

Foundation ring: Using colour A, make a Magic Ring.

Round 1: Ch 1, 8dc into the ring, change to colour B when joining with sl st in first dc. (8 sts)

Round 2: Ch 1, 2dc in same place, *2dc in next st; rep from * a further 6 times, change to colour A when joining with sl st in first dc. (16 sts)

Round 3: Beg PS in same place, *ch 3, skip 1 st, PS in next st; rep from * a further 6 times, ch 3, join with sl st in top of first PS made.

Round 4: Ch 1, 1dc in same place, *3dc in next ch-3 sp, 1dc in next PS; rep from * a further 6 times, 3dc in next 3ch-sp, change to colour C when joining with sl st in first dc.

Round 5: *Ch 4, [2dtr in next st] twice, ch 4, sl st in next st**, sl st in next st; rep from * a further 6 times, then from * to ** once again, sl st in first ch of ch-4. Break colour C.

Round 6: Join colour B through the back loop of sl st between two petals from Round 5, ch 6 (counts as 1tr and ch 3), 1tr in same sp, *ch 3, 1dc in next sl st between two petals ch 3**, [1tr, ch 3, 1tr] through back loop of sl st between two petals; rep from * twice more and then from * to ** once again, join with sl st in 3rd ch of ch-6. (12 sts and 12 ch-sp)

Round 7: Ch 3 (counts as 1tr), *[3tr, 1dtr, 3tr] in ch-3 corner sp, 1tr in next tr, 4tr in 3ch-sp, 1tr in next dc 4tr in 3ch-sp**, 1tr in next tr; rep from * twice more and then from * to ** once again, join with sl st in 3rd ch of ch-3.

Round 8: Ch 3 (counts as 1tr), 1tr in each tr and [1tr, 1dtr, 1tr] in each corner dtr to end of round, change to colour A when joining with sl st in 3rd ch of ch-3.

Round 9: Ch 3 (counts as 1tr), 1tr in each tr and [1tr, 1dtr, 1tr] in each corner dtr to end of round, change to colour C when joining with sl st in 3rd ch of ch-3.

Round 10: Ch 3 (counts as 1tr), 1tr in each tr and [1tr, 1dtr, 1tr] in each corner dtr to end of round, join with sl st in 3rd ch of ch-3.

Fasten off and weave in ends.

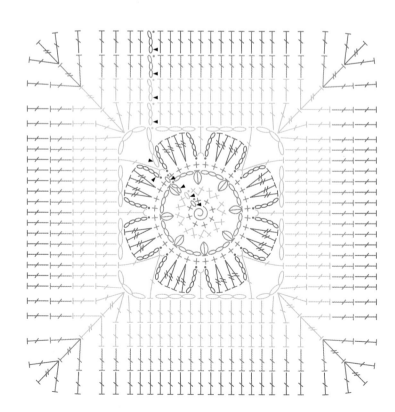

✪ ✪ Origami Flower

See page 33

A=Bleached
B=Greengage
C=Bubbles

SPECIAL STITCHES
3ch-P (3 chain picot): Sl st in st at base of 3 ch.

Foundation ring: Using colour A, ch 5 and join with sl st in first ch to form a ring.
Round 1: Ch 3, 15tr into the ring, change to colour B when joining with sl st in 3rd ch of ch-3.
Round 2: Sl st into space between next 2tr, 2dc in same sp, [2tr in space between next 2tr] 15 times, change to colour C when joining with sl st in first dc.

Round 3: Ch 5 (counts as 1dtr), 4trtr tog in back loops of next 4dc, *ch 6, 5trtr tog over back loops of [same dc as last insertion and foll 4dc], ch 7, 5trtr as before; rep from * twice more, ch 6, 5trtr tog making last insertion at base of ch-5, ch 7, sl st in top of 4trtr tog. Break colour C. (8 petals made)
Round 4: Join colour B to any 7ch-sp. Ch 4, sl st in first of these ch 4, *5dc in same 7ch-sp, 1dc in top of petal, 7dc in ch-6 sp, 1dc in next petal, 5dc in 7ch-sp, 3ch-P: rep from * ending 4dc in 7ch-sp, sl st in first of ch-4.

Round 5: Sl st in 3ch-P, ch 5 (counts as 1dtr and ch 2), 1dtr in same ch-3P, *1dtr in each of next 17tr, [1dtr, ch 2, 1dtr] in 3ch-P, rep from * twice more, 1dtr in each of next 17tr, change to yarn A when joining with sl st in 3rd ch of ch-5.
Round 6: Sl st in 2ch-sp, ch 5 (counts as 1dtr and ch 2), 1tr in same 2ch-sp, *ch 1, [1tr in next tr, ch 1, skip next tr] 9 times, 1tr in next tr, ch 1**, [1tr, 2ch, 1tr] in 2ch-sp; rep from * twice more and from * to ** once again, join with sl st in 3rd ch of ch-5.

Round 7: Sl st in 2ch-sp, ch 5 (counts as 1tr and ch 2), 1tr in same 2ch-sp, *1tr in each tr and 1ch-sp, and [1tr, ch 2, 1tr] in each 2ch-sp, to end of round, change to colour C when joining with sl st in 3rd ch of ch-5.
Round 8: Sl st into ch-2 sp, ch 4 (counts as 1htr and ch 2), 1htr in same 2ch-sp, 1htr in each tr and [1htr, ch 2, 1htr] in each ch-2 corner sp, to end of round, join with sl st in 3rd ch of ch-4.
Fasten off and weave in ends.

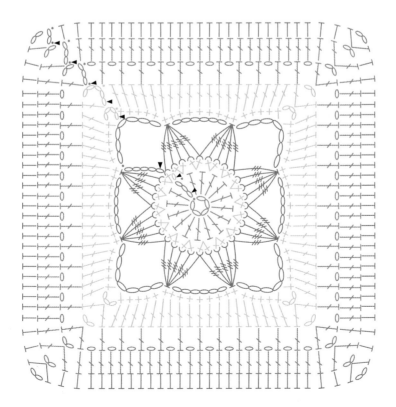

Raised Petal Flower
See page 35

A=Shell
B=Bubbles
C=Bleached
D=Greengage

Foundation ring: Using colour A make a Magic Ring.

Round 1: Ch 1, 3dc into the ring, [ch 3, 3dc into ring] 3 times, ch 3, join with sl st in first dc. Break colour A.

Round 2: Join colour B to any 3ch-sp, ch 1, [1dc, 1htr, 3tr, 1htr, 1dc] in each 3ch-sp to end of round, join with sl st in first dc. Break colour B.

Round 3: Join colour C between any two dc, ch 1, 1dc in same place, [ch 5, 1dc between next 2dc] 3 times, ch 5, join with sl st in first dc.

Round 4: Sl st in first 5ch-sp, ch 3 (counts as 1tr), [tr2tog, ch 2, tr3tog, ch 3, tr3tog, ch 2, tr3tog] in same 5ch-sp, *ch 2, [tr3tog, ch 2, tr3tog, ch 3, tr3tog, ch 2, tr3tog] in

next 5ch-sp; rep from * twice more, join with sl st in top of first cluster. Break colour C.

Round 5: Join colour D to any 3ch-sp, ch 3 (counts as 1tr), [1tr, ch 2, 2tr] in same 2ch-corner-sp, *[ch 1, 2tr in next 2ch-sp] 3 times, ch 1**, [2tr, ch 2, 2tr] in 3ch-corner-sp; rep from * twice more then from * to ** once again, join with sl st in 3rd ch of ch-3.

Round 6: Sl st in next tr, sl st in 2ch-corner-sp, ch 1, [1dc, ch 1, 1dc] in same 2ch-corner-sp, 1dc in every tr and 1ch-sp, working [1dc, ch 1, 1dc] in each 2ch-corner-sp to end of round, join with sl st in first dc.

Fasten off and weave in ends.

Six-petal Flower
See page 33

A=Bubbles
B=Shell
C=Bleached
D=Greengage

Foundation ring: Using colour A, make a magic ring.

Round 1: Ch 2 (counts as 1htr), 5htr into the ring, join with sl st in 2nd ch of ch-2. (6 sts)

Round 2: Ch 2 (counts as 1htr), 1htr into same place, 2htr in every st from Round 1, change to colour B when joining with sl st in 2nd ch of ch-2. Break colour A. (12 sts)

Round 3: Ch 1, 1dc in same place, *ch 3, skip next st**, 1dc in next st; rep from * a further 4 times, then from * to ** once again, join with sl st in first dc.

Round 4: Sl st in first 3ch-sp, *[1dc, 1htr, 1tr, 1dtr, 1tr, 1htr, 1dc] in next 3ch-sp**, sl st in next dc; rep from * a further 4 times, then from * to ** once again, change to colour C when joining with sl st in first sl st. Break colour B.

Round 5: *Sl st in next dc, 1dc in htr, 1htr in tr, [2tr, ch 2, 2tr] in dtr, 1htr in tr, 1dc in htr, sl st in next dc, sl st in next sl st; rep from * 5 more times, join with sl st in first sl st. Break colour C.

Round 6: Join colour D to any dc from Round 3, *ch 3, sl st in next dc from Round 3, [ch 4, sl st in next dc from Round 3] twice; rep from * once

more, join with sl st in first sl st.

Round 7: Sl st in first 3ch-sp, ch 3 (counts as 1tr), 3tr in same 3ch-sp, [2tr, ch 2, 4tr] in next 4ch-sp, [4tr, ch 2, 2tr] in next 4ch-sp, 4tr in next 3ch-sp, [2tr, ch 2, 4tr] in next 4ch-sp, [4tr, ch 2, 2tr] in next 4ch-sp, join with sl st in 3rd ch of ch-3.

Round 8: Ch 3 (counts as 1tr), *1tr in each st to corner, [2tr, ch 2, 2tr] in next 2ch-corner-sp; rep from * 3 more times, 1tr in each st to end of round, join with sl st in 3rd ch of ch-3.

Round 9: Ch 3 (counts as 1tr), 1tr in next st, *1tr through ch-2 sp at top of petal from Round 5 and into next st from Round 8, 1tr in next 5 sts, [2tr, ch 2, 2tr] in next 2ch-corner-sp, 1tr in next st, 1tr through ch-2 sp at top of petal from Round 5 and into next st from Round 8, 1tr in next 8 sts, 1tr through ch-2 sp at top of petal from Round 5 and into next st from Round 8, 1tr in next st, [2tr, ch 2, 2tr] in next 2ch-corner-sp**, 1tr in next 6 sts; rep from * to ** once more, 1tr in next 4 sts, join with sl st in 3rd ch of ch-3.

Fasten off and weave in ends.

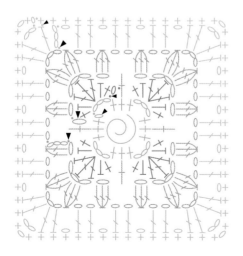

✪✪✪ Ruffled Flower

See page 32

A=Shell
B=Bleached
C=Bubbles

Foundation ring: Using colour A, ch 6 and join with sl st in first ch to form a ring.

Round 1: Ch 3 (counts as 1tr), 3tr into ring, ch 3, turn; 1tr in first tr, 1tr in next 2tr, 1tr in 3rd ch of ch-3, turn; *working across back of petal just made, 4tr into ring, ch 3, turn; 1tr in first tr, 1tr in next 3tr, ch 3, turn; rep from * a further 6 times, join with sl st in 3rd ch of ch-3. Break colour A. (8 petals made)

Round 2: Join colour B to any 3ch-sp behind one of the petals, ch 3 (counts as 1tr), [2tr, 2 ch, 3tr] in same sp, 3tr in next 3ch-sp, *[3tr, ch 2, 3tr] in next 3ch-sp, 3tr in next 3ch-sp; rep from * twice more, join with sl st in 3rd ch of ch-3. Break colour B.

Round 3: Join colour C to any ch-2 corner sp, ch 3 (counts as 1tr), [2tr, ch 3, 3tr] in same sp, *1tr in each of next 9tr**, [3tr, ch 3, 3tr] in next 3ch-sp; rep from * twice more and from * to ** once again, join with sl st in 3rd ch of ch-3. Break colour C.

Round 4: Join colour D to any ch-3 corner sp, ch 2 (counts as 1htr), [2htr, 1tr, 3htr] in same sp, *1htr in each of next 15tr**, [3tr, ch 3, 3tr] in same sp; rep from * twice more and from * to ** once again, join with sl st to 2nd ch of ch-2.

Fasten off and weave in ends.

✪✪ Raised Rose

See page 32

A=Rose
B=Bleached
C=Greengage
D=Blackcurrant

Foundation ring: Using colour A, ch 6 and join with sl st in first ch to form a ring.

Round 1: Ch 3 (counts as 1tr), 11tr into the ring, join with sl st in 3rd ch of ch-3.)

Round 2: Ch 2 (counts as 1htr), 1htr in same place, 2htr in each of the next 11tr, join with sl st in 2nd ch of ch-2.

Round 3: Ch 1, 1dc in same place, *ch 5, skip next 2htr, 1dc in next htr; rep from * a further 6 times, ch 5, join with sl st in first dc. Break colour A.

Round 4: Join colour B in any 5ch-sp, ch 1, [1dc, 1htr, 5tr, 1htr, 1dc] in same 5ch-sp, [1dc, 1htr, 5tr, 1htr, 1dc] in each of next 5ch-sps, join with sl st in back loop of first dc.

Round 5: Working behind petals of previous round, [ch 5, 1BPdc round next dc] 8 times, do not join the round.

Round 6: Sl st in next 5ch-sp, [1dc, 1htr, 7tr, 1htr, 1dc] in same 5ch-sp, [1dc, 1htr, 7tr, 1htr, 1dc] in each of next seven 5ch-sps, join with sl st to back loop of first dc. Break colour B.

Round 7: Join colour C in 3rd tr of any 7tr group from previous round, ch 1, 1dc in same place, 1dc in each of next 2tr, *ch 5, 1dc in 3rd, 4th and 5th tr of next 7tr group, ch 8**, 1dc in 3rd, 4th and 5th tr of next 7tr group; rep from * twice more and from * to ** once again, join with sl st in first dc.

Round 8: Ch 3 (counts as 1tr), 1tr in each dc of previous round, working 5tr in each 5ch-sp and [5tr, ch 3, 5tr] in each 8ch-sp, join with sl st in 3rd ch of ch-3.

Round 9: Ch 3 (counts as 1tr), 1tr in each tr of previous round, working [2tr, ch 2, 2tr] in each ch-3 corner sp, change to colour D when joining with sl st in 3rd ch of ch-3.

Round 10: Ch 1, 1dc in same place, 1dc in each tr of previous round, working 3dc in each ch-2 corner sp, join with sl st in first dc.

Fasten off and weave in ends.

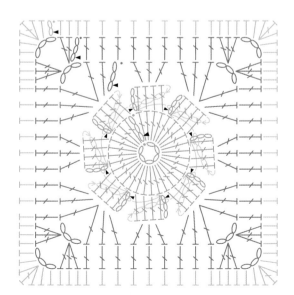

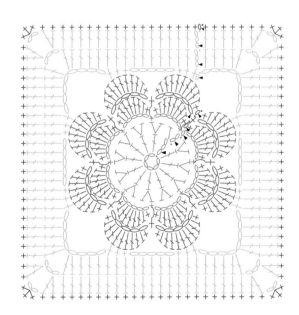

✪ ✪ Cluster Flower

See page 33

A=Shell
B=Blackcurrant
C=Dijon

SPECIAL STITCHES

tr3tog (beg cl): Work three treble sts tog: [yrh, draw up a loop in next st, (yrh, pull through 2 loops on hook) 3 times] twice, yrh and draw through all 4 loops on hook.

tr4tog (cl): Work four treble sts tog: [yrh, draw up a loop in next st, (yrh, pull through 2 loops on hook) 4 times] twice, yrh and draw through all 5 loops on hook.

Foundation chain: Using colour A, ch 6 and join with a sl st to form a ring.

Round 1: Ch 5 (counts as 1tr and 2ch), [1tr into ring, ch 2] 7 times, join with sl st in 3rd ch of ch-5.

Round 2: Ch 3 (counts as 1tr), tr3tog in next 2ch-sp, [ch 5, tr4tog in next 2ch-sp] 7 times more, ch 5, change to colour B when joining with sl st in 3rd ch of ch-3.

Round 3: Ch 1, 1dc in the same place, *ch 2, work over 5ch-sp and enclose it by working 1tr in the next tr of Round 1, ch 2, 1dc in top of next cl; rep from * to end of round, omitting last dc, join with sl st in first dc.

Round 4: Sl st in next ch, ch 1, 1dc in same place, *ch 3, 1dc in next 2ch-sp; rep from * to end of round, omitting last dc, join with sl st in first dc.

Round 5: Sl st in next ch, ch 3 (counts as 1tr), [1tr, ch 2, 2tr] in same sp, *ch 2, 1dc in next ch-3 sp, [ch 3, 1dc in next ch-3 sp] twice, ch 2**, [2tr, ch 2, 2tr] in next 3ch-sp; rep from * twice and from * to ** once again, join with sl st in 3rd ch of ch-3. Break colour B.

Round 6: Join colour C to any ch-2 corner sp, ch 3 (counts as 1tr), [1tr, ch 2, 2tr] in same space, *ch 2 [1dc in next ch-sp, ch 3] 3 times, 1dc in next

ch-sp, ch 2**, [2tr, ch 2, 2tr] in ch-2 corner sp; rep from * twice and from * to ** once more, join with sl st in 3rd ch of ch-3.

Round 7: Sl st in next ch-2 corner sp, ch 3 (counts as 1tr), [1tr, ch 2, 2tr] in the same space, *ch 2, [1dc in next ch-sp, ch 3] 4 times, 1dc in next ch-sp, ch 2**, [2tr, ch 2, 2tr] in ch-2 corner sp; rep from * twice and from * to ** once more, join with sl st in 3rd ch of ch-3.

Round 8: Sl st in next ch-2 corner sp, ch 3 (counts as 1tr), [1tr, ch 2, 2tr] in same space, *ch 2, [1dc in next ch-sp, ch 3] 5 times, 1dc in next ch-sp, ch 2**, [2tr, ch 2, 2tr] in ch-2 corner sp; rep from * twice and from * to ** once more, join with sl st in 3rd ch of ch-3.

Round 9: Sl st in next ch-2 corner sp, ch 3 (counts as 1tr), [1tr, ch 2, 2tr] in same space, *ch 2, [1dc in next ch-sp,

ch 3] 6 times, 1dc in next ch-sp, ch 2**, [2tr, ch 2, 2tr] in ch-2 corner sp; rep from * twice and from * to ** once more, join with sl st in 3rd ch of ch-3. Break colour C.

Round 10: Join colour A to any ch-2 corner sp, ch 2 (counts as 1htr, [1htr, ch 2, 2htr] in same space, *3htr in next 2ch-sp, 3htr in each of next 6 3ch-sps, 3htr in next 2ch-sp**, [2htr, ch 2, 2htr] in corner 2ch-sp; rep from * twice more and from * to ** once again, join with sl st to 2nd ch of ch-2. Break colour A.

Round 11: Join colour B to any ch-2 corner sp, ch 3 (counts as 1tr), 4tr into same same sp, 1tr in every htr from previous round, working 5tr into every ch-2 corner sp to end of round, join with sl st to 3rd ch of ch-3.

Fasten off and weave in ends.

Lacy Daisy

See page 34

A=Heather
B=Shell
C=Blackcurrant

Foundation ring: Using colour A, ch 6 and join with sl st in first ch to form a ring.

Round 1: Ch 1, 12dc into the ring, change to colour B when joining in back loop of first tr with sl st. Break colour A. (12 sts)

Round 2: Ch 6 (counts as 1trtr and ch 1), 1trtr in back loop of same dc, ch 1, [1trtr, ch 1] twice in back loop of every dc to end of round, join with sl st in 5th ch of ch-6. Break colour B.

Round 3: Join colour C to any 1ch-sp, ch 5 (counts as 1tr and ch 2), 1tr in same ch-sp, *ch 1, 1htr in next ch-sp, [ch 1, 1dc in next ch-sp] 3 times, ch 1, 1htr in next ch-sp, ch 1**, [1tr, ch 2, 1tr] in next ch-sp; rep from * twice more and then from * to ** once again, join with sl st in 3rd ch of ch-5.

Round 4: *Sl st in next 2ch-sp, ch 5, sl st in same ch-sp, ch 4, skip [1tr, ch 1, 1htr], sl st in next 1ch-sp, ch 4, skip [1dc, ch 1], sl st in next dc, ch 4, skip [ch 1, 1dc], sl st in next ch, ch 4, skip [1htr, ch 1, 1tr], sl st in next 2ch-sp; rep from * a further 3 times, join with sl st in first sl st.

Round 5: Sl st in each of next 2 ch, sl st under rem 3 ch, *ch 5, sl st in same ch-sp, [ch 4, sl st in next 4ch-sp] 5 times; rep from * a further 3 times, join with sl st in first 5ch-sp.

Round 6: Sl st in each of next 2 ch, sl st under rem 3 ch, *ch 5, sl st in same ch-sp, [ch 4, sl st in next ch-sp] 6 times; rep from * a further 3 times, join with sl st in first 5ch-sp.

Round 7: Sl st in each of next 2 ch, sl st under rem 3 ch, ch 6 (counts as 1tr and ch 3), 1tr in same ch-sp, *[ch 2, 1tr in next ch-sp] 7 times, ch 3, 1tr in same ch-sp; rep from * twice more, [ch 2, 1tr in next ch-sp] 6 times, ch 2, join with sl st in 3rd ch of ch-6.

Round 8: Sl st in 3ch-sp, ch 6 (counts as 1tr and ch 3), 1tr in same ch-sp, 3tr in each 2ch-sp and [1tr, ch 3, 1tr] in each 3ch-corner-sp to end of round, join with sl st in 3rd ch of ch-6. (23tr on each side)

Round 9: Sl st in 3ch-sp, ch 2, 1dc in same ch-sp, 1dc in each dc and [1dc, ch 2, 1dc] in each corner-sp to end of round, join with sl st in 2nd ch of ch-3. (25dc on each side)

Round 10: Sl st in 2ch-sp, ch 2, 1dc in same ch-sp, 1dc in each dc and [1dc, ch 2, 1dc] in each corner-sp to end of round, change to colour A when joining with sl st to 2nd ch of ch-3. (27dc on each side)

Round 11: Sl st in 2ch-sp, ch 2, 1dc in same ch-sp, 1dc in each dc and [1dc, ch 2, 1dc] in each corner-sp to end of round, change to colour A when joining with sl st to 2nd ch of ch-3. (29dc on each side)

Round 12: Sl st in 2ch-sp, ch 2, 1dc in same ch-sp, 1dc in each dc and [1dc, ch 2, 1dc] in each corner-sp to end of round, join with sl st in 2nd ch of ch-3. (31dc on each side)

Fasten off and weave in ends.

Poppy

See page 34

A=Blackcurrant
B=Heather
C=Shell

Foundation ring: Using colour A, ch 4 and join with sl st in first ch to form a ring.

Round 1: Ch 1, 8dc into the ring, join with sl st to first dc. (8dc)

Round 2: Ch 3 (counts as 1htr and ch 1), [1htr in front loop of next dc, ch 1] 7 times, join with sl st in 3rd ch of ch 3. Break colour A.

Round 3: Join colour B in back loop of any htr, ch 3 (counts as 1tr), [2tr in ch-1 sp, 1tr blo in next htr] 7 times, 2tr in 1ch-sp, join with sl st in 3rd ch of ch-3.

Round 4: [Ch 3, 1dtr in next htr, 2trtr in next htr, 1trtr in next htr, 2trtr in next htr, 1dtr in next htr, ch 3, sl st in next htr] 4 times, working final sl st in same place as base of first ch-3. Break colour B. (4 petals)

Round 5: Ch 5 (counts as 1tr and ch 2), 1tr in same trtr, *ch 5, [1tr, ch 3, 1tr] in sl st between petals, ch 5**, [1tr, ch 2, 1tr in centre trtr of next petal, * rep from * twice more and from * to ** once again, join with sl st in 3rd ch of ch-5.

Round 6: Sl st in 2ch-sp, ch 5 (counts as 1tr and ch 2), 1tr in same ch-sp, * ch 5, 1dc in 5ch-sp, [3tr, ch 1, 3tr] in next 3ch-sp, 1dc in next 5ch-sp, ch 5**, [1tr, ch 2, 1tr] in next 2ch-sp; rep from * twice and from * to ** once again, join with sl st in 3rd ch of ch-5.

Round 7: Sl st in 2ch-sp, ch 5 (counts as 1tr and ch 2), 1tr in same 5ch-sp, *ch 5, 1dc in 5ch-sp, ch 5, 1dc in next 1ch-sp, ch 5, 1dc in next 5ch-sp, ch 5**, [1tr, ch 2, 1tr] in next 2ch-sp; rep from * twice more and from * to ** once again, join with sl st in 3rd ch of ch-5.

Round 8: Sl st in 2ch-sp, ch 5 (counts as 1tr and ch 2), 1tr in same ch-sp, *[ch 5, 1dc in 5ch-sp] 4 times, ch 5**, [1tr, ch 2, 1tr] in next 2ch-sp; rep from * twice more and from * to ** once again, ch 5, join with sl st in 3rd ch of ch-5.

Round 9: Sl st in 2ch-sp, ch 5 (counts as 1tr and ch 2), 1tr in same ch-sp, *4tr in next 5ch-sp, [5tr in next 5ch-sp] 3 times, 4tr in next 5ch-sp**, [1tr, ch 2, 1tr] in next 2ch-sp; rep from * twice more and from * to ** once again, change to colour B when joining with sl st in 3rd ch of ch-5.

Round 10: Ch 3 (counts as 1tr), 1tr in every tr from previous round and [1tr, ch 2, 1tr] in next and each 2ch-sp to end of round, change to colour A when joining with sl st in 3rd ch of ch-3.

Round 11: Ch 3 (counts as 1tr), 1tr in every tr from previous round and [1tr, ch 2, 1tr] in next and each 2ch-sp to end of round, join with sl st in 3rd ch of ch-3.

Fasten off and weave in ends.

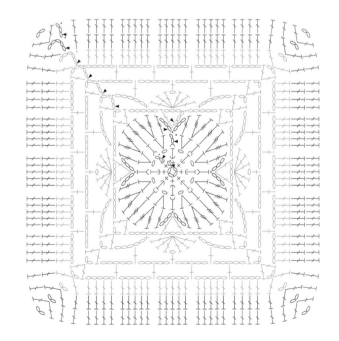

⊛ ⊛ *Marigold*

See page 33

A=Rose
B=Bleached
C=Blackcurrant
D=Greengage

Foundation ring: Using colour A, ch 6 and join with sl st in first ch to form a ring.

Round 1: Ch 5 (counts as 1tr and 2ch), [1tr into ring, ch 2] 7 times, join with sl st in 3rd ch of ch-5.

Round 2: Sl st in next 2ch-sp, ch 1, [1dc, 1htr, 1tr, 1htr, 1dc] in same sp (petal made), [1dc, 1htr, 1tr, 1htr, 1dc] in each rem 2ch-sp to end of round, join with sl st in first dc. Break colour A.

Round 3: Working behind the petals of the previous round, join colour B between two petals, ch 3, [sl st in back loop of first dc of next petal, ch 3] 7 times, join with sl st in first of ch-3.

Round 4: Sl st in next 3ch-sp, ch 1, [1dc, 2htr, 1tr, 2htr, 1dc] in same sp, [1dc, 2htr, 1tr, 2htr, 1dc] in each rem 3ch-sp to end of round, join with sl st in first dc. Break colour B.

Round 5: Working behind the petals of the previous round, join colour C between two petals, ch 4, [sl st in back loop of first dc of next petal, ch 4] 7 times, join with sl st in first ch of ch-4.

Round 6: Sl st in next 4ch-sp, ch 1, [1dc, 2htr, 3tr, 2htr, 1dc] in same sp, [1dc, 2htr, 3tr, 2htr, 1dc] in each rem 4ch-sp to end of round, join with sl st in first dc. Break colour C.

Round 7: Working behind the petals of the previous round, join colour D between two petals, ch 5, [sl st in back loop of first dc of next petal, ch 5] 7 times, join with sl st in first of ch-5.

Round 8: Sl st in next 5ch-sp, ch 3 (counts as 1tr), 5tr in same sp, *[3tr, ch 2, 3tr] in next 5ch-sp, (corner made)**, 6tr in next 5ch-sp; rep from * twice more and from * to ** once again, join with sl st in first tr.

Round 9: Ch 3 (counts as 1tr), 1tr in each tr of previous round, working [2tr, ch 2, 2tr] in each 2ch-corner-sp, join with sl st in 3rd ch of ch-3.

Round 10: Sl st in next tr, ch 5 (counts as 1tr and ch 2), skip 2tr, 1tr in next tr, ch 2, skip 2tr, 1tr in next tr, skip 3tr, *[3tr, ch 2, 3tr] in next 2ch-corner-sp, skip 3tr**, [1tr in next tr, ch 2, skip 2tr] 3 times, 1tr in next tr; rep from * twice more and from * to ** once again, 1tr in next tr, ch 2, skip 2tr, join with sl st in 3rd ch of ch-5.

Round 11: Ch 5 (counts as 1tr and ch 2), [1tr in next tr, ch 2] twice, 1tr in next tr, *[3tr, ch 2, 3tr] in next 2ch-corner-sp, 1tr in next tr**, ch 2, skip 2tr, [1tr in next tr, ch 2] 4 times, 1tr in next tr; rep from * twice and from * to ** once again, ch 2, 1tr in next tr, ch 2, join with sl st in 3rd ch of ch-5.

Round 12: Ch 5 (counts as 1tr and ch 2), [1tr in next tr, ch 2] 3 times, 1tr in next tr, *[3tr, ch 2, 3tr] in next 2ch-corner-sp, 1tr in next tr, ch 2, skip 2tr**, [1tr in next tr, ch 2] 6 times, skip 2tr, 1tr in next tr; rep from * twice and from * to ** once again, [1tr in next tr, ch 2] twice, join with sl st in 3rd ch of ch-5.

Round 13: Ch 5 (counts as 1tr and ch 2), [1tr in next tr, ch 2] 4 times, skip 2tr, 1tr in next tr, *[3tr, ch 2, 3tr] in next 2ch-corner-sp, 1tr in next tr, ch 2, skip 2tr**, [1tr in next tr, ch 2] 8 times, skip 2tr, 1tr in next tr; rep from * twice more and from * to ** once again, [1tr in next tr, ch 2] 3 times, join with sl st in 3rd ch of ch-5.

Round 14: Ch 1, 1dc in same place, 1dc in each tr of previous round, working 2dc in each 2ch-sp along sides of square and 3dc in each 2ch-corner-sp, join with sl st to first dc.

Fasten off and weave in ends.

Flame Flower

See page 32

A=Bleached
B=Rose
C=Greengage
D=Blackcurrant

Foundation ring: Using colour A, ch 4 and join with sl st in first ch to form a ring.

Round 1: Ch 4 (counts as 1tr and ch 1), [1tr into ring, ch 1] 7 times, join with sl st in 3rd ch of ch-4. (8 sts, 8 ch-sp)

Round 2: Ch 1 and dc in same sp, *sl st in next 1ch-sp, ch 9, sl st in same 1ch-sp**, 1dc in next tr; rep from * a further 6 times then from * to ** once again, join with sl st in first dc. (8 sts, 8 ch-sp)

Round 3: Ch 1, *(5dc, ch 2, 5dc) in ch-9 sp**, sl st in next dc; rep from * 6 more times and from * to ** once again, change to colour B when joining with sl st to first sl st. (80 sts, 16 sl sts, 8 ch-sp.) Break colour A.

Round 4: Ch 1, *1dc in first dc of petal, 1htr in next 2 sts, 1tr in next 2dc, (2tr, ch 2, 2tr) in 2ch-sp, 1tr in next 2 sts, 1htr in next 2sts, 1dc in next st**, FPdc around tr from Round 1; rep from * 6 more times and from * to ** once again, change to colour C when joining

with sl st to first dc of petal. Break colour B. (120 sts, 8 ch-sp)

Round 5: Join colour C with a BP sl st around tr from Round 1, ch 3, skip 1dtr, *BP sl st around tr from Round 1, ch 3, skip 1tr; rep from * 3 more times, join with sl st in first sl st made. (4 BP sl sts, 4ch-sp)

Round 6: Sl st in 3ch-sp, ch 3 (counts as 1tr), 2tr, ch 2, 3tr in same ch-sp, ch 1, *(3tr, ch 2, 3tr) in next 3ch-sp, ch 1; rep from * twice more, join with sl st in 3rd ch of ch-3. (24 sts, 8 ch-sp)

Round 7: Sl st to next 2ch-sp, ch 3 (counts as 1tr), 2tr, ch 2, 3tr in same 1ch-sp, ch 1, *3tr in 1ch-sp, ch 1**, (3tr, ch 2, 3tr) in next 2ch-sp, ch 1; rep from * twice more and then from * to ** once again join with sl st in 3rd ch of ch-3. (36 sts, 12ch-sp)

Round 8: Sl st to next 2ch-sp, ch 3 (counts as 1tr), 2tr, ch 2, 3tr in same ch-sp, ch 1, *[3tr in 1ch-sp, ch 1] twice**, [3tr, ch 2, 3tr] in next 2ch-sp, ch 1; rep from * twice more and then

from * to ** once again join with sl st in 3rd ch of ch-3. (48 sts, 16ch-sp)

Round 9: Sl st to next 2ch-sp, ch 3 (counts as 1tr), 2tr, ch 2, 3tr in same ch-sp, ch 1, *[3tr in 1ch-sp, ch 1] 3 times**, [3tr, ch 2, 3tr] in next 2ch-sp, ch 1; rep from * twice more and then from * to ** once again, join with sl st in 3rd ch of ch-3. (60 sts, 20ch-sp)

Round 10: Ch 1, 1dc in same sp, 1dc in each of next 2 sts, *(1dc, 1htr, 1dc) in 2ch-sp, 1dc in each of next 5 sts and ch-sp, 1dc through 2ch-sp of Round 4 petal and in next st, 1dc in next 7 sts and ch-sp, 1dc through 2ch-sp of Round 4 petal and in next st**, 1dc in each of next 5 sts and ch-sp to 2ch-corner-sp; rep from * twice more and from * to ** once again, dc to end of round, join with sl st in first dc made. (88 sts)

Round 11: Sl st to next 2ch-sp, ch 3 (counts as 1tr), 2tr, ch 3, 3tr in same sp, *[ch 1, skip next st, 1tr in each of

next 3 sts] 5 times, ch 1, skip next st**, [3tr, ch 3, 3tr] in next ch-2 corner sp; rep from * twice more and from * to ** once again, join with sl st in 3rd ch of ch-3.

Round 12: Sl st to next 3ch-sp, ch 3 (counts as 1tr), [2tr, ch 3, 3tr] in same sp, *[ch 1, 3tr in next 1ch-sp] 6 times, ch 1**, [3tr, ch 3, 3tr] in next 3ch-corner-sp; rep from * twice more and from * to ** once again, join with sl st in 3rd ch of ch-3.

Round 13: Sl st to next 3ch-sp, ch 3 (counts as 1tr), [2tr, ch 3, 3tr] in same sp, *[ch 1, 3tr in next 1ch-sp] 7 times, ch 1**, [3tr, ch 3, 3tr] in next 3ch-corner-sp; rep from * twice more and from * to ** once again, change to colour D when joining with sl st in 3rd ch of ch-3.

Round 14: Ch 1, 1dc in every tr and ch-sp, from previous round, working 3dc in every 3ch-corner-sp, join with sl st in first dc.

Fasten off and weave in ends.

American Beauty

See page 35

A=Rose
B=Shell
C=Dark Forest

Foundation ring: Using colour A, ch 12 and join with sl st to form a ring.
Round 1: Ch 1, 18dc into the ring, join with a sl st in first dc. (18 dc)
Round 2: Ch 1, 1dc in same place, [ch 3, skip 2dc, 1dc into next dc] 5 times, ch 3, skip 2dc, join with sl st in first dc. (6 ch-3 loops)
Round 3: Ch 1, [1dc, ch 3, 5tr, ch 3, 1dc] in each of next 6 ch-3 loops, join with sl st in first dc. (6 petals)
Round 4: Ch 1, 1dc in same place, [ch 5 behind petal of previous round, 1dc between 2dc] 5 times, ch 5

behind petal of previous round, join with sl st in first dc. (6 ch-5 loops)
Round 5: Ch 1, [1dc, ch 3, 7tr, ch 3, 1dc] in each of next 6 ch-5 loops, join with sl st in first dc. (6 petals)
Round 6: Ch 1, 1dc in same place, [ch 7 behind petal of previous round, 1dc between 2dc] 5 times, ch 7 behind petal of previous round, join with sl st in first dc. (6 ch-7 loops)
Round 7: Ch 1, [1dc, ch 3, 9tr, ch 3, 1dc] in each of next 6 ch-7 loops, join with sl st in first dc. (6 petals). Break colour A.

Round 8: Join colour B between any 2dc, ch 1, [1dc between 2dc, ch 8 behind petal of previous round] 6 times, join with sl st in first dc. (6 ch-8 loops)
Round 9: Sl st in next ch-8 loop, ch 3 (counts as 1tr), [7tr, ch 2, 3tr] in same loop, *10tr in next ch-8 loop, [3tr, ch 2, 8tr] in next ch-8 loop**, [8tr, ch 2, 3tr] in next ch-8 loop; rep from * to ** once more, join with sl st in 3rd ch of ch-3. (16tr along each side of square)
Round 10: Ch 3 (counts as 1tr), 1tr in

each tr of previous round, working [3tr, ch 2, 3tr] in each 2ch-corner-sp, change to colour C when joining with sl st in 3rd ch of ch 3.
Rounds 11–13: Ch 3 (counts as 1tr), 1tr in each tr of previous round, working [2tr, ch 2, 2tr] in each 2ch-corner-sp, join with sl st in 3rd ch of ch 3.
Round 14: Ch 1, 1dc in each tr of previous round, working 3dc in each 2ch-corner-sp, join with sl st in first dc.
Fasten off and weave in ends.

✦ ✦ ✦ *Chrysanthemum*

See page 34

A=Blackcurrant
B=Bleached
B=Rose

Central flower

Using A, ch 6, sl st in 3rd ch from hook, ch 2, skip 2ch, 1dc in first ch, do not turn, [ch 5, sl st in 3rd ch from hook, ch 2, skip 2 ch, 1dc in side edge of dc, do not turn] 8 times, [ch 7, sl st in 3rd ch from hook, ch 4, skip 4 ch, 1dc in side edge of dc, do not turn] 9 times, [ch 9, sl st in 3rd ch from hook, ch 6, skip 6 ch, 1dc in side edge of dc, do not turn] 9 times, do not turn. Count along side edge, sl st in 8th dc. Fasten off colour A.

Block

Round 1: Turn central flower over and join colour B to back loop of any dc in the ring just made, ch 3, 2tr in back loop of each of next 7 sts, 1tr in base of ch 3, sl st in 3rd ch of of ch-3. (16 tr)

Round 2: Ch 3, 2tr in each tr, 1tr in base of ch 3, sl st in 3rd ch of ch-3. (32 tr)

Round 3: Ch 3, [1tr in next tr, 2tr in next tr] 15 times, 1tr in last tr, 1tr in base of ch 3, sl st in 3rd ch of ch-3. (48 tr)

Round 4: Ch 3, [1tr in next tr, 2tr in next tr] 15 times, 1tr in last tr, 1tr in base of ch 3, sl st in 3rd ch of ch-3. Break colour B. (64 tr)

Round 5: Join colour C to any tr, ch 3, tr3tog in same place as base of ch-3, [ch 4, skip 3tr, tr4tog in next tr] 15 times, ch 4, skip 3tr, sl st in first tr3tog. Break colour C. (80 sts)

Round 6: Join colour B in any 4ch-sp, ch 6 (counts as 1dtr and ch 2), [2dtr, 1tr] in same 4ch-sp, *[2tr, 3htr] in next 4ch-sp, 5htr in next 4ch-sp, [3htr, 2tr] in next 4ch-sp, [1tr, 2dtr, ch 2, 2dtr, 1tr] in next 4ch-sp; rep from * a further 3 times ending last rep with [1tr, 1dtr] in first ch-sp, sl st in 4th ch of ch-6. (21 sts on each side)

Round 7: Sl st in 2ch-sp, ch 5 (counts as 1tr and ch 2), 2tr in same 2ch-sp, *1tr in each of next 21 sts, [2tr, ch 2, 2tr] in 2ch-sp; rep from * a further 3 times ending last rep with 1tr in first 2ch-sp, sl st in 3rd ch of ch-5. (25 sts on each side)

Round 8: Sl st into 2ch-sp, ch 5 (counts as 1tr and ch 2), 2tr in same 2ch-sp, *1tr in each of next 25 sts, [2tr, ch 2, 2tr] in 2ch-sp; rep from * a further 3 times, ending last rep with 1tr in first ch-sp, sl st in 3rd ch of ch-5. (29 sts on each side)

Round 9: Sl st into 2ch-sp, ch 5 (counts as 1tr and ch 2), 2tr in same 2ch-sp, *1tr in each of next 29 sts, [2tr, ch 2, 2tr] in 2ch-sp; rep from * a further 3 times, ending last rep with 1tr in first ch-sp, sl st in 3rd ch of ch-5. (33 sts on each side)

Fasten off and weave in ends.

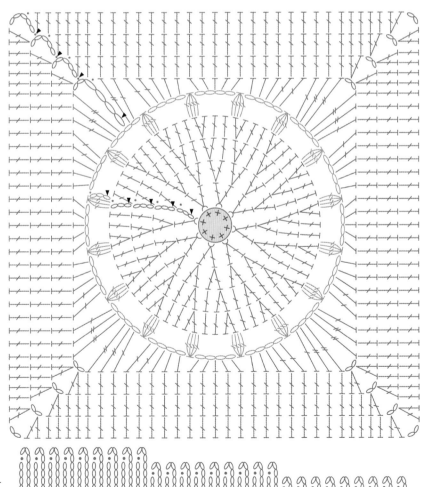

Central flower

Primrose Square

See page 33

A=Shell
B=Bleached
C=Greengage

SPECIAL STITCHES

1gp (2 linked sts together): Yarn round hook twice, insert hook into designated st, [yarn round hook, pull 2 loops through] twice, yarn round hook, insert hook in lowest link of st just made, yarn round hook, pull through link, yarn round hook, pull through 2 loops, yarn round hook, pull through 3 loops on hook.

5chP (5-ch picot): Ch 5, sl st to first of ch-5.

7chP (7-ch picot): Ch 7, sl st to first of ch-7.

First primrose

Using colour A make a Magic Ring.
Round 1: Sl st into ring, ch 1, 4dc into ring, join with sl st to first ch. Break colour A. (5 sts)
Round 2: Join colour B to to any dc, ch 3, 1tr in first of these ch 3, ch 1, 1gp in same dc, *ch 3, [1gp, ch 1, 1gp] in next dc; rep from * a further 3

times, ch 3, join with sl st in first tr of the round. Break colour B.
Round 3: Join colour C to any 3ch-sp, ch 1, 2dc in same ch-sp, *dc2tog over [same 3ch-sp and next 1ch-sp], 5-chP, dc2tog over [same ch-1 sp and next 3ch-sp], 4dc in same 3ch-sp**; rep from * once more, dc2tog as set, 7-chP, dc2tog as set, 4dc in same 3ch-sp; rep from * to ** twice more ending 1dc in first ch-sp, join with sl st in first ch of round.
Fasten off.

Second primrose

Work as first primrose, joining to first primrose on last round by linking the second 5chP and the 7chP to corresponding picots.

Third primrose

Work as first primrose, linking to second primrose as before.

Fourth primrose

Work as first primrose without fastening off colour C, joining to first,

second and third primroses on last round by linking the second 5chP, the 7chP and the next 5chP forming a square. Do not fasten off. Rejoin colour C to last sl st of Round 3 of first primrose.
Round 4: Ch 5 (counts as 1tr and ch 2), *1tr in next dc, ch 3, sl st in 5chP, ch 3, [1dtr, ch 3, 1dtr] in st linking two 5chP, ch 3, sl st in next ch 5P, ch 3**, 1tr in 2nd ch of 4dc, ch 2; rep from * twice more then from * to ** once again join with sl st in 3rd ch of ch-5.
Round 5: Sl st in next 2ch-sp, ch 5 (counts as 1tr and ch 2), 2tr in same ch-sp, *4tr in each of next two 3ch-sp, 3tr in next 3ch-sp (between dtr), 4tr in each of next two 3ch-sp**, [2tr, ch 2, 2tr] in 2ch-corner-sp; rep from * twice more then from * to ** once again, 1tr in first corner ch-sp, join with sl st in 3rd ch of ch-5. (23 tr on each side.)
Round 6: Sl st in next 2ch-sp, ch 5

(counts as 1tr and ch 2), 1tr in same ch-sp, *1tr in each of next 23tr**, [1tr, ch 2, 1tr] in 2ch-corner-sp; rep from * twice more then from * to ** once again, join with sl st in 3rd ch of ch-3. (25 tr on each side.)
Round 7: Sl st in next 2ch-sp, ch 5 (counts as 1tr and ch 2), 1tr in same ch-sp, *1tr in each of next 25tr**, [1tr, ch 2, 1tr] in 2ch-corner-sp; rep from * twice more then from * to ** once again, join with sl st in 3rd ch of ch-3. (25 tr on each side.)
Round 8: Sl st in next 2ch-sp, ch 1, [1dc, ch 2, 1dc] in same ch-sp, *1dc in each tr around and work [1dc, ch 2, 1dc] in 2ch-corner-sp, join with sl st in 3rd ch of ch-3. (29 tr on each side)
Fasten off and weave in ends.

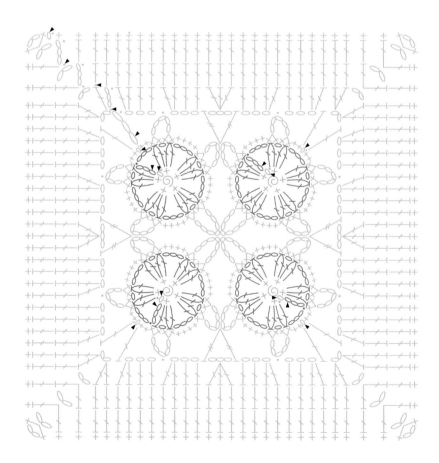

Waterlily

See page 35

A=Shell
B=Bleached
C=Greengage

Foundation ring: Using colour A, ch 8 and join with sl st in first ch to form a ring.

Round 1: Ch 6 (counts as 1tr and ch 3), [1tr into the ring, ch 3] 7 times, join with sl st in 3rd ch of ch-3. Break colour A. (8 spaced tr)

Round 2: Join colour B to any ch-3 sp, ch 1, [1dc, ch 2, 3tr, ch 2, 1dc] in same sp, *[1dc, ch 2, 3tr, ch 2, 1dc] in next ch-3 sp; rep from * 7 times, do not join. (8 petals)

Note: Rounds 3–6 are worked in a continuous spiral. You might find it helpful to use a stitch marker to keep track of the start of the round.

Round 3: Ch 5 working behind petal, skip 1 petal, 1dc in top of next dc of Round 1, [ch 5, working behind petal, skip 1 petal, 1dc in top of next dc of round 1] 7 times, do not join. (8 ch-5 loops)

Round 4: *[1dc, ch 2, 5tr, ch 2, 1dc] in next ch-5 loop; rep from * to end of round, do not join. (8 petals)

Round 5: Ch 7 working behind petal, skip1 petal, 1dc in top of next dc of round 3, [ch 7, working behind petal, skip1 petal, 1dc in top of next dc of round 3] 7 times, do not join. (8 ch-7 loops)

Round 6: *[1dc, ch 2, 7tr, ch 2, 1dc] in next ch-7 loop; rep from * to end of round, do not join. Break colour B. (8 petals)

Round 7: Working behind petals, join colour C to any dc on Round 5, ch 3 (counts as 1tr), 2tr in same dc, ch 3, *[3tr, ch 3, 3tr] in next dc of Round 5 to make corner, ch 3**, 3tr in next dc, ch 3; rep from * twice more and from * to ** once again, join with sl st in 3rd ch of ch-3.

Round 8: Ch 3 (counts as 1tr), 1tr in every tr and 3tr in each 3ch-sp of previous round, working [2tr, ch 3, 2tr] in each ch-3 corner sp, join with sl st in 3rd ch of ch-3.

Round 9: Ch 3 (counts as 1tr), 1tr in every tr of previous round, working [2tr, ch 3, 2tr] in each ch-3 corner sp, with sl st in 3rd ch of ch-3.

Round 10: Ch 1, 1dc in every tr of previous round, working [2dc, ch 1, 2dc] in each 3ch-corner-sp, changing to colour B when joining with sl st in first dc.

Round 11: Ch 1, 1dc in every dc of previous round, working [1dc, ch 1, 1dc] in each 1ch-corner-sp, join with sl st in first dc.

Round 12: Ch 1, 1dc in every dc of previous round, working [1dc, ch 1, 1dc] in each 1ch-corner-sp, changing to colour A when joining with sl st in first dc.

Rounds 13–14: Ch 1, 1dc in every dc of previous round, working [1dc, ch 1, 1dc] in each 1ch-corner-sp, join with sl st in first dc.

Fasten off and weave in ends.

Filet Flower

See page 34

A=Rose

SPECIAL STITCHES

Tr2tog (work two treble sts tog): [Yrh draw up a loop in next st, (yrh, pull through 2 loops on hook) twice] twice, yrh and draw through all 3 loops on hook.

Foundation ring: Using colour A, ch 6 and join with sl st in first ch to form a ring.

Round 1: Ch 1, 12dc into the ring, join with a sl st in first dc.

Round 2: Ch 3 (counts as 1tr), 4tr in same place, [ch 3, skip 2dc, 5tr in next dc] 3 times, ch 3, join with sl st in 3rd ch of ch-3.

Round 3: Ch 3 (counts as 1tr), 1tr in next tr, 5tr in next tr, 1tr in each of next 2tr, *ch 3, skip 3ch, 1tr in each of next 2tr, 5tr in next tr, 1tr in each of next 2tr; rep from * twice more, ch 3, skip 3ch, join with sl st in 3rd ch of ch-3.

Round 4: Ch 3 (counts as 1tr), 1tr in each of next 3tr, 5tr in next tr, 1tr in each of next 4tr, *ch 3, skip 3ch, 1tr in each of next 4tr, 5tr in next tr, 1tr in each of next 4tr; rep from * twice more, ch 3, skip 3ch, join with sl st in 3rd ch of ch-3.

Round 5: Ch 2, 1tr in each of next 4tr, *tr2tog over next 2tr, ch 7, tr2tog over [same tr as last insertion and next tr], 1tr in each of next 3tr, tr2tog over next 2tr, ch 5, skip 3ch**, tr2tog over next 2tr, 1tr in each of next 3tr; rep from * twice more and then from * to ** once

again, join with sl st in first tr.

Round 6: Ch 2, 1tr in each of next 2tr, *tr2tog over next 2 sts, ch 3, skip 2ch, 1tr in next ch, ch 3, skip 1ch, 1tr in next ch, ch 3, skip next 2ch, tr2tog over next 2sts, 1tr in next tr, tr2tog over next 2 sts, ch 3, skip 2ch, 1tr in next ch, ch 3, skip 2ch**, tr2tog over next 2 sts, 1tr in next tr; rep from * twice more and from * to ** once again, join with sl st in first tr.

Round 7: Ch 4 (counts as 1tr and ch 1), skip first 2tr, 1tr in tr2tog, ch 1, skip 1ch, 1tr in next ch, ch 1, skip 1ch, 1tr in next tr, *ch 5, skip 3ch, 1tr in next tr, ch 1, skip 1ch, 1tr in next ch, ch 1, skip 1ch, 1tr in next tr2tog, ch 1, skip 1tr, 1tr in next tr2tog, ch 1, skip 1ch, 1tr in next ch, ch 1, skip 1ch, 1tr in next tr, ch 1, skip 1ch, 1tr in next tr2tog, ch 1, skip 1ch, 1tr in next ch**, 1tr in next tr2tog, ch 1, skip 1tr, 1tr in next tr2tog, ch 1, skip 1ch, 1tr in next ch, skip 1 ch, 1tr in next tr; rep from * twice more and from * to ** once again, join with sl st in 3rd ch of ch-4.

Round 8: Ch 2 (counts as 1htr), 1htr in every tr and 1ch-sp and [2htr, ch 3, 2htr] in every 5ch-corner sp to end of round, join with sl st in 2nd ch of ch-2.
Fasten off and weave in ends.

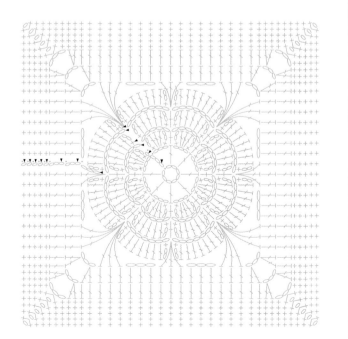

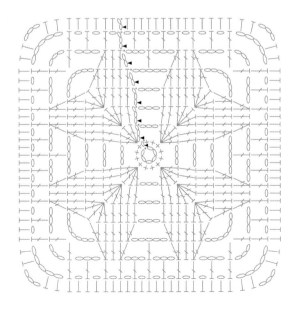

Rosetta

See page 35

A=Shell
B=Rose
C=Dark Forest

SPECIAL STITCHES

Trtr (triple treble crochet): Yarn round hook 3 times before inserting in designated st or space, yrh and pull through st or space, [yrh and pull through 2 loops on hook] 4 times.

Dc2tog (double crochet 2 sts together): Insert hook through next st, yrh and pull through st, skip 2 sts, insert hook through next st, yrh and pull through st, yrh and pull through all 3 loops on hook.

Spike htr (spiked half tr): Yrh and insert hook in skipped dc from previous round, pull loop through so that it is level with current round, yrh and pull through all 3 loops on hook.

Foundation ring: Using colour A, work 8 ch and join with sl st to form a ring.

Round 1: Ch 1, 12dc in ring, join with a sl st to first dc. (12 dc)

Round 2: Ch 5 (counts as 1tr and ch 2), [1tr, ch 2] in every dc, join with sl st to 3rd ch of beg ch-5. (12 ch-2 sps)

Round 3: Ch 1, 1dc in same st, *3dc in next ch-2 sp**, 1dc in next tr; rep from * a further 10 times and from * to ** once more, change to colour D when joining with a sl st to first dc. (48 sts)

Round 4: Join colour B, ch 5 (counts as trtr), 1trtr in each of next 3dc, *ch 6, 1trtr in each of next 4dc; rep from * a further 10 times, ch 6, join with a sl st to 5th ch of beg ch-5.

Round 5: Ch 1, dc2tog across first 4trtr, *8dc in next ch-6 sp**, dc2tog across next 4trtr; rep from * a further 10 times and from * to ** once more,

join with a sl st to first dc2tog. Fasten off colour B.

Round 6: Join colour C to any dc2tog from previous round, ch 4 (counts as 1dtr), 1dtr in same place (half corner made), [ch 2, skip next 3dc, 1dc in each of next 2dc, ch 2, skip next 3dc, 1tr in next dc2tog] twice, ch 2, skip next 3dc, 1dc in each of next 2dc, ch 2, skip next 3dc**, [2dtr, ch 3, 2dtr in next dc2tog] (corner made); rep from * twice more and from * to ** once again, 2dtr in first dc2tog of round, ch 3, join with sl st to 4th ch of beg ch-4.

Round 7: Ch 1, 1dc in same place, 1dc in every st, 2dc in every ch-2 sp, [2dc, ch 3, 1dc] in every ch-3 corner sp to end of round, changing to colour A when joining with sl st to first dc.

Round 8: Join colour C, ch 1, 1dc in

same place, 1dc in every st, [1dc, ch 1, 1dc] in every ch-3 corner sp to end of round, join with sl st to first dc.

Round 9: Ch 1, 1dc in same place, ch 1, skip next dc, work [1dc in next st, ch 1, skip next dc to next corner sp] and [2dc, ch 1, 2dc] in every ch-1 corner sp to end of round, changing to colour B when joining with sl st to first dc.

Round 10: Ch 2 (counts as 1htr), skip next dc, *[spike htr in next skipped dc of previous round, ch 1**, skip 1dc] to corner sp, [1dc, ch 1, 1dc] in ch-1 corner sp, ch 1, skip next dc; rep from * twice more times and then from * to ** once again, join with sl st to 2nd ch of beg ch-2.

Fasten off and weave in ends.

Poinsettia

See page 34

A=Rose

SPECIAL STITCHES

tr2tog (work two treble sts tog):
[Yrh draw up a loop in next st, (yrh, pull through 2 loops on hook) twice] twice, yrh and draw through all 3 loops on hook.

tr5tog (work five treble sts tog):
[Yrh draw up a loop in next st, (yrh, pull through 2 loops on hook) twice] 5 times, yrh and draw through all 6 loops on hook.

Foundation chain: Using colour A, ch 6 and join with sl st in first ch to form a ring.

Round 1: Ch 3 (counts as 1tr), 15tr into the ring, join with sl st to 3rd of ch-3.

Round 2: Ch 4 (counts as 1tr and ch 1), *5tr in next tr, ch 1**, 1tr in next tr, ch 1; rep from * a further 6 times and from * to ** once more, join with sl st in 3rd ch of ch-4.

Round 3: Ch 4 (counts as 1tr and ch 1), 1tr in same place, *ch 1, 2tr in each of next 5tr, ch 1**, [1tr, ch 1, 1tr] in next tr, ch 1; rep from * a further 6 times and from * to ** once more, join with sl st in 3rd ch of ch-4.

Round 4: Ch 3 (counts as 1tr), 1tr in same place, ch 1, 2tr in next tr, ch 1, *[tr2tog over next 2 sts] 5 times, ch 1**, [2tr in next tr, ch 1] twice; rep from * 6 more times and from * to ** once more, join with sl st in 3rd ch of ch-3.

Round 5: Ch 4 (counts as 1tr and ch 1), [1tr, ch 1] in each of next 3tr, *tr5tog over next 5 sts, ch 1**, [1tr, ch 1] in each of next 4tr; rep from * a further 6 times and from * to ** once more, join with sl st in 3rd ch of ch-4.

Round 6: Ch 4 (counts as 1tr and ch 1), *1tr in next tr, ch 1, [2dtr, ch 3, 2dtr] in next 1ch-sp, [ch 1, 1tr] in each of next 2tr, ch 1, 1htr in next tr5tog, [ch 1, 1dc] in each of next 4tr, ch 1, 1htr in next tr5tog, ch 1**, 1tr in next tr, ch 1; rep from * twice more and from * to ** once again, join with sl st in 3rd ch of ch-4.

Round 7: Ch 3 (counts as 1tr), 1tr in every st and 1ch-sp around, working [2tr, ch 2, 2tr] in each 3-ch corner sp, join with sl st in 3rd ch of ch-3.

Round 8: Ch 2 (counts as 1htr), 1htr in every st around, working 3tr in every ch-2 corner sp, join with sl st in 2nd ch of ch-2.

Fasten off and weave in ends.

⊛ ⊛ *Mitered Increase*

See page 37

A=Rose
B=Ecru
C=Ultramarine
D=Oyster

Foundation chain: Using colour A, make 6ch.

Row 1: 1tr in 4th ch from hook, 1tr in each of next 2 ch, turn.

Row 2: Ch 3 (counts as 1tr), 1tr in each of next 2tr, 4tr in loop made between tch and first tr of previous row, turn.

Row 3: Ch 3 (counts as 1tr), 1tr in each of next 2tr, [2tr, ch 2, 2tr] in next tr, 1tr in each of next 2tr, 1tr in 3rd ch of tch, turn.

Row 4: Ch 3 (counts as 1tr), 1tr in each of next 4tr, [2tr, ch 2, 2tr] in 2ch-sp, 1tr in each of next 4tr, change to colour B when working 1tr in 3rd ch of tch, turn.

Row 5: Ch 3 (counts as 1tr), 1tr in each of next 6tr, [2tr, ch 2, 2tr] in 2ch-sp, 1tr in each of next 6tr, 1tr in 3rd ch of tch, turn.

Row 6: Ch 3 (counts as 1tr), 1tr in each of next 8tr, [2tr, ch 2, 2tr] in 2ch-sp, 1tr in each of next 8tr, change to colour C when working 1tr in 3rd of tch, turn.

Row 7: Ch 3 (counts as 1tr), 1tr in each of next 10tr, [2tr, ch 2, 2tr] in 2ch-sp, 1tr in each of next 10tr, change to colour D when working 1tr in 3rd ch of tch, turn.

Row 8: Ch 3 (counts as 1tr), 1tr in each of next 12tr, [2tr, ch 2, 2tr] in 2ch-sp, 1tr in each of next 12tr, 1tr in 3rd ch of tch, turn.

Row 9: Ch 3 (counts as 1tr), 1tr in each of next 14tr, [2tr, ch 2, 2tr] in 2ch-sp, 1tr in each of next 14tr, 1tr in 3rd ch of tch, turn.

Row 10: Ch 3 (counts as 1tr), 1tr in each of next 16tr, [2tr, ch 2, 2tr] in 2ch-sp, 1tr in each of next 16tr, change to colour A when working 1tr in 3rd ch of tch, turn.

Row 11: Ch 3 (counts as 1tr), 1tr in each of next 18tr, [2tr, ch 2, 2tr] in 2ch-sp, 1tr in each of next 18tr, 1tr in 3rd ch of tch, turn.

Row 12: Ch 3 (counts as 1tr), 1tr in each of next 20tr, [2tr, ch 2, 2tr] in 2ch-sp, 1tr in each of next 20tr, 1tr in 3rd ch of tch, turn.

Row 13: Ch 3 (counts as 1tr), 1tr in each of next 22tr, [2tr, ch 2, 2tr] in 2ch-sp, 1tr in each of next 22tr, change to colour B when working 1tr in 3rd ch of tch, turn.

Row 14: Ch 3 (counts as 1tr), 1tr in each of next 24tr, [2tr, ch 2, 2tr] in 2ch-sp, 1tr in each of next 24tr, change to colour C when working 1tr in 3rd ch of tch, turn.

Row 15: Ch 3 (counts as 1tr), 1tr in each of next 26tr, [2tr, ch 2, 2tr] in 2ch-sp, 1tr in each of next 26tr, 1tr in 3rd ch of tch, do not turn.

Border

Round 1: Ch 1, 1dc in same place, [2dc in every row end to last row end, [3dc in top ch of corner st] twice, 1dc in every tr to corner, 3dc in ch-2 corner sp, 1dc in every tr to last tr, 3dc in last tr, join with sl st to first dc.

Fasten off and weave in ends.

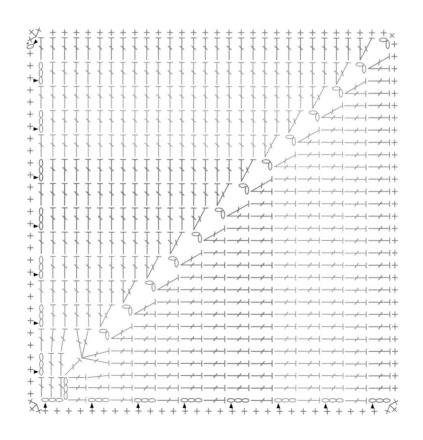

✪ ✪ Mitered Decrease

See page 37

A=Oyster
B=Ultramarine
C=Ecru
D=Rose
E=Bleached

SPECIAL STITCHES

Dc3tog: Decrease 2 sts by working the next 3 sts together.

Foundation chain: Using colour A, work 58 ch.
Foundation row (WS): 1dc in 2nd ch from hook, 1dc in every ch to end of row, turn. (57 dc)
Row 1 (RS): Ch 1, 1dc in next 27dc, dc3tog, 1dc in each of rem 27dc, turn. (55 dc)
Row 2: Ch 1, 1dc in next 26dc, dc3tog, 1dc in each of rem 26dc, turn. Break colour A. (53 dc)

Row 3: Join colour B, ch 1, 1dc in next 25dc, dc3tog, 1dc in each of rem 25dc, turn. (51 dc)
Row 4: Ch 1, 1dc in next 24dc, dc3tog, 1dc in each of rem 24dc, turn. (49 dc)
Continue in pattern as set, working dc3tog over 3 centre sts on every row. At the same time change colours in the following sequence.
2 more rows in B.
4 rows in C.
3 rows in D.
2 rows in E.
4 rows in A.

2 rows in B.
1 row in C.
2 rows in D.
1 row in E.
1 row in B.
Next row: Dc3tog. Fasten off.
Border
Join colour D to end of Foundation row with sl st.
Row 1 (RS): Ch 1, 1dc in same place, 1dc in next 26 row ends, 3dc in corner, 1dc in following 27 row ends, turn. (57 dc)
Row 2: Ch 1, 1dc in next 28dc, 3dc in centre st of 3dc corner, 1dc in rem

27dc, turn. (59 dc)
Row 3: Ch 1, 1dc in next 29dc, 3dc in centre st of 3dc corner, 1dc in rem 28dc, turn. (61 dc)
Row 4: Join colour A, ch 2 (counts as 1htr), 1htr in next 30dc, 3htr in centre st of 3dc corner, htr in rem 28dc, turn. Break colour A. (63 htr)
Row 5: Join colour B, ch 3 (counts as 1tr), 1tr in next 30dc, 3tr in centre st of 3htr corner, 1tr in rem 29dc, turn. (65 tr)
Fasten off and weave in ends.

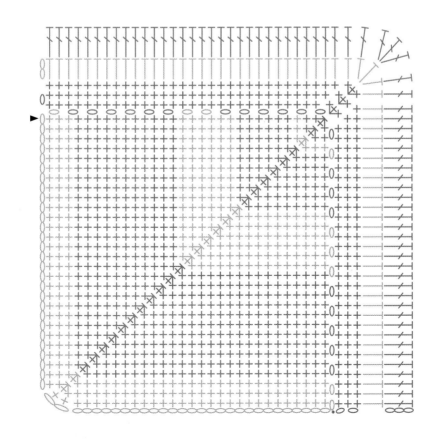

⭐⭐ *Log Cabin Granny*   See page 39

A=Greengage
B=Bleached
C=Sky
D=Blackcurrant
E=Oyster
F=Persimmon
G=Burnt Orange

Foundation ring: Using colour A, ch 6 and join with sl st in first ch to form a ring.
Section 1: Ch 3, (counts as 1tr throughout), 2tr into ring, ch 3, *3tr into ring, ch 3; rep from * twice more, join with sl st in 3rd ch of ch-3. Break colour A.
Section 2: Join colour B to any ch-3 corner sp, ch 3 (counts as 1tr), 2tr in same sp, 3tr in next ch-3 corner sp, ch 3, turn, 3tr between 2 clusters from previous row, 1tr in 3rd ch of ch-3. Fasten off.
Section 3: Join colour C to ch-3 sp from previous section, ch 3, 2tr in same sp, 3tr in each sp between two clusters to end of row, ch 3, 3tr in each sp between two clusters to end of row, 1tr in 3rd ch of ch-3. Fasten off.

Section 4: As Section 3 in colour D.
Section 5: As Section 3 in colour E.
Section 6: As Section 3 in colour F.
Section 7: As Section 3 in colour G.
Section 8: As Section 3 in colour A.
Section 9: As Section 3 in colour B.
Section 10: As Section 3 in colour C.
Section 11: As Section 3 in colour D.
Section 12: As Section 3 in colour E.
Section 13: As Section 3 in colour F.
Section 14: As Section 3 in colour G.
Section 15: As Section 3 in colour A.
Section 16: As Section 3 in colour B.
Section 17: As Section 3 in colour C.
Fasten off and weave in ends.

⭐ *Vertical Woven Block*   See page 37

A=Rose
B=Blackcurrant
C=Oyster

Foundation chain: Using colour A, ch 33.
Row 1: 1tr in 4th ch from hook, 1tr in next ch, *ch 1, skip next ch, 1tr in each of next 3tr; rep from * to end of row, turn.
Row 2: Ch 3, skip first tr, 1tr in each of next 2tr, *ch 1, skip 1ch, 1tr in each of next 3tr; rep from * to end of row, 1tr in 3rd of tch, turn. Rep Row 2 a further 12 times. Do not fasten off.
Border
Round 1: Ch 1, 1dc in same place, 1dc in same row-end post, *2dc in each of next 12 row-end posts, [2dc, 1htr, 2dc] in last row-end post**, 1dc in each foundation ch to corner, [2dc, 1htr, 2dc] in next row-end post; rep from * to **, 1dc in each tr to end of round, [1htr, 2dc] in first row-end post, join with sl st in first dc.
Round 2: Ch 2, 1htr in each dc and 1tr in each tr from previous round, join with sl st in 2nd ch of ch-2.
Fasten off and weave in ends.
Weaving
*Cut three strands of colour B approx. 23cm (9in) long and weave over and under the bars created by the ch-sps**.
Cut three strands of colour C approx. 23cm (9in) long and weave under and over the bars created by the ch-sps. Rep from * twice more and from * to ** once again.
Gently stretch the block in both directions to ensure that the weaving is not too tight before weaving in the ends.

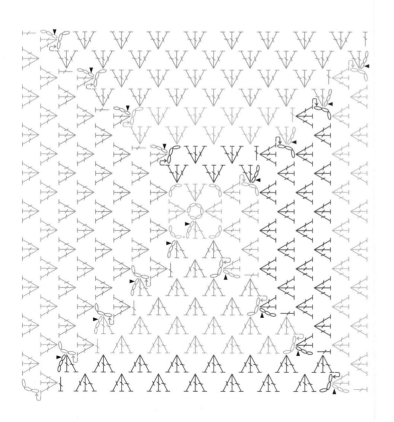

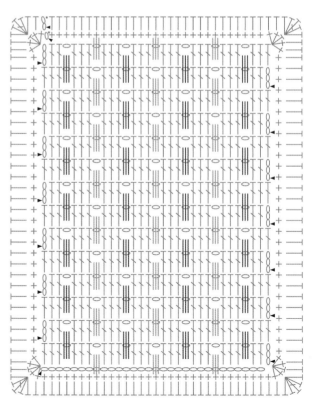

Corner Log Cabin

See page 39

A=Greengage
B=Bleached
C=Sky
D=Blackcurrant
E=Oyster
F=Persimmon

Section 1
Using colour A, ch 11.
Row 1: 1tr in 4th ch from hook,
1tr in every ch to end of row, turn.
Row 2: Ch 2, skip first tr, 1tr in sp
between first and second tr, *skip next
tr, 1tr in foll sp; rep from * to last tr,
skip last tr, 1tr in ch-sp, turn.
Rows 3–6: As Row 2, ending colour
A at end of Row 6 and joining colour
B.
Rows 7–12: As Row 2, ending colour
B at end of Row 12 and joining colour
C.

Section 2
Row 1: Ch 3, 1tr in each of next 11
row-ends, 2tr in last row-end, turn.
Row 2: Ch 2, skip first tr, 1tr in sp
between first and second tr, skip next
tr, 1tr in next sp, skip next tr, *2tr in
next sp, skip next tr, 1tr in next sp,
skip next tr; rep from * to end, 1tr in
ch-sp, turn.
Row 3: Ch 2, skip first tr, 1tr in sp
between first and second tr, *skip next
tr, 1tr in next sp; rep from * to last tr,
skip last tr, 1tr in ch-sp, turn.
Rows 4–6: As Row 3, ending colour
C at end of Row 6 and joining colour
D.

Section 3
Row 1: Ch 3, 1tr in same row-end sp
as ch 3, 1tr in each of next 5 row-
ends, skip next tr, 1tr in every sp
between tr to end of row, 1tr in ch-sp,
turn.
Row 2: Ch 2, skip first tr, 1tr in sp
between first and second tr, skip next
tr, [1tr in next sp, skip next tr] 6 times,
[2tr in next sp, skip next tr, 1tr in next
sp, skip next tr] 3 times, 1tr in ch-sp,
turn.

Row 3: Ch 2, skip first tr, 1tr in sp
between first and second tr, *skip next
tr, 1tr in next sp; rep from * to last tr,
skip last tr, 1tr in ch-sp, turn.
Rows 4–6: As Row 3, ending colour
D at end of Row 6 and joining colour
E.

Section 4
Row 1: Ch 3, 1tr in same row-end sp
as ch 3, 1tr in each of next 5 row-
ends, skip next tr, 1tr in every sp
between tr to end of row, 1tr in ch-sp,
turn.
Row 2: Ch 2, skip first tr, 1tr in sp
between first and second tr, skip next
tr, [1tr in next sp, skip next tr] 16 times,
[2tr in next sp, skip next tr, 1tr in next
sp, skip next tr] 3 times, 1tr in ch-sp,
turn.
Row 3: Ch 2, skip first tr, 1tr in sp
between first and second tr, *skip next

tr, 1tr in next sp; rep from * to last tr,
skip last tr, 1tr in ch-sp, turn.
Rows 4–6: As Row 3.
Fasten off.

Border
Round 1: Join colour F to any tr from
Section 4 with a sl st, ch 2, 1htr in
every tr to last tr, 3htr in last tr, [1htr in
next row-end sp, 2htr in next row-end
sp] 3 times, 1htr in each of next 16tr,
3htr in next tr, [1htr in next row-end sp,
2htr in next row-end sp] 9 times, 3htr
in first foundation ch, 1htr in each of
next 8 foundation ch, [2htr in next
row-end sp, 1htr in next row-end sp] 6
times, 3htr in next tr, 1htr in every rem
tr to end of round, join with sl st in 2nd
ch of ch-2.
Fasten off and weave in ends.

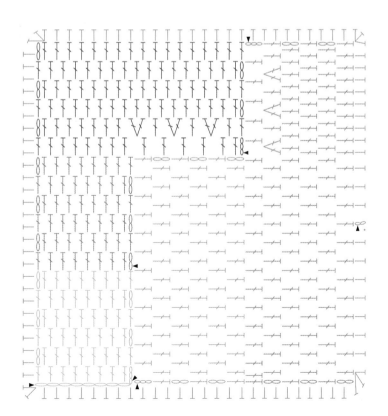

⊛⊛ *Log Cabin*

See page 39

A=Greengage
B=Bleached
C=Sky
D=Blackcurrant

E=Oyster
F=Persimmon
G=Dark Forest

Centre
Using colour A, make 11ch.

Row 1: (RS): 1dc in 2nd ch from hook, 1dc in every ch to end of row, turn.
(10 sts)

Row 2: Ch 1 (does not count as st throughout), 1dc in every dc to end of row, turn.

Rows 3–10: As Row 2. Fasten off.

Section 1
With RS facing, join colour B with a sl st to first dc at top right of centre block.

Row 1: Ch 1, 1dc in same place as sl st, 1dc in each of next 8dc, 3dc in next dc, 1dc in each of next 9 row-ends, turn.

Row 2: Ch 1, 1dc in each of next 10dc, 3dc in next dc, 1dc in each of last 10dc, turn.

Row 3: Ch 1, 1dc in each of next 11dc, 3dc in next dc, 1dc in each of last 11dc, turn.

Row 4: Ch 1, 1dc in each of next 12dc, 3dc in next dc, 1dc in each of last 12dc. Fasten off.

Section 2
With RS facing and first section at lower right, join colour C with a sl st to first row end.

Row 1: Ch 1, 1dc in same place as sl st, 1dc in each of next 3 row-ends, 1dc in each of next 9ch, 3dc in next ch, 1dc in each of next 13 row-ends, turn.

Row 2: Ch 1, 1dc in each of next 14dc, 3dc in next dc, 1dc in each of last 14dc, turn.

Row 3: Ch 1, 1dc in each of next 15dc, 3dc in next dc, 1dc in each of last 15dc, turn.

Row 4: Ch 1, 1dc in each of next 16dc, 3dc in next dc, 1dc in each of last 16dc. Fasten off.

Section 3
With RS facing and second section at lower right, join colour D with a sl st to first row end.

Row 1: Ch 1, 1dc in same place as sl st, 1dc in each of next 3 row-ends, 1dc in each of next 13dc, 3dc in next ch, 1dc in each of last 13dc, turn.

Row 2: Ch 1, 1dc in each of next 18dc, 3dc in next dc, 1dc in each of last 18dc, turn.

Row 3: Ch 1, 1dc in each of next 19dc, 3dc in next dc, 1dc in each of last 19dc, turn.

Row 4: Ch 1, 1dc in each of next 20dc, 3dc in next dc, 1dc in each of last 20dc. Fasten off.

Section 4
With RS facing and third section at lower right, join colour E with a sl st to first row end.

Row 1: Ch 1, 1dc in same place as sl st, 1dc in each of next 3 row-ends, 1dc in each of next 17dc, 3dc in next ch, 1dc in each of last 17dc, turn.

Row 2: Ch 1, 1dc in each of next 22dc, 3dc in next dc, 1dc in each of last 22dc, turn.

Row 3: Ch 1, 1dc in each of next 23dc, 3dc in next dc, 1dc in each of last 23dc, turn.

Row 4: Ch 1, 1dc in each of next 24dc, 3dc in next dc, 1dc in each of last 24dc. Fasten off.

Section 5
With RS facing and fourth section at lower right, join colour F with a sl st to first row end.

Row 1: Ch 1, 1dc in same place as sl st, 1dc in each of next 3 row-ends, 1dc in each of next 21dc, 3dc in next ch, 1dc in each of last 21dc, turn.

Row 2: Ch 1, 1dc in each of next 26dc, 3dc in next dc, 1dc in each of last 26dc, turn.

Row 3: Ch 1, 1dc in each of next 27dc, 3dc in next dc, 1dc in each of last 27dc, turn.

Row 4: Ch 1, 1dc in each of next 28dc, 3dc in next dc, 1dc in each of last 28dc. Fasten off.

Section 6
With RS facing and fifth section at lower right, join colour G with a sl st to first row end.

Row 1: Ch 1, 1dc in same place as sl st, 1dc in each of next 3 row-ends, 1dc in each of next 25dc, 3dc in next ch, 1dc in each of last 25dc, turn.

Row 2: Ch 1, 1dc in each of next 30dc, 3dc in next dc, 1dc in each of last 30dc, turn.

Row 3: Ch 1, 1dc in each of next 31dc, 3dc in next dc, 1dc in each of last 31dc, turn.

Row 4: Ch 1, 1dc in each of next 32dc, 3dc in next dc, 1dc in each of last 32dc. Fasten off.

Section 7
With RS facing and sixth section at lower right, join colour C with a sl st to first row end.

Row 1: Ch 1, 1dc in same place as sl st, 1dc in each of next 3 row-ends, 1dc in each of next 29dc, 3dc in next ch, 1dc in each of last 29 dc, turn.

Row 2: Ch 1, 1dc in each of next 34dc, 3dc in next dc, 1dc in each of last 34dc, turn.

Row 3: Ch 1, 1dc in each of next 35dc, 3dc in next dc, 1dc in each of last 35dc, turn.

Row 4: Ch 1, 1dc in each of next 36dc, 3dc in next dc, 1dc in each of last 36dc.

Fasten off and weave in ends.

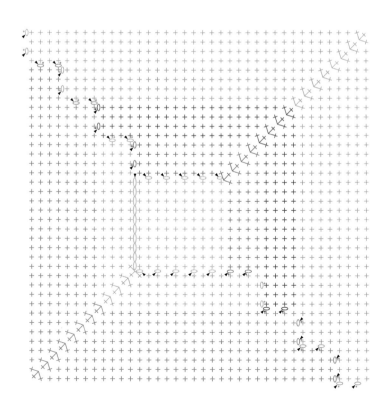

★★ *Beaded Double Crochet*   See page 38

A=Sky
261 size 6 glass beads

SPECIAL STITCHES

Bdc (beaded double crochet):
insert hook as directed, yrh, pull loop through, slide bead up yarn close to work, yrh (catching yarn beyond bead), pull through both loops on hook.

Foundation chain: Start by threading beads onto colour A. Make 34 ch.
Row 1 (WS): 1dc in 2nd ch from hook, 1dc in every ch to end of row, turn. (33 sts)
Row 2: Ch 1, skip first st, [1dc in every st to end of row, 1dc in tch, turn.
Row 3: Ch 1, skip first st, 1dc in each of next 2dc, *1Bdc in next dc, 1dc in next dc; rep from * to end, 1dc in tch, turn.
Row 4: As Row 2.
Row 5: Ch 1, 1dc in each of next 3dc, *1Bdc in next dc, 1dc in next dc; rep from * to last 2 sts, 1dc in each of last 2 sts, turn.

Rep Rows 2–5 a further 8 times then Row 2 once more.

Fasten off and weave in ends.

★★ *Sequinned Double Crochet*   See page 38

A=Sky
261 7mm flat sequins

SPECIAL STITCHES

SQdc (sequined double crochet):
insert hook as directed, yrh, pull loop through, slide sequin up yarn close to work, yrh (catching yarn beyond sequin), pull through both loops on hook.

Foundation chain: Start by threading sequins onto colour A. Make 34 ch.
Row 1 (WS): 1dc in 2nd ch from hook, 1dc in every ch to end of row, turn. (33 sts)
Row 2: Ch 1, skip first st, [1dc in every st to end of row, 1dc in tch, turn.
Row 3: Ch 1, skip first st, 1dc in each of next 2dc, *1SQdc in next dc, 1dc in next dc; rep from * to end, 1dc in tch, turn.
Row 4: As Row 2.
Row 5: Ch 1, 1dc in each of next 3dc, *1SQdc in next dc, 1dc in next dc; rep from * to last 2 sts, 1dc in each of last 2 sts, turn.

Rep Rows 2–5 a further 8 times then Row 2 once more.

Fasten off and weave in ends.

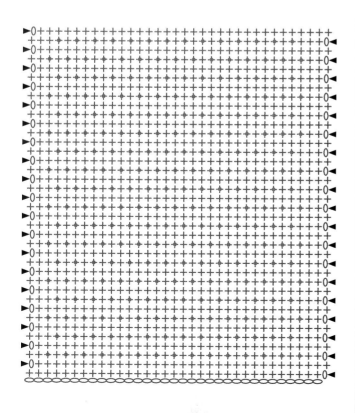

Loop Stitch Columns

See page 38

A=Sky

SPECIAL STITCHES

Loop st: Use the left hand to control the size of the loop, insert hook into designated stitch, pick up both threads of the loop and pull through, yarn over hook, draw through all loops on the hook.

Foundation chain: Using colour A, make 34 ch.
Row 1 (RS): 1tr in 4th ch from hook, 1tr in every ch to end of row, turn.

(31 sts and ch-3)
Row 2: Ch 1, 1dc in each of first 2tr, *1 Loop st in each of next 4tr**, 1dc in each of next 4tr; rep from * ending last repeat at **, 1dc in last tr, 1dc in 3rd ch of ch-3, turn.
Row 3: Ch 3 (counts as 1tr), skip first tr, 1tr in every st to end of the row, turn.
Rep Rows 2–3 a further 10 times.
Fasten off and weave in ends.

Chain Loops Flower

See page 38

A=Persimmon
B=Ecru

Foundation ring: Using colour A, make a Magic Ring.
Round 1: Ch 1, 12dc into ring, change to colour B when joining with sl st in first dc. (12 dc)
Round 2: Ch 13, *sl st in next dc, ch 13; rep from * a further 10 times, join with sl st in first ch. Break colour B.
Round 3: Join colour A in any 13ch-sp, ch 1, 1dc in same sp, ch 4, *1dc in next 13ch-sp, ch 4; rep from * to end of round, change to colour B when joining with sl st in first dc.
Round 4: Sl st in next 4ch-sp, ch 3, [1tr, ch 4, tr2tog] in same sp, *[ch 4, 1dc in next 4ch-sp] twice, ch 4**, [tr2tog, ch 4, tr2tog] in next 4ch-sp; rep from * twice more, then from * to ** once again, change to colour A when joining with sl st in 3rd ch of ch-3.
Round 5: Ch 1, 1dc in same place,

*[2dc, ch 2, 2dc] in next 4ch-sp, 1dc in next st, [3dc in next 4ch-sp, 1dc in next dc] twice, 3dc in next 4ch-sp, 1dc in next cluster; rep from * to end of round, omitting last dc and change to colour B when joining with sl st in first dc.
Round 6: Ch 3 (counts as 1tr), 1tr in every st from previous round and 3tr in every 2ch-corner-sp, change to colour A when joining with sl st in 3rd ch of ch 3.
Round 7: Ch 3 (counts as 1tr), 1tr in every st from previous round and 3tr in centre tr of each 3tr corner-sp, change to colour B when joining with sl st in 3rd ch of ch 3.
Round 8: Ch 3 (counts as 1tr), 1tr in every st from previous round and 3tr in centre tr of each 3tr corner-sp, join with sl st in 3rd ch of ch 3.
Fasten off and weave in ends.

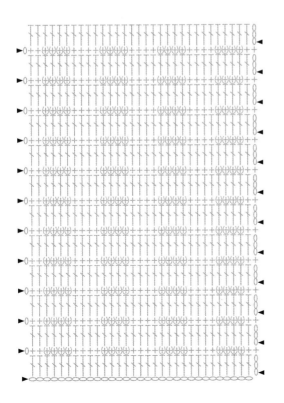

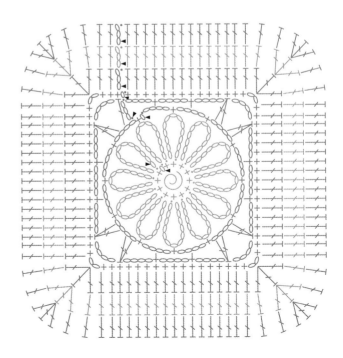

Horizontal Woven Block

See page 37

A=Rose
B=Blackcurrant
C=Oyster

Foundation chain: Using colour A, ch 33.
Row 1: 1tr in 4th ch from hook, 1tr in next ch, *ch 1, skip next ch, 1tr in each of next 3tr; rep from * to end of row, turn.
Row 2: Ch 3, skip first tr, 1tr in each of next 2tr, *ch 1, skip 1ch, 1tr in each of next 3tr; rep from * to end of row, 1tr in 3rd of tch, turn.
Rep Row 2 a further 12 times. Do not fasten off.
Border
Round 1: Ch 1, 1dc in same place, 1dc in same row-end post, *2dc in each of next 12 row-end posts, [2dc, 1htr, 2dc] in last row-end post**, 1dc in each foundation ch to corner, [2dc, 1htr, 2dc] in next row-end post; rep from * to **, 1dc in each tr to end of round, [1htr, 2dc] in first row-end post, join with sl st in first dc.

Round 2: Ch 2, 1htr in each dc and 1tr in each tr from previous round, join with sl st in 2nd ch of ch-2.
Fasten off and weave in ends.
Weaving
*Cut three strands of colour B approx. 23cm (9in) long and starting at the bottom right hand corner, weave over and under the 3tr clusters by working in and out of the ch-sps**.
Cut three strands of colour C approx. 23cm (9in) long and weave under and over the 3tr clusters by working in and out of the ch-sps.
Rep from * twice more and from * to ** once again.
Gently stretch the block in both directions to ensure that the weaving is not too tight before weaving in the ends.

Harlequin

See page 38

A=Shell
B=Lavender
C=Bleached
D=Blackcurrant

Foundation chain: Using colour A, ch 6 and join with sl st in first ch to form a ring.
Round 1: Ch 1, 12dc into the ring, join with a sl st in first dc.
Round 2: [Sl st in next dc, ch 4, 1tr in each of next 2dc, ch 4] 4 times, join with sl st in first sl st. Fasten off. (4 blocks made)
Round 3: Join colour B to 1st ch of last ch-4 of previous round *ch 4, 1tr in each of next 2 ch, sl st in top of next ch-4 of previous round, ch 4, 1tr in each of next 2tr, ch 4, sl st in top of next ch-4 of previous round; rep from * a further 3 times. Fasten off.
Round 4: Join colour C to 1st ch of last ch-4 of previous round, *ch 4, 1tr in each of next 2 ch, sl st to top of next ch-4 of previous round, ch 4, 1tr in each of next 2tr, sl st to top of next ch-4 of previous round, ch4; rep from * to end of round. Fasten off.
Round 5: Join colour A to to 1st ch of last ch-4 of previous round, *ch 4, 1tr in each of next 2 ch, sl st to top of next ch-4 of previous round, [ch 4, 1tr in each of next 2tr, sl st to top of next ch-4 of previous round, ch 4] twice, ch 4, 1tr in each of next 2tr, ch 4, sl st to top of next ch-4 of previous

round; rep from * to end of round. Fasten off.
Round 6: Join colour A to to 1st ch of last ch-4 of previous round, *ch 4, 1tr in each of next 2 ch, sl st to top of next ch-4 of previous round, [ch 4, 1tr in each of next 2tr, sl st to top of next ch-4 of previous round, ch4] 3 times, ch 4, 1tr in each of next 2tr, ch 4, sl st to top of next ch-4 of previous round; rep from * to end of round. Fasten off.
Round 7: Join colour A to to 1st ch of last ch-4 of previous round, *ch 4, 1tr in each of next 2 ch, sl st to top of next ch-4 of previous round, [ch 4, 1tr in each of next 2tr, sl st to top of next ch-4 of previous round, ch 4] 4 times, ch 4, 1tr in each of next 2tr, ch 4, sl st to top of next ch-4 of previous round; rep from * to end of round. Fasten off.
Round 8: Join colour D to to 1st ch of last ch-4 of previous round, ch1, *1dc in first ch, 1htr in next ch, 1tr in next ch, 1dtr in next ch, [1dc in top of next ch-4, 1htr in next dtr, (1tr, 1dtr in next dtr)] 5 times, [1dc, 1htr] in top of next ch-4, [1tr, ch 2, 1tr] in next tr, [1htr, 1dc] in next dtr; rep from * a further 3 times, join with sl st in first dc.
Fasten off and weave in ends.

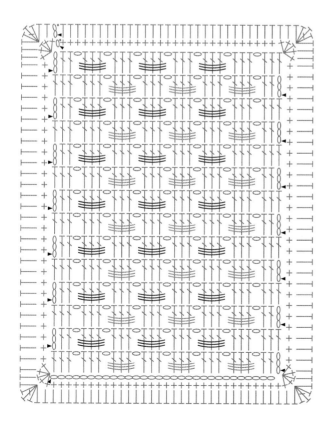

⭐⭐ *Two-sided Granny*

See page 37

A=Shell
B=Lavender

Foundation ring: Using colour A, make a Magic Ring.

Round 1: Using colour A, ch 3 (counts as 1tr throughout), 2tr into the ring, ch 2, 3tr into the ring, ch 1, using colour B, ch 1, 3tr into the ring, ch 2, 3tr into the ring, ch 1, join with a htr in 3rd ch of ch-3, turn.

Round 2: Using B, ch 3, 2tr in same sp, ch 1, [3tr, ch 2, 3tr] in next sp, ch 1, 3tr in next ch-3 sp, ch 1; using A, ch 1, 3tr in same sp, ch 1, [3tr, ch 2, 3tr] in next sp, ch 1, 3tr in next sp, ch 1, join with a htr in 3rd ch of ch-3, turn.

Round 3: Using A, ch 3, 2tr in same sp, ch 1, 3tr in next ch-1 sp, ch 1, (3tr, ch 3, 3tr) in next sp, ch 1, 3tr in next ch-1 sp, ch 1, 3tr in next ch sp, ch 2; using B, ch 1, 3tr in same sp, ch 1,

3tr in next ch-1 sp, ch 1, [3tr, ch 2, 3tr] in next sp, ch 1, 3tr in next sp, ch 1, join with a htr in 3rd ch of ch-3, turn.

Round 4: Using B, ch 3, 2tr in same sp, [ch 1, 3tr in next sp] twice, ch 1, [3tr, ch 3, 3tr] in next sp, [ch 1, 3tr in next sp] 3 times, ch 2; using A, ch 1, 3tr in same sp, [ch 1, 3tr in next sp] twice, ch 1, [3tr, ch 3, 3tr] in next sp, [ch 1, 3tr in next sp] 3 times, ch 1, join with a htr in 3rd ch of ch-3, turn.

Round 5: Using A, ch 3 (counts as 1tr), 2tr in same sp, ch 1, 3tr in next ch-1 sp, ch 1, [3tr, ch 3, 3tr] in next sp, ch 1, 3tr in next ch-1 sp, ch 1, 3tr in next ch sp, ch 2; using B, ch 1, 3tr in same sp, ch 1, 3tr in next ch-1 sp, ch 1, [3tr, ch 2, 3tr] in next sp, ch 1, 3tr in next sp, ch 1, join with a htr in 3rd ch of ch-3, turn.

Round 6: Using B, ch 3, 2tr in same sp, [ch 1, 3tr in next sp] 3 times, ch 1, [3tr, ch 3, 3tr] in next sp, [ch 1, 3tr in next sp] 4 times, ch 2; using A, ch 1, 3tr in same sp, [ch 1, 3tr in next sp] 3 times, ch 1, [3tr, ch 3, 3tr] in next sp, [ch 1, 3tr in next sp] 4 times, ch 1, join with a htr in 3rd ch of ch-3, turn.

Round 7: Using A, ch 3, 2tr in same sp, [ch 1, 3tr in next sp] 4 times, ch 1, [3tr, ch 3, 3tr] in next sp, [ch 1, 3tr in next sp] 5 times, ch 2; using B ch 1, 3tr in same sp, [ch 1, 3tr in next sp] 4 times, ch 1, [3tr, ch 3, 3tr] in next sp, [ch 1, 3tr in next sp] 5 times, ch 1, join with a htr in 3rd ch of ch-3, turn.

Round 8: Using B, ch 3, 2tr in same sp, [ch 1, 3tr in next sp] 5 times, ch 1, [3tr, ch 3, 3tr] in next sp, [ch 1, 3tr in next sp] 6 times, ch 2; using A ch 1,

3tr in same sp, [ch 1, 3tr in next sp] 5 times, ch 1, [3tr, ch 3, 3tr] in next sp, [ch 1, 3tr in next sp] 6 times, ch 1, join with a htr in 3rd ch of ch-3, turn.

Round 9: Using A, ch 3, 2tr in same sp, [ch 1, 3tr in next sp] 6 times, ch 1, [3tr, ch 3, 3tr] in next sp, [ch 1, 3tr in next sp] 7 times, ch 2; using B ch 1, 3tr in same sp, [ch 1, 3tr in next sp] 6 times, ch 1, [3tr, ch 3, 3tr] in next sp, [ch 1, 3tr in next sp] 7 times, ch 1, join with a htr in 3rd ch of ch-3.

Fasten off and weave in ends.

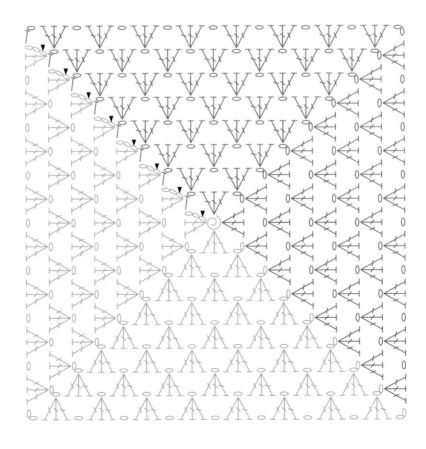

⭐ ✪ *Shell Border*

See page 36

A=Ecru
B=Greengage

SPECIAL STITCHES

V-st: [1tr, ch 1, 1tr] in next st.
Open shell: [ch 1, (2tr, ch1, 2tr)].

Centre block

Foundation ring: Using colour A, ch 4 and join with sl st in first ch to form a ring.

Round 1: Ch 3 (counts as 1tr), 11tr in the ring, join with sl st in 3rd ch of ch-3.

Round 2: Ch 3 (counts as 1tr), *[2tr, 1dtr] in next tr, [1dtr, 2tr] in next tr**, 1tr in next tr; rep from * twice more and from * to ** once again, join with sl st in 3rd ch of ch-3.

Round 3: Ch 3 (counts as 1tr), 1tr in each of next 2tr, *[2tr, 1dtr] in next dtr, [1dtr, 2tr] in next dtr**, 1tr in each of next 5tr; rep from * twice more and from * to ** once again, 1tr in each of next 2tr, join with sl st in 3rd ch of ch-3.

Round 4: Ch 3 (counts as 1tr), 1tr in each of next 4tr, *[2tr, 1dtr] in next dtr, [1dtr, 2tr] in next dtr**, 1tr in each of next 9tr; rep from * twice more and from * to ** once again, 1tr in each of next 4tr, join with sl st in 3rd ch of ch-3. Fasten off.

Border

Join colour B 4 sts to the left of the corner st.

Round 1: Ch 4 (counts as 1tr and ch 1), 1tr in same st, *ch 2, skip 3 sts, 1tr in next st, ch 2, skip 3 sts, V-st in next st, ch 2, skip 3 sts, [1tr, (ch 1, 1tr) 4 times] in middle dtr, ch 2, skip 3 sts**, V-st in next st; rep from * twice more and from * to ** once again, join with sl st in 3rd ch of ch-4.

Round 2: Sl st in next 1ch-sp, ch 4 (counts as 1tr and ch 1), 1tr in same sp, ch 2, *[1tr in next tr, ch 2, V-st in ch-sp of next V-st, ch 2, 1tr in next tr, ch 2, skip next tr, [V-st in next ch-sp, ch1] twice, ch 1, skip 1tr**, [1tr in next tr, ch 2, V-st in ch-sp of next V-st, ch 2] twice; rep from * twice more and from * to ** once again, 1tr in next tr, ch 2, join with sl st in 3rd ch of ch-4.

Round 3: Sl st in next 1ch-sp, ch 3 (counts as 1tr), 1tr, ch 1, 2tr in same sp, ch 1, skip 1tr, 1tr in next tr, *[open shell in ch-sp of V-st, ch 1, skip 1tr, 1tr in next tr] twice, ch 1, skip 1ch-sp, open shell in ch-sp of V-st, ch 3, skip 1ch-sp, open shell in ch-sp of V-st, ch 1, skip 1tr, 1tr in next tr**, ch 1, open shell in ch-sp of next V-st; rep from * twice more and from * to ** once again, join with sl st in 3rd ch of ch-3.

Round 4: Ch 1, 1dc in last tr, skip joining st and 2tr, [5tr in ch-sp of next open shell, 1dc in next tr] twice, 5tr in ch-sp of next open shell, *1dc in corner ch-1 sp, [5tr in ch-sp of next open shell, 1dc in next tr] three times, 5tr in ch-sp of next open shell; rep from * twice more, 5tr in ch-sp of next open shell, join with sl st in first dc.

Fasten off and weave in ends.

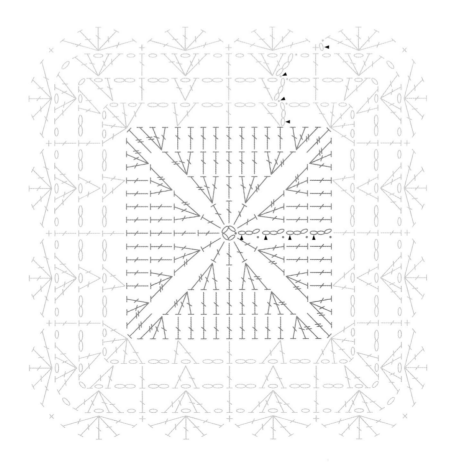

Shell and Bar Border

See page 36

A=Ecru
B=Greengage

Centre block

Foundation ring: Using colour A, ch 4 and join with sl st in first ch to form a ring.

Round 1: Ch 3 (counts as 1tr throughout), 11tr into the ring, join with sl st in 3rd ch of ch-3.

Round 2: Ch 3, *[2tr, 1dtr] in next tr, [1dtr, 2tr] in next tr**, 1tr in next tr; rep from * twice more and from * to ** once again, join with sl st in 3rd ch of ch-3.

Round 3: Ch 3, 1tr in each of next 2tr, *[2tr, 1dtr] in next dtr, [1dtr, 2tr] in next dtr**, 1tr in each of next 5tr; rep from * twice more and from * to ** once again, 1tr in each of next 2tr, join with sl st in 3rd ch of ch-3.

Round 4: Ch 3, 1tr in each of next 4tr, *[2tr, 1dtr] in next dtr, [1dtr, 2tr] in next dtr**, 1tr in each of next 9tr; rep from * twice more and from * to ** once again, 1tr in each of next 4tr, join with sl st in 3rd ch of ch-3.

Round 5: Ch 3, 1tr in each of next 6tr, *[2tr, 1dtr] in next dtr, 1dtr in sp before next tr, [1dtr, 2tr] in next dtr**, 1tr in each of next 13tr; rep from * twice more and from * to ** once again, 1tr in each of next 6tr, join with sl st in 3rd ch of ch-3. Fasten off.

Border

Join colour B, 2 sts to the left of the corner st.

Round 1: Ch 3 (counts as 1tr), *1tr in each of next 2 sts, ch 5, skip 5 sts, 1tr in next st, ch 5, skip 5 sts, 1tr in each of next 3 sts, ch 3, skip 1 st, 1tr in corner st, ch 3, skip 1tr, 1tr in next st; rep from * to end of round, omitting last tr, join with sl st in 3rd ch of ch-3.

Round 2: Ch 3 (counts as 1tr), *1tr in each of next 2tr, ch 3, [1tr, ch 2, 1tr] in next tr, ch 3, 1tr in each of next 3tr, ch 3, [1tr, ch 3, 1tr] in next tr, ch 3, 1tr in next tr; rep from * to end of round, omitting last tr, join with sl st in 3rd ch of ch-3.

Round 3: Ch 3 (counts as 1tr), *1tr in each of next 2tr, ch 2, skip 1tr, 7tr in next ch-2 sp, ch 2, skip 1tr, 1tr in each of next 3tr, ch 2, 9tr in 3-ch corner sp, ch 2, skip 1tr, 1tr in next tr; rep from * to end of round, omitting last tr, join with sl st in 3rd ch of ch-3.

Fasten off and weave in ends.

Picot Border

See page 36

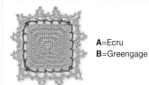

A=Ecru
B=Greengage

SPECIAL STITCHES

Picot-3: Ch 3, sl st in 3rd ch from hook.

Picot-5: Ch 5, sl st in 5th ch from hook.

Centre block

Foundation ring: Using colour A, ch 4 and join with sl st in first ch to form a ring.

Round 1: Ch 3 (counts as 1tr), 11tr in the ring, join with sl st in 3rd ch of ch-3.

Round 2: Ch 3 (counts as 1tr), *[2tr, 1dtr] in next tr, [1dtr, 2tr] in next tr**, 1tr in next tr; rep from * twice more and from * to ** once again, join with sl st in 3rd ch of ch-3.

Round 3: Ch 3 (counts as 1tr), 1tr in each of next 2tr, *[2tr, 1dtr] in next dtr, [1dtr, 2tr] in next dtr**, 1tr in each of next 5tr; rep from * twice more and from * to ** once again, 1tr in each of next 2tr, join with sl st in 3rd ch of ch-3.

Round 4: Ch 3 (counts as 1tr), 1tr in each of next 4tr, *[2tr, 1dtr] in next dtr, [1dtr, 2tr] in next dtr**, 1tr in each of next 9tr; rep from * twice more and from * to ** once again, 1tr in each of next 4tr, join with sl st in 3rd ch of ch-3.

Round 5: Ch 3 (counts as 1tr), 1tr in each of next 6tr, *[2tr, 1dtr] in next dtr, 1dtr in space before next st, [1dtr, 2tr] in next dtr**, 1tr in each of next 13tr; rep from * twice more and from * to ** once again, 1tr in each of next 6tr, join with sl st in 3rd ch of ch-3. Fasten off.

Border

Join colour B, 4 sts to the left of the corner st.

Round 1: Ch 1, 1dc in same place, ch 5, skip 3 sts, [1dc in next st, ch 5, skip 3 sts] 3 times, *[1dc, ch 3, 1dc] in corner st, ch 5**, skip 3 sts, [1dc in next st, ch 5, skip 3 sts] 4 times; rep from * twice more and from * to ** once again, changing to colour A when joining with sl st to first dc. Break colour B.

Round 2: Ch 1, 1dc in same place, ch 5, *1dc in next dc, ch 5; rep from * to end of round, join with sl st in first dc.

Round 3: Sl st in 5ch-sp, ch 3 (counts as 1tr), [3tr, Picot-3, Picot-5, Picot-3, 4tr] in same sp, *[2dc, ch 3, 2dc] in next ch-sp**, [4tr, Picot-3, Picot-5, Picot-3, 4tr] in next ch-sp; rep from * twice more and from * to ** once again, join with sl st in 3rd ch of ch-3.

Fasten off and weave in ends.

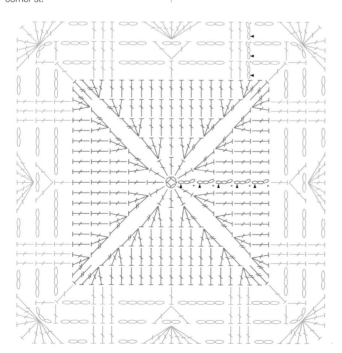

Fan Border

See page 36

A=Ecru
B=Greengage
C=Winsor

SPECIAL STITCHES
V-st: (1tr, ch 1, 1tr) in next st.
Shell: 9tr in next st.

Centre block
Foundation ring: Using colour A, ch 4 and join with sl st in first ch to form a ring.
Round 1: Ch 3 (counts as 1tr throughout), 11tr into the ring, join with sl st in 3rd ch of ch-3.
Round 2: Ch 3, *[2tr, 1dtr] in next tr, [1dtr, 2tr] in next tr**, 1tr in next tr; rep from * twice more and from * to ** once again, join with sl st in 3rd ch of ch-3.
Round 3: Ch 3, 1tr in each of next 2tr, *[2tr, 1dtr] in next tr, [1dtr, 2tr] in next tr**, 1tr in each of next 5tr; rep from * twice more and from * to ** once again, 1tr in each of next 2tr, join with sl st in 3rd ch of ch-3.
Round 4: Ch 3, 1tr in each of next 4tr, *[2tr, 1dtr] in next tr, 1dtr in sp before next st, [1dtr, 2tr] in next tr**, 1tr in each of next 9tr; rep from * twice more and from * to ** once again, 1tr in each of next 4tr, join

with sl st in 3rd ch of ch-3.
Fasten off.

Border
Join colour B in second st to left of corner st.
Round 1: Ch 1, 1dc in same place, *[skip 3 sts, shell in next st, skip 3 sts, 1dc in next st] twice, skip 1 st, 7tr in corner dtr, skip 1st, 1dc in next st; rep from * to end of round, omitting last dc, change to colour C when joining with sl st in first dc. Break colour B.
Round 2: Ch 4 (counts as 1tr and ch-1), 1tr in same st, *[ch 2, skip 4tr, 1dc in next tr (fifth tr of shell), skip 4tr, ch 2, V-st in next dc] twice, ch 2, skip 3tr, [1dc, ch 1, 1dc] in corner tr, ch 2, V-st in next dc; rep from * to end of round, omitting last V-st, join with sl st in 3rd ch of ch-4.
Round 3: Sl st into next ch-1 sp, ch 3 (counts as 1tr), 8tr in same sp, 1dc in next dc, *[shell in ch-sp of next V-st, 1dc in next dc twice, 7tr in corner ch-sp, 1dc in next dc; rep from * to end of round, join with sl st in 3rd ch of ch-3.
Fasten off and weave in ends.

 ## Arched Border

See page 36

A=Ecru
B=Dawn Grey
C=Winsor

SPECIAL STITCHES
Partial tr: Yarn round hook, insert hook into stitch or space indicated and pull a loop through, yarn round hook and pull through two loops on the hook.

Centre block
Foundation ring: Using colour A, ch 4 and join with sl st in first ch to form a ring.
Round 1: Ch 3 (counts as 1tr throughout), 11tr into the ring, join with sl st in 3rd ch of ch-3.
Round 2: Ch 3, *[2tr, 1dtr] in next tr, [1dtr, 2tr] in next tr**, 1tr in next tr; rep from * twice more and from * to ** once again, join with sl st in 3rd ch of ch-3.
Round 3: Ch 3, 1tr in each of next 2tr, *[2tr, 1dtr] in next dtr, [1dtr, 2tr] in next dtr**, 1tr in each of next 5tr; rep from * twice more and from * to ** once again, 1tr in each of next 2tr, join with sl st in 3rd ch of ch-3.
Round 4: Ch 3, 1tr in each of next 4tr, *[2tr, 1dtr] in next dtr, [1dtr, 2tr] in next dtr**, 1tr in each of next 9tr; rep from * twice more and from * to ** once again, 1tr in each of next 4tr, join with sl st in 3rd ch of ch-3.

Border
Join colour B in eighth st to left of corner st.
Round 1: Ch 5 (counts as 1dtr and ch-1), 1tr in same place, ch 7, skip 7 sts, *[1tr, ch 1, 1tr, ch 7, 1tr, ch 1, 1tr] in corner dtr, ch 7, skip 7 sts**, [1tr,

ch1, 1dtr, ch1, 1tr] in next st ch 7, skip 7 sts; rep from * twice more and then from * to ** once again, 1tr in st at base of ch-5, join with sl st in 4th ch of ch-5.
Round 2: Ch 1, 1dc in same place, [4tr, ch 1, 4tr] in next 7ch-sp, *[1dc in 1ch-sp, [4tr, ch 1, 4tr] in corner sp, 1dc in next ch-sp, [4tr, ch 1, 4tr] in next 7ch-sp**, 1dc in next dtr, [4tr, ch 1, 4tr] in next 7ch-sp; rep from * twice more and from * to ** once again, join with sl st in first dc. Break colour B.
Round 3: Join colour C to last ch-sp, ch 1, 1dc in same sp, ch 7, 1dc in next ch-sp, ch 7, *[1dc in corner ch-1 sp, ch 7**, [1dc in next ch-sp, ch7] twice; rep from * twice more and from * to ** once again, join with sl st in first dc.
Round 4: Sl st in next ch-sp, ch 2 (counts as Partial tr), [4tr, ch 3, 4tr] in same sp, Partial tr in same sp, Partial tr in next sp, yrh and pull through all 3 loops on hook, [(4tr, ch 3, 4tr) in same ch-sp], *1dc in corner-sp, [5tr, ch 3, 4tr] in next sp**, [Partial tr in same sp, yrh and pull through all 3 loops on hook, [4tr, ch 3, 4tr] in same ch-sp] twice; rep from * twice more then from * to ** once again, Partial tr in last ch-sp, insert hook in top of ch-2 and pull up a loop, yrh and pull through all 3 loops.
Fasten off and weave in ends.

Cluster Border

See page 39

A=Ecru
B=Dawn Grey
C=Winsor

SPECIAL STITCHES

Dtr2tog (work two double treble sts tog): [(Yrh) twice, draw up a loop in next st, (yrh, pull through 2 loops on hook) twice] twice, yrh and draw through all 3 loops on hook.

Dtr3tog (work three double treble sts tog): [(Yrh) twice, draw up a loop in next st, (yrh, pull through 2 loops on hook) 3 times] twice, yrh and draw through all 4 loops on hook.

Centre block

Foundation ring: Using colour A, ch 4 and join with sl st in first ch to form a ring.

Round 1: Ch 3 (counts as 1tr), 11tr in the ring, join with sl st in 3rd ch of ch-3.

Round 2: Ch 3 (counts as 1tr), *[2tr, 1dtr] in next tr, [1dtr, 2tr] in next tr**, 1tr in next tr; rep from * twice more and from * to ** once again, join with sl st in 3rd ch of ch-3.

Round 3: Ch 3 (counts as 1tr), 1tr in each of next 2tr, *[2tr, 1dtr] in next dtr, [1dtr, 2tr] in next dtr**, 1tr in each of next 5tr; rep from * twice more and from * to ** once again, 1tr in each of next 2tr, join with sl st in 3rd ch of ch-3.

Round 4: Ch 3 (counts as 1tr), 1tr in each of next 4tr, *[2tr, 1dtr] in next dtr, [1dtr, 2tr] in next dtr**, 1tr in each of next 9tr; rep from * twice more and from * to ** once again, 1tr in each of next 4tr, join with sl st in 3rd ch of ch-3.

Round 5: Ch 3 (counts as 1tr), 1tr in each of next 6tr, *[2tr, 1dtr] in next dtr, 1dtr in space before next st, [1dtr, 2tr] in next dtr**, 1tr in each of next 13tr; rep from * twice more and from * to ** once again, 1tr in each of next 6tr, join with sl st in 3rd ch of ch-3. Fasten off.

Border

Join colour B, 1 st to the left of the corner st.

Round 1: Ch 1, 1dc in same place, *[ch 4, skip 2 sts, dtr3tog in next st, ch 4, skip 2 sts, 1dc in next st] 3 times, ch 4, dtr3tog in corner st, ch 4, 1dc in next st; rep from * to end of round, omitting last dc, join with sl st in first dc.

Round 2: Ch 1, 1dc in same place, *ch 4, 1dc in top of cluster, ch 4, 1dc in next dc; rep from * to end of round, omitting last dc, change to colour C when joining with sl st to first dc. Break colour B.

Round 3: Ch 4, dtr2tog in same place, *ch 4, 1dc in next dc, ch 4, dtr3tog in next dc; rep from * to end of round, omitting last dtr3tog, join with sl st in 4th ch of ch-4.

Round 4: Ch 1, 1dc in same place, *ch 4, 1dc in next dc, ch 4, 1dc in top of cluster; rep from * to end of round, omitting last dc, join with sl st in first dc.

Fasten off and weave in ends.

✪✪ *Cross-stitched Border*

See page 39

A=Ecru
B=Winsor
C=Dawn Grey
D=Greengage

SPECIAL STITCHES

Tr5tog (work five treble sts tog):
[Yrh draw up a loop in next st, (yrh, pull through 2 loops on hook) 5 times] twice, yrh and draw through all 6 loops on hook.
Crossed tr: Skip 1 st, 1tr in next st; working behind previous st, 1tr in the skipped st.

Centre block

Foundation ring: Using colour A, ch 4 and join with sl st in first ch to form a ring.
Round 1: Ch 3 (counts as 1tr), 11tr in the ring, join with sl st in 3rd ch of ch-3.
Round 2: Ch 3 (counts as 1tr), *[2tr, 1dtr] in next tr, [1dtr, 2tr] in next tr**, 1tr in next tr; rep from * twice more and

from * to ** once again, join with sl st in 3rd ch of ch-3.
Round 3: Ch 3 (counts as 1tr), 1tr in each of next 2tr, *[2tr, 1dtr] in next dtr, [1dtr, 2tr] in next dtr**, 1tr in each of next 5tr; rep from * twice more and from * to ** once again, 1tr in each of next 2tr, join with sl st in 3rd ch of ch-3.
Round 4: Ch 3 (counts as 1tr), 1tr in each of next 4tr, *[2tr, 1dtr] in next dtr, [1dtr, 2tr] in next dtr**, 1tr in each of next 9tr; rep from * twice more and from * to ** once again, 1tr in each of next 4tr, join with sl st in 3rd ch of ch-3.
Round 5: Ch 3 (counts as 1tr), 1tr in each of next 6tr, *[2tr, 1dtr] in next dtr, 1dtr in space before next st, [1dtr, 2tr] in next dtr**, 1tr in each of next 13tr; rep from * twice more and from * to **

once again, 1tr in each of next 6tr, join with sl st in 3rd ch of ch-3. Fasten off.
Border
Join colour B in third st to the left of corner st.
Round 1: Ch 3 (counts as 1tr), 1tr in st to the right of the last st, *[work Crossed tr in next 2 sts] to corner (working first tr of final Crossed tr pair in corner dtr), ch 3, work Crossed tr pair in next st and corner st; rep from * to end of round, join with sl st in first Crossed tr. Break colour B.
Round 2: Join colour C to space between a Crossed tr pair, *ch 1, skip 1 Crossed tr pair, [1dc in sp between Crossed tr pairs, ch 1, skip 1 Crossed tr pair] to corner sp**, [1dc, ch 1, 1dc, ch 1, 1dc] in corner sp; rep from * twice more and from * to **

once more, change to colour D when joining with sl st in first dc. Break colour C.
Round 3: Ch 3 (counts as 1tr), *tr5tog in next ch-sp, [1tr in next dc, tr5tog in next ch-sp]** to corner dc, 3tr in corner dc, tr5tog in next ch-sp; rep from * a further 3 times and from * to ** once again, change to colour B when joining with sl st in 3rd ch of ch-3. Break colour D.
Round 4: Ch 1, 1dc in same place, *[ch 1, skip 1 st, 1dc in next tr] to corner st, ch 1, [1dc, ch 1] twice in corner tr, 1dc in next tr; rep from * to end of round, ending last rep [ch 1, skip 1 st, 1dc in next tr] twice, skip 1 st, join with 1dc to last dc.
Fasten off and weave in ends.

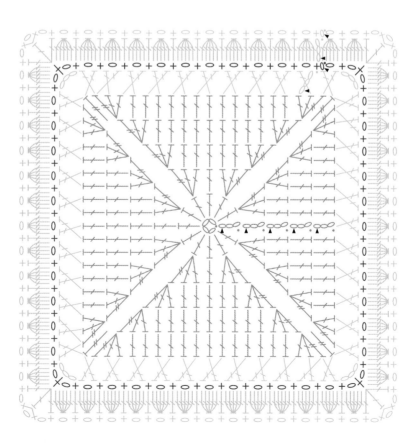

The projects

The blocks in this book can be used to
decorate a whole host of different items.
These inspirational projects demonstrate
just a few ideas including homewares,
toys, and stationery.

Floor Cushion

A boldly patterned cushion is a great way to brighten an interior. I have combined a simple geometric pattern with hard-wearing yarn to make this useful accessory.

WORKING THE CROCHET
Tension: After blocking, one square will measure 18 × 18cm (7 × 7in)

Finished size: 60 × 60cm (24 × 24in)
Work: 4 × Spiky Square (see page 107), where A=Blue, B=White, C=Grey, and D=Red (BSS)
Work: 4 × Spiky Square, where A=Red, B=White, C=Grey, and D=Blue (RSS)

BASIC DOUBLE CROCHET SQUARE
Ch 29.
Row 1: 1dc in 2nd ch from hook, 1dc in every ch to end of row, turn.
Row 2: Ch 1, 1dc in every dc to end of row, turn.
Rep Row 2 until work is square. Fasten off.
Join contrast yarn to any ch along Foundation edge.
Round 1: Ch 3 (counts as 1tr), 1tr in every ch and row end, working 3tr in each corner to end of round, join with a sl st to 3rd of ch-3. Fasten off.
Work 4 x double crochet squares in blue with grey border. (BDC)
Work 4 x double crochet squares in red with grey border. (RDC)

FINISHING
Weave in any loose ends and block according to ball band instructions. Arrange blocks in the following sequence:
Row 1: RDC, RSS, BDC, BSS
Row 2: RSS, BDC, BSS, RDC
Row 3: BDC, BSS, RDC, RSS
Row 4: BSS, RDC, RSS, BDC
Join all seams using slip stitch.
Stitch backing fabric to the crocheted panel along three sides.
Insert cushion pad and close with a slipstitch.

YOU WILL NEED

- ☐ 1 × 50g (2oz) ball 4ply/fingering-weight cotton yarn in colour of choice
- ☐ 2.5mm (C/2) crochet hook
- ☐ Clean glass jar approx 8cm (3¼in) in diameter and 26cm (10in) tall

Vase Cover

Use your crochet skills to turn throwaway items, such as glass jars, into something useful or decorative. The lacy panels would look attractive with the light from a candle shining through. Alternatively, fill with water and add a bunch of flowers.

WORKING THE CROCHET
Make: 2 × Old Vienna (see page 62)
Tension: After blocking, one square will measure 13 x 13cm (5 × 5in)
Finished size: According to jar size

FINISHING
Weave in any loose ends and block according to ball band instructions. Slip stitch side seams together. Using 2.5mm (C/2) hook, join yarn to bottom edge and work four rounds of double crochet, decreasing stitches where necessary to ensure a snug fit. Fasten off. Using 2.5mm (C/2) hook, join yarn to top edge and work four rounds of double crochet, decreasing stitches where necessary to ensure a snug fit. Continue to work in rounds of double crochet without further decreases so that the top of the jar is covered—this will be typically 6–8 rounds. Fasten off.

Journal Cover

A journal is a very personal item. A cover made from small blocks will make this item unique for your own use or it could add an extra special touch for the journal's recipient.

WORKING THE CROCHET

Tension: After blocking, one square will measure 7 × 7cm (3 × 3in)
Finished size: 15 × 22cm (6 × 9in)
Work: 15 × Raised Petal (see page 112), where A=Hot Pink, B=Mulberry, C=White, and D=Pale Pink

FINISHING

Weave in any loose ends and block according to ball band instructions. Arrange blocks in the three rows of five squares and join together with slip stitch.
Join colour D to any dc.
Round 1: Ch 1, 1dc in every dc and 3dc in every corner dc to end of round, join with sl st to first dc. Fasten off.
Join color B to centre dc at top right-hand corner edge.
Row 1: Ch 1, 1dc in every dc to centre dc at top left-hand corner. Fasten off.
Join colour B to centre dc at bottom left-hand corner edge.
Row 2: Ch 1, 1dc in every dc to centre dc at bottom right-hand corner. Fasten off.

FLAPS

Join color D to bottom right-hand corner.
Row 1: Ch 1, 1dc in every dc to end of row, turn.
Rep last row, 8 more times. Fasten off.
Join colour D to top left-hand corner.
Row 2: Ch 1, 1dc in every dc to end of row, turn.
Rep last row, 8 more times. Fasten off.
Fold flaps over and stitch to top and bottom edges of main fabric; insert journal.

Baby Block

A soft toy for a new baby is always welcome. I have used two blocks that feature bobbles so that the toy is interesting, yet still soft to touch. The bobbles will also help a young child develop a sense of pattern and early counting skills.

WORKING THE CROCHET

Make: 1 × Candy Stripe Bobbles (see page 50), where A=Brown, B=Orange, and C=Cream
Make: 1 × Candy Stripe Bobbles, where A=Orange, B=Cream, and C=Brown
Make: 1 × Candy Stripe Bobbles, where A=Cream, B=Brown, and C=Orange
Make: 3 × Alternating Bobbles (see page 50)—one in each colour.
Tension: After blocking, one square will measure 15cm x 15cm (6 x 6in)
Finished size: 6 × 6 × 6in (15 × 15 × 15cm)

FINISHING

Weave in any loose ends and block according to ball band instructions. Arrange blocks so that all Candy Stripe Bobbles form one strip. Use slip stitch to join first Alternating Bobble block to top edge of centre block. Join second and third Alternating blocks and then join with a slip stitch to bottom edge of centre Candy Stripe Bobble block. Join side seams so that you start to form a cube, but insert foam before joining last four seams around the base.

Lap Blanket

A small blanket is always handy and can be used at home, in the car, or on the beach. The design is made up of alternating crosses. One is made from chain spaces and the other by working clusters on the diagonal.

WORKING THE CROCHET
Tension: After blocking, one square will measure 23 x 23cm (9 × 9in)
Finished size: Approx. 69 x 115cm (27 × 45in)
Make: 7 x Lacy Cross (see page 86) and 8 x Wisteria (see page 95)

FINISHING
Weave in any loose ends and block according to ball band instructions.
Arrange blocks in the following sequence. Rows 1, 3, and 5: 75, 71, 75. Rows 2 and 4: 71, 75, 71.
Join all seams using slip stitch.

Crochet Refresher Course

For readers who are new to crochet (and those who could use a review), this section provides instruction on the stitches used in this book.

HOLDING THE HOOK AND YARN

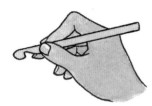

1 Holding the hook as if it were a pen is the most widely used method. Centre the tips of your right thumb and forefinger over the flat section of the hook.

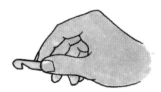

2 An alternative way to hold the hook is to grasp the flat section of the hook between your right thumb and forefinger as if you were holding a knife.

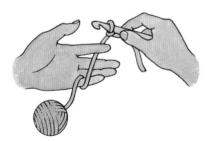

3 To control the supply and keep an even tension on the yarn, hold the short end of the yarn in place with your right thumb. Take the yarn coming from the ball loosely around the little finger of your left hand and loop it over the left forefinger. Use the middle finger on the same hand to help hold the work. If you are left-handed, hold the hook in the left hand and the yarn in the right.

MAKING A SLIP KNOT

1 Loop the yarn as shown, insert the hook into the loop, catch the yarn with the hook, and pull it through to make a loop over the hook.

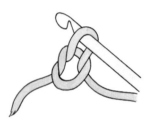

2 Gently pull the yarn to tighten the loop around the hook and complete the slip knot.

WORKING A SLIP STITCH (SL ST)

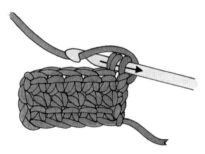

The main uses of slip stitches are for joining rounds but also for making seams and carrying the hook and yarn from one place to another. Insert the hook from front to back into the required stitch. Wrap the yarn round the hook (yrh) and draw it through both the work and the loop on the hook. One loop remains on the hook and one slip stitch has been worked.

WORKING A FOUNDATION CHAIN (CH)

The foundation chain is the equivalent of casting on in knitting and it's important to make sure that you have made the required number of chains for the pattern you are going to work. Count each V-shaped loop on the front of the chain as one chain stitch, except for the loop on the hook, which is not counted. You may find it easier to turn the chain over and count the stitches on the back of the chain. When working the first row of stitches (usually called the foundation row) into the chain, insert the hook under one thread or two, depending on your preference.

1 Holding the hook with the slip knot in your right hand and the yarn in your left, wrap the yarn over the hook. Draw the yarn through to make a new loop and complete the first chain stitch.

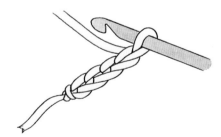

2 Repeat this step, drawing a new loop of yarn through the loop already on the hook until the chain is the required length. Move the thumb and second finger that are grasping the chain upward after every few stitches to keep the tension even. When working into the chain, insert the hook under one thread (for a looser edge) or two (for a firmer edge), depending on your preference.

WORKING A DOUBLE CROCHET (DC)

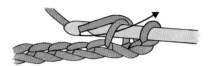

1 Begin with a foundation chain (see left) and insert the hook from front to back into the second chain from the hook. Wrap the yarn round the hook (yrh) and draw it through the first loop, leaving two loops on the hook.

2 To complete the stitch, yarn round hook and draw it through both loops on the hook, leaving one loop on the hook. Continue in this way, working one double crochet into each chain.

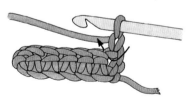

3 At the end of the row, turn and work one chain for the turning chain (remember that this chain does not count as a stitch). Insert the hook into the first double crochet at the beginning of the row. Work a double crochet into each stitch of the previous row, being careful to work the final stitch into the last stitch of the row, but not into the turning chain.

WORKING A HALF TREBLE CROCHET (HTR)

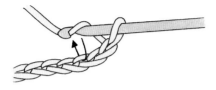

1 Begin with a foundation chain (see page 147), wrap the yarn round the hook (yrh), and insert the hook into the third chain from the hook.

2 Draw the yarn through the chain, leaving three loops on the hook. Yarn round hook and draw through all three loops on the hook, leaving one loop on the hook. One half treble crochet complete.

3 Continue to work one half treble crochet into each chain. At the end of the row, work two chains to turn. Skip the first stitch and work a half treble crochet into each stitch on the previous row. At the end of the row, work the last stitch into the top of the turning chain.

WORKING A TREBLE CROCHET (DC)

1 Begin with a foundation chain (see page 147), wrap the yarn round the hook, and insert the hook into the fourth chain from the hook.

2 Draw the yarn through the chain, leaving three loops on the hook. Yarn round hook again and draw the yarn through the first two loops on the hook, leaving two loops on the hook.

3 Yarn round hook and draw the yarn through the two loops on the hook leaving one loop on the hook. One treble crochet complete. Continue along the row, working one treble crochet stitch into each chain. At the end of the row, work three chains to turn. Skip the first stitch and work a treble crochet into each stitch made on the previous row. At the end of the row, work the last stitch into the top of the turning chain.

WORKING A DOUBLE TREBLE CROCHET (DTR)

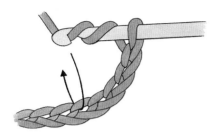

1 Begin with a foundation chain (see page 147), wrap the yarn round the hook twice (yrh twice), and insert the hook into the fifth chain from the hook.

4 Yarn round hook again and draw through the two remaining loops, leaving one loop on the hook. Double treble crochet is now complete.

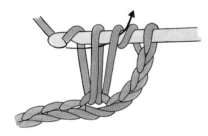

2 Draw the yarn through the chain, leaving four loops on the hook. Yarn round hook again and draw the yarn through the first two loops on the hook, leaving three loops on the hook.

5 Continue along the row, working one double treble crochet stitch into each chain. At the end of the row, work four chains to turn. Skip the first stitch and work a double treble crochet into each stitch made on the previous row. At the end of the row, work the last stitch into the top of the turning chain.

3 Yarn round hook again and draw through the first two loops on the hook leaving two loops on the hook.

LONG TREBLES

A triple treble or quadruple treble (or an even longer stitch) may be made in a similar way to a treble, above. At step 1, wrap the yarn three, four, or more times around the hook. Work step 2, then repeat step 3 as many times as necessary, until two loops remain on the hook. Work step 5 to complete the long treble. For any long treble, the number of turning chains required at the beginning of a row is two more than the number of times the yarn is wrapped around the hook.

POPCORN (PC)

A popcorn is formed when several complete treble crochet stitches (or longer stitches) are worked in the same place, and the top of the first stitch is joined to the last to make a "cup" shape. A four-treble crochet popcorn is shown here.

1 Work four trebles (or the number required) in the same place.

2 Slip the last loop off the hook. Reinsert the hook in the top of the first treble of the group, as shown, and catch the empty loop. (On a wrong-side row, reinsert the hook from the back, to push the popcorn to the right side of the work.)

PUFF

A puff is normally a group of three or more half treble crochet stitches joined at both top and bottom (a three-half-treble puff [Hdc3tog] is demonstrated below).

1 *Wrap the yarn round the hook, insert the hook where required, draw through a loop, repeat from * two (or more) times in the same place. You now have seven loops (or more) on the hook. Wrap the yarn round the hook again, and pull through all the loops on the hook.

2 Often, one chain is worked in order to close the puff.

SPIKE STITCHES

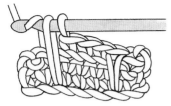

Many pattern variations may be made by inserting the hook one or more rows below the previous row. The insertion may be directly below the next stitch, or one or more stitches to the right or left. Insert the hook as directed, wrap the yarn round the hook, and pull the loop through the work, lengthening the loop to the height of the working row. Complete the stitch as instructed. (Double crochet spike shown here.)

WORKING INTO THE FRONT AND BACK OF THE STITCHES

Unless pattern details instruct you otherwise, it's usual to work crochet stitches under both loops of the stitches made on the previous row.

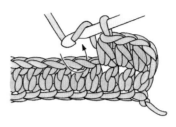

Working into the front When instructions tell you to work into the front of the stitches, insert the hook only under the front loops of stitches on the previous row.

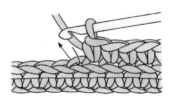

Working into the back Likewise, to work into the back of the stitches, insert the hook only under the back loops of stitches on the previous row.

CHANGING COLOUR

Often when you are working a pattern, you will need to change yarn colour.

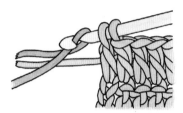

1 To make a neat join between colours, leave the last stitch of the old colour incomplete so there are two loops on the hook and wrap the new colour around the hook.

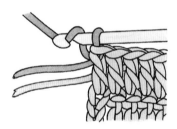

2 Draw the new colour through to complete the stitch and continue working in the new colour. The illustrations show a colour change in a row of treble crochet stitches—the method is the same for double treble crochet and other stitches.

BLOCKING

A trim that is crocheted separately and then sewn into place lacks a base to anchor it, and may tend to curl or spiral. (This is particularly true of edgings that are crocheted lengthwise.) You can correct this by blocking: soak the edging in cold water, press it flat and straight, and set it on a towel until it is completely dry. You will then be able to handle, sew, or glue it more easily.

Working in Rounds

Some features are worked in rounds, which means that they are worked outward from a central ring called a foundation ring.

MAKING A FOUNDATION RING

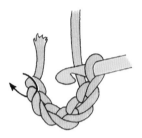

1 Work a short length of foundation chain (see page 147) as specified in the pattern. Join the chains into a ring by working a slip stitch into the first stitch of the foundation chain.

WORKING INTO THE RING

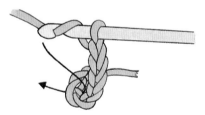

1 Work the number of turning chains specified in the pattern—three chains are shown here (counting as a treble crochet stitch). Inserting the hook into the space at the centre of the ring each time, work the number of stitches specified in the pattern into the ring. Count the stitches at the end of the round to check you have worked the correct number.

2 Join the first and last stitches of the round together by working a slip stitch into the top of the turning chain.

MAKING A MAGIC RING

A Magic Ring can be used in place of a Foundation Ring for crocheting in the round. The benefit of this method is that after pulling the yarn tail to draw the stitches together there is no hole at the centre of your work.

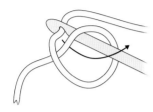

1 Wind the yarn around your finger once, leaving the yarn tail on the left and the working yarn on the right.

2 Insert your hook under the strands of the ring and draw through a loop of the working yarn.

3 Now work the number of starting chains required in the pattern.

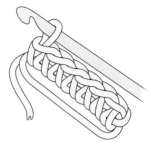

4 Continue in the same manner as for working into a Foundation Ring.

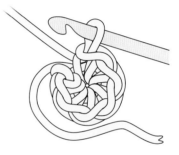

5 When the first round is complete, pull tightly on the yarn tail to close the Magic Ring.

Symbols & Abbreviations

These are the abbreviations and symbols used in the charts and patterns in this book. Charts represent how a stitch pattern is constructed, and may not bear much resemblance to the appearance of the finished stitch. Always read the written instructions as well as the chart.

BASIC STITCHES, ABBREVIATIONS & SYMBOLS

British crochet terms are used throughout this book, abbreviated as shown. For detailed methods of working, see pages 146–153.

Stitch	Abbreviation	Symbol
chain	ch	
slip stitch	sl st	
double crochet	dc	
extended double crochet	EXdc	
half treble	htr	
treble	tr	
double treble	dtr	
triple treble	trtr	
quintuple treble	quintr	

ADDITIONAL SYMBOLS

These are used on some charts to clarify the meaning.

Stitch	Abbreviation	Symbol
direction of working	-	
stitch worked in front loop only	-	
stitch worked in back loop only	-	
beaded double crochet	Bdc	
beaded double crochet	Bdc	
sequined double crochet	Sqdc	
sequined double crochet	Sqdc	
work in back loop (left); work in front loop (right)	-	

SPECIAL STITCHES

In addition, various patterns use special stitch constructions and, where these occur in this book, the abbreviation is indicated in the Special Stitches instructions for that pattern. Always refer to Special Stitches instructions where they occur.

Stitch	Abbreviation	Symbol	Stitch	Abbreviation	Symbol
front raised double crochet	**FRdc**		spike cluster	**Scl**	
back raised double crochet	**BRdc**		pineapple	**Ps**	
front raised treble (left); back raised treble (right)	**FRtr, BRtr**		raised pineapple	**Rps**	
front raised double treble	**FRdtr**		puff stitch	-	
front raised triple treble	**FRtrtr**		popcorn	**PC**	
spiked double crochet	**Sdc**		bullion stitch	**Bs**	
group	**Gp**		loop stitch	-	
extended half treble	**EXhtr**		surface crochet	-	
magic ring	-		joining bar	-	

ARRANGEMENT OF SYMBOLS

Description	Abbreviation	Explanation
symbols joined at top		A group of symbols may be joined at the top, indicating that these stitches should be worked together as a cluster.
symbols joined at base		Symbols joined at the base should all be worked into the same stitch below.
symbols joined at top and bottom		Sometimes a group of stitches is joined at both top and bottom, making a puff, bobble, or popcorn, as page 150.
symbols on a curve		Sometimes symbols are drawn along a curve, depending on the construction of the stitch pattern.
distorted symbols		Some symbols may be lengthened, curved, or spiked to indicate where the hook is inserted below, as for spike stitches, page 151.

COMMON ABBREVIATIONS

Term	Abbreviation	Term	Abbreviation
stitch(es)	st(s)	yarn over	yo
chain space	ch sp	right side	RS
turning chain	tch	wrong side	WS
together	tog	yarn round hook	yrh

BRITISH/AMERICAN EQUIVALENT TERMS

Some American terms differ from the British system, as shown below: patterns
you may encounter that are published using American terminology can be very
confusing unless you understand the difference.

British	American	American abbreviation	Symbol
double crochet	single crochet	sc	+
extended double crochet	extended single crochet	exsc	
half treble	half double	hdc	
treble	double	dc	
double treble	treble	tr	
triple treble	double treble	dtr	
sextuple treble	quintuple treble	quintr	

Index

A

abbreviations 154–156
American/British equivalent terms 157
Aligned Railing Block 13, 57
Alternating Bobbles 13, 50
Alternative Granny 10, 46
American Beauty 35, 118
Anemone 27, 88
Arched Border 36, 135

B

baby block 144
Basket Weave 15, 54
Beaded Double Crochet 38, 129
Belgian Lace 18, 60
Big Bloom 12, 59
blanket 145
blocking 152
bobbles
    Alternating Bobbles 13, 50
    Bobble Stripes 12, 51
    Bobbles on the Diagonal 14, 52
    Candy Stripe Bobbles 15, 50
Bold Block 31, 104
borders
    Arched Border 36, 135
    Cluster Border 39, 136
    Cross-stitched Border 39, 137
    Fan Border 36, 135
    Picot Border 36, 134
    Shell and Bar Border 36, 134
    Shell Border 36, 133
Butterfly Garden 17, 66

C

cables
    Celtic Cable 12, 53
    Classic Cable 15, 58
    Candy Stripe Bobbles 15, 50
    Cartwheel Flower 32, 110
    Catherine Wheel 26, 92
    Celtic Cable 12, 53

Chain Loops Flower 38, 130
Chrysanthemum 34, 119
circles
    Circle in a Hexagon 20, 84
    Circle in a Square 23, 74
    Cluster Circle 20, 76
    Framed Circle 20, 78
    Fretwork Circle 21, 76
    Squaring the Circle 22, 75
    Starflower Circle 20, 77
Classic Cable 15, 58
clusters
    Cluster Border 39, 136
    Cluster Circle 20, 76
    Cluster Flower 33, 114
    Pineapple Cluster 13, 55
colour, changing 152
Compass Cross 26, 94
Corner Log Cabin 39, 127
Criss Cross 27, 86
crochet refresher course 146
    blocking 152
    changing colour 152
    holding the hook and yarn 146
    long trebles 149
    making a foundation ring 152
    making a magic ring 153
    making a slip knot 146
    popcorn (pc) 150
    puff 150
    spike stitches 151
    working a double crochet (dc) 147
    working a double treble crochet (dtr) 149
    working a foundation chain (ch) 147
    working a half treble crochet (htr) 148
    working a slip stitch (sl st) 146
    working a treble crochet (tr) 148
    working in rounds 152–153
    working into the front and back of the stitches 151
    working into the ring 152
Cross-stitched Border 39, 137

crosses
    Compass Cross 26, 94
    Criss Cross 27, 86
    Crossroads 27, 91
    Dip Stitch Cross 29, 107
    Double Popcorn Cross 25, 94
    Embossed Cross 24, 91
    Interlocking Cross 25, 90
    Italian Cross 24, 89
    Lacy Cross 25, 86
    Looped Cross 26, 90
    Popcorn Cross 26, 87
    Sunray Cross 24, 87
    Treble Cross 26, 93
Crossroads 27, 91
cushion 140

D

Daisy Chain Square 18, 71
Darts 30, 102
diagonals
    Bobbles on the Diagonal 14, 52
    Diagonal Raised Treble 12, 54
Diamonds 22, 83
    Danish Diamond 27, 96
    Diamond in a Square 23, 80
    Double Diamonds 21, 85
Dip Stitch Cross 29, 107
double crochet (dc) 147
Double Filet Mesh 19, 73
Double Popcorn Cross 25, 94
double treble crochet (dtr) 149

E

Edwardian Fancy 22, 81
Eight-petal Flower 32, 108
Embossed Cross 24, 91
Eyelet Lace in the Round 19, 64

F

Fan Border 36, 135
filet squares
    Double Filet Mesh 19, 73

Filet Flower 34, 121
Filet Flower Square 17, 67
Filet Mesh Center 18, 73
Fine Texture 15, 48
Flame Flower 32, 117
Fleur 19, 68
floor cushion 140
Florentine Tile 28, 105
flower squares
    Cartwheel Flower 32, 110
    Chain Loops Flower 38, 130
    Cluster Flower 33, 114
    Eight-petal Flower 32, 108
    Filet Flower 34, 121
    Filet Flower Square 17, 67
    Flame Flower 32, 117
    Flower Granny 11, 45
    Flower in a Web 21, 79
    Framed Flower 35, 109
    Octagon Framed Flower 22, 82
    Origami Flower 33, 111
    Raised Flower Granny 11, 47
    Raised Petal Flower 35, 112
    Ruffled Flower 32, 113
    Six-petal Flower 33, 112
Flying Carpet 30, 104
foundation chain (ch) 147
foundation ring 152
    working into the ring 152
Four-patch Granny 10, 44
Framed Circle 20, 78
Framed Flower 35, 109
Fretwork Circle 21, 76

G

Gothic Square 25, 92
granny squares
    Alternative Granny 10, 46
    Flower Granny 11, 45
    Four-patch Granny 10, 44
    Granny in the Middle 10, 42
    Granny Stripes 11, 43
    Log Cabin Granny 39, 126
    Mitered Granny 11, 45
    Nine-patch Granny 11, 47

Plain Granny 10, 42
Raised Flower Granny 11, 47
Rectangle Granny 10, 43
Two-sided Granny 37, 132

H
Half and Half 29, 102
half treble crochet (htr) 148
Harlequin 38, 131
hexagons
    Circle in a Hexagon 20, 84
    Hexagon in a Square 22, 84
holding the hook and yarn 146
Honeycomb 14, 55
Horizontal Woven Block 37, 131
Hourglass 28, 103

I
Intarsia Steps 28, 98
Interlocking Cross 25, 90
Interlocking Stripes 31, 100
Interwoven Block 15, 57
Isabella 16, 67
Italian Cross 24, 89

J
Jaquard Checks 31, 101
Jaquard Stripes 29, 101
journal cover 143

L
lace squares
    Belgian Lace 18, 60
    Eyelet Lace in the Round 19, 64
    Lacy Cross 25, 86
    Lacy Daisy 34, 115
    Lacy Wheel 16, 61
    Old Vienna 17, 62
    Pineapple Lace 18, 65
    Popcorns & Lace 19, 68
    Queen Anne's Lace 16, 63
    Spiralling Lace 16, 72

Sunshine Lace 19, 70
    Victorian Lace 17, 62
lap blanket 145
Lemon Peel 14, 49
Log Cabin 39, 128
Log Cabin Granny 39, 126
loops
    Chain Loops Flower 38, 130
    Loop Stitch Columns 38, 130
Looped Cross 26, 90

M
magic ring 153
Marigold 33, 116
Mitered Curve 23, 83
Mitered Decrease 37, 125
Mitered Granny 11, 45
Mitered Increase 37, 124

N
Nine-patch Granny 11, 47

O
Octagon Framed Flower 22, 82
Octagon Tile 23, 82
Old Vienna 17, 62
Openwork 16, 60
Origami Flower 33, 111

P
Picot Border 36, 134
Picot Rose 17, 69
Pineapple Cluster 13, 55
Pineapple Lace 18, 65
Plain Granny 10, 42
Poinsettia 34, 123
popcorn (pc) 150
    Double Popcorn Cross 25, 94
    Popcorn Cross 26, 87
    Popcorn Square 18, 69
    Popcorns & Lace 19, 68
Poppy 34, 115
Primrose Square 33, 120

projects
    baby block 144
    floor cushion 140
    journal cover 143
    lap blanket 145
    vase cover 142
puff 150

Q
Quartet 30, 98
Queen Anne's Lace 16, 63

R
Raised Flower Granny 11, 47
Raised Petal Flower 35, 112
Raised Rose 32, 113
Random Patches 28, 99
Rectangle Granny 10, 43
Rose of Sharon 30, 106
Rosetta 35, 122
rounds 152–153
Ruffled Flower 32, 113

S
Seminole 28, 100
Sequined Double Crochet 38, 129
Seville 25, 88
Shell and Bar Border 36, 134
Shell Border 36, 133
Six-petal Flower 33, 112
slip knots 146
slip stitch (sl st) 146
Snowflake in a Square 23, 79
spike stitches 151
Spiky Square 29, 107
Spinner 20, 74
Spiralling Lace 16, 72
Squaring the Circle 22, 75
St. Petersburg 24, 97
Stacking Squares 31, 105
Star in a Square 21, 80
Starburst in a Square 21, 75
Starflower Circle 20, 77

stripes
    Bobble Stripes 12, 51
    Candy Stripe Bobbles 15, 50
    Interlocking Stripes 31, 100
    Jaquard Stripes 29, 101
    Striped Knot 14, 49
    Textured Stripes 12, 48
Sunray Cross 24, 87
Sunshine Lace 19, 70
symbols 154–156
    American/British equivalent
        terms 157

T
texture
    Fine Texture 15, 48
    Textured Stripes 12, 48
treble crochet (tr) 148
    long trebles 149
    Treble Cross 26, 93
Tricolour Square 27, 97
Tricolour Trinity 13, 56
Trio 29, 103
Tuscan Tile 30, 106
Two-colour Raised Ripple 14, 56
Two-sided Granny 37, 132

V
vase cover 142
Vertical Woven Block 37, 126
Victorian Lace 17, 62

W
Waterlily 35, 121
Winter Blueberry Patch 13, 52
Wisteria 24, 95
working into the front and back
    of stitches 151

Z
Zig Zag 31, 99

Credits

Quarto are grateful to Rowan Yarns who supplied all the yarns used in this book and a special thanks must go to David MacLeod and Vicky Sedgewick.

The author wishes to thank Amanda Golland and Jools Yeo for their enthusiasm and beautiful crochet work.

All photographs and illustrations are the copyright of Quarto Publishing plc. While every effort has been made to credit contributors, Quarto would like to apologise should there have been any omissions or errors – and would be pleased to make the appropriate correction for future editions of the book.

To my husband Paul, who supports me in knit, crochet, love and life.